STUDIES
IN CATULLAN VERSE

AN ANALYSIS OF WORD TYPES AND PATTERNS
IN THE POLYMETRA

BY

JULIA W. LOOMIS

LUGDUNI BATAVORUM E. J. BRILL MCMLXXII

STUDIES
IN CATULLAN VERSE

MNEMOSYNE

BIBLIOTHECA CLASSICA BATAVA

COLLEGERUNT

W. DEN BOER • W. J. VERDENIUS • R. E. H. WESTENDORP BOERMA

BIBLIOTHECAE FASCICULOS EDENDOS CURAVIT

W. J. VERDENIUS, HOMERUSLAAN 53, ZEIST

SUPPLEMENTUM VICESIMUM QUARTUM

JULIA W. LOOMIS

STUDIES
IN CATULLAN VERSE

LUGDUNI BATAVORUM E. J. BRILL MCMLXXII

STUDIES
IN CATULLAN VERSE

AN ANALYSIS OF WORD TYPES AND PATTERNS
IN THE POLYMETRA

BY   ▸ P 2 1   ◀

JULIA W. LOOMIS

LUGDUNI BATAVORUM E. J. BRILL MCMLXXII

ISBN 90 04 03429 3

PRINTED IN THE NETHERLANDS

AVI MEI
F. J. E. WOODBRIDGE
MANIBUS
PIE
HOC OPUSCULUM DEDICAVI

TABLE OF CONTENTS

PREFACE

This book was originally presented as a doctoral dissertation to the Faculty of Philosophy of Columbia University in the spring of 1968. Since then a number of books and articles on the subject of Catullus' poetry have appeared. None of them, however, has any direct bearing on the basic purpose of this book, which is to present a radically new approach to Greek and Latin quantitative metrics, as developed by Professor Howard Porter of Columbia University. I have therefore not felt it necessary to make any revision in the text, although I have enlarged the bibliography to include important recent publications. I would have liked to have presented my statistical material to the Dartmouth College Computer center, since there is certainly much that can be ascertained in the field of metrics by modern computer methods. The small number of lines to be considered, however, made the project unrealistic.

Much of the material of the book was derived form a course given under the joint sponsorship of the Department of Linguistics and the Department of Greek and Latin at Columbia in the spring of 1967 entitled "Language and Poetry." Thus I am deeply indebted to Professor John Lotz for many of the definitions as expressed in linguistic terminology, and to Professor Robert Austerlitz for his assistance with charts. The greatest single debt I owe to Professor Howard Porter. His perception that the aesthetic elements of a poem, its vocabulary, perfectly chosen turns of phrase, deep human truths, were so many lifeless *disiecta membra* without the unifying vibrant immediacy of the metrical pattern chosen by the poet as the medium of expression, was the prime mover for this book.

Many other individuals have been of invaluable assistance. Chief of these are Professor Gilbert Highet, Mark Jupiter of the Columbia University library staff, and the two foreign scholars who sent me copies of their own works: Professor Ernst Zinn of the University of Tübingen and Professor Francesco della Corte of the University of Genoa. Lastly thanks are due to Patricia Horowitz, not only for her painstaking care in the preparation of the typescript, but for her never failing enthusiasm and cheerfulness in the face of all the frustrations and changes such a task entails.

New York, October 1971   J. W. L.

PRINCIPAL TEXTS *

Aischylos	G. Murray, *Aeschyli septem quae supersunt tragoediae* (Oxford 1952) (OCT)
Alkaios	E. Lobel & D. Page, *Poetarum Lesbiorum Fragmenta* (Oxford 1955) *PLF*
Anakreon	D. Page, *Poetae Melici Graeci* (Oxford 1962) *PMG*
Anthologia Graeca	W. R. Paton, *The Greek Anthology* (New York 1918-1927) (LCL) *AP*
Anthologia Latina	F. Bücheler, A. Riese, E. Lommatzsch, *Anthologia Latina* 1-2 (Amsterdam reprint 1964) *AL*
Archilochos	F. Lasserre et A. Bonnard, *Archiloque: Fragments* (Paris 1958) *L &B*
Aristophanes	F. W. Hall & W. M. Geldart, *Aristophanis Comoediae* 1 (Oxford 1952) (OCT)
Ausonius	R. Peiper, *Decimi Magni Ausonii Opuscula* (Leipzig 1886) (Teubner)
Bibaculus	W. Morel, *Fragmenta Poetarum Latinorum* (Stuttgart 1963) (Teubner) *M*, Morel *FPL*
Boethius	R. Peiper, *Anicii Manlii Severini Boetii Philosophiae Consolationis* (Leipzig 1871) (Teubner)
Calvus	(see supra Bibaculus)
Catullus	W. Kroll, *C. Valerius Catullus* (Stuttgart 1959)
Cinna	(see supra Bibaculus)
Cornificius	(see supra Bibaculus)
Diogenes Laertius	H. S. Long, *Diogenes Laertius Vitae Philosophorum* (Oxford 1964) (OCT)
Euripides	G. Murray, *Euripides Fabulae* 1-3 (Oxford 1949) (OCT)
Gellius	J. C. Rolfe, *The Attic Nights of Aulus Gellius* (Harvard 1934) (LCL)
Grammatici Latini	H. Keil, *Grammatici Latini* 1 (Leipzig 1857), 6 (Hildesheim reprint 1961) *Gr. Lat.*
Herondas	W. Headlam & A. D. Knox, *Herodas, The Mimes and Fragments* (Cambridge 1966 [2])
Hephaistion	M. Consbruch, *Hephaestionis Enchiridion* (Leipzig 1906) (Teubner) Consbr. *Ench.*
Hipponax	O. Masson, *Les Fragments du Poète Hipponax* (Paris 1962)
Horace	F. Klingner, *Horatius* (Leipzig 1959) (Teubner) C. Bennett & J. Rolfe, *Horace, Complete Works* (New York 1963)
Kallimachos	R. Pfeiffer, *Callimachus* 1 & 2 (Oxford 1949-1953) Pf.

* Italicized initials represent the abbreviations used for the texts. Initials in brackets represent the chief textual series: LCL standing for the Loeb Classical Library, and OCT for the Oxford Classical Texts.

Abbreviations for the individual works of classical authors are those found in *The Oxford Classical Dictionary* 1949 ix-xix.

Laevius	(see supra Bibaculus)
Lucilius	F. Marx, *C. Lucilii Carminum Reliquiae* (Leipzig 1904-1905)
Martial	W. Gilbert, *M. Valerii Martialis Epigrammaton Libri* (Leipzig 1886) (Teubner)
Matius	(see supra Bibaculus)
Nonius	W. M. Lindsay, *Nonius Marcellus De Compendiosa Doctrina* (Hildesheim reprint 1964) (Teubner) *Nonius*
Petronius	F. Bücheler, *Petronii Saturae* (Berlin 1963[8])
Pindar	A. Turyn, *Pindari Carmina* (Harvard 1952[2])
Plautus	W. M. Lindsay, *T. Macci Plauti Comoediae* 1 & 2 (Oxford 1903-1913) (OCT)
Poetae Latini Aevi Carolini	E. Dümmler, L. Traube, P. Winterfeld, K. Strecker, *Monumenta Germaniae Historica*: *Poetae Latini Aevi Carolini* (Berlin, Leipzig 1881-1937) 1-5 *PLAC*
Poetae Lyrici Graeci	T. Bergk, *Poetae Lyrici Graeci* 3 (Leipzig 1914) (Teubner) *PLG*
Priapea	L. Müller, *Catulli Tibulli Properti Carmina Accedunt Laevii Calvi Cinnae Aliorum Reliquiae et Priapea* (Leipzig 1880) (Teubner) *CTP*
Quintilian	L. Radermacher, *M. Fabii Quintiliani Institutionis Oratoriae* 1 and 2 (Leipzig 1965) (Teubner)
Sappho	(see supra Alkaios)
Seneca	R. Peiper & G. Richter, *L. Annaei Senecae Tragoediae* (Leipzig 1902) (Teubner)
Sidonius Apollinaris	W. B. Anderson, *Sidonius*: *Poems and Letters* 1 (Cambridge 1936) (LCL)
Statius	E. Bährens, *P. Papinii Statii Silvae* (Leipzig 1876) (Teubner)
Sophokles	A. C. Pearson, *Sophocles Fabulae* (Oxford 1950) (OCT)
Theokritos	A. F. S. Gow, *Bucolici Graeci* (Oxford 1952) (OCT)
Ticidas	(see supra Bibaculus)
Varro	F. Bücheler, *Petronii Saturae adiectae sunt Varronis et Senecae Saturae Similesque Reliquiae* (Berlin 1936[8]) *VMR*
Vergil	R. Ellis, *Appendix Vergiliana* (Oxford 1950) (OCT)

PRINCIPAL ABBREVIATIONS

Fordyce	C. J. Fordyce, *Catullus, a Commentary* (Oxford 1961)
Koster, *Traité*	W. J. W. Koster, *Traité de Métrique Grecque* (Leyden 1966⁴)
Lindsay, *ELV*	W. M. Lindsay, *Early Latin Verse* (Oxford 1922)
Lindsay, *LL*	W. M. Lindsay, *The Latin Language* (Oxford 1894)
PLF	E. Lobel & D. Page, *Poetarum Lesbiorum Fragmenta* (Oxford 1955)
PLG	T. Bergk, *Poetae Lyrici Graeci 3, Poetae Melici* (Leipzig 1914)
PMG	D. Page, *Poetae Melici Graeci* (Oxford 1962)
Raven, *LM*	D. S. Raven, *Latin Metre* (London 1965)
Wilkinson, *GLA*	L. P. Wilkinson, *Golden Latin Artistry* (Cambridge 1963)
Wilamowitz, *GV*	U. von Wilamowitz-Möllendorff, *Griechische Verskunst* (Berlin 1921)
Wilamowitz, *HD*	U. von Wilamowitz-Möllendorff, *Hellenistische Dichtung in der Zeit des Kallimachos* (Berlin 1962²)

Abbreviations for titles of periodicals follow the list published in "Notes for Contributors and Abbreviations," *AJA* 69, 1965, 199-206. Those abbreviations which are not in this list are found in J. Marouzeau and J. Ernst, *L'Année Philologique* (Paris) for the appropriate year.

INTRODUCTION

I. Propositions

This study has a two-fold, interrelated purpose. The first is to illustrate the value of describing Greek and Latin quantitative meters in terms of semantic colometry, a method of description developed by Professor Howard Porter,[1] instead of using the foot-metron terminology inherited from the ancient grammarians, which has little relationship to semantic or phonetic phrasing and hence possesses minimal descriptive utility. The secondary and related purpose is to show how the Greek colometric frames were assimilated and developed in the *polymetra*[2] of the Latin poet, Catullus, the earliest of the Romans who attempted to impose a variety of strict Greek metrical patterns on the Latin language,[3] and whose works survive in sufficient quantity to provide significant statistics. In order to make this study intelligible, it is imperative that I set forth basic definitions of terms as I have used them, even though they may not be acceptable to every scholar in metrics. If even such long established terms as "thesis" and "arsis"[4] are subject to controversy, it is inevitable that there will be disagree-

---

[1] H. Porter, "The Early Greek Hexameter," *YCS* 12, 1951, 3-63. Porter uses the term "semantic" to denote linguistic and phonetic units perceptible to the intelligence (6).

[2] I use this term to include all Catullus' meters except the dactylic hexameter and pentameter which I have not covered in this study for two reasons. The first is that they have received extensive coverage already, see infra 9 n. 1. The second reason is the fact that the great number of lines would require a work equal to or longer than this, which time did not permit.

[3] I am not disregarding the role of Plautus who attempted a great variety of meters throughout his plays. However, his use of Greek meter is extremely difficult to analyze in terms of strict numerical or quantitative regulation of syllables, and thus falls outside the scope of this study which deals with strict Greek colometry in Latin. However, it seems to me that a study of his colometric patterns is one that should be made, particularly since almost the whole focus of attention on Plautine metrics has been on the problem of the Latin word accent (see infra 71 n. 6).

[4] A recent work by A. Kabell, "Metrische Studien II, Antiker Form sich nährend," *UppsÅrsskr* 1960, no. 6, illustrates the continuing disagreement about these and other terms in the first chapter entitled, "Das Labyrinth." See also P. Maas, *Greek Metre*, transl. by H. Lloyd-Jones (Oxford 1962) 6-7, who wants to abolish the terms altogether.

ment concerning the following definitions. They are relevant to Greek and Latin quantitative meters only.

1. Meter, metrical

the organization of units of linguistic expression, such as word, phrase, clause, into numerically regulated systems of short and long syllabic pulses.

2. Metrics

the study of meter, particularly in cataloguing the elements of coherence, and discovering the maximal order.

3. Frame

a syntactically coherent unit, regulated in the field of metrics by number, composed of hierarchical lengths beginning with the smallest unit, the colon, to the line, stanza, strophe, triad,[1] and poem.

4. Colon, colometric, colometry

the smallest indivisible metrical unit of syllabic sequences ≥ three syllables, ≤ eight syllables, defined by word-end, and conforming to linguistic norms or "patterns of expectancy" [2] conditioned within a cultural unconscious over a long period of time; sometimes, but not necessarily, a semantic unit; can also be called a segment.[3]

5. Line

a metrical unit composed of one or more cola, defined by word-end, *brevis in longo*, and hiatus.

6. Stanza

a grouping of three or more lines in a standardized unit which can be repeated within the same poem, or used in others.

7. Strophe

a grouping anew for each poem of standardized cola into line patterns which are repeated in the same poem, as in the anti-strophe, but generally not repeated in different poems.

8. Thesis

a fixed long syllabic pulse.

9. Arsis

a "free" syllabic pulse between theses, free in the sense that it has four values:

---

[1] Triad will not be defined, as it does not occur in Latin poetry. Strophe is also a term only valid for Greek verse.

[2] Porter, *op. cit.* (supra 1 n. 1) 8.

[3] J. Lotz, "Notes on Structural Analysis in Metrics," *Helikon* 4, 1942, 132.

A o nothing[1]
B ⌣ one short syllabic pulse
C × a syllabic pulse which can be short or long: anceps
D ⌣⌣ two short syllabic pulses for which one long syllabic pulse may occasionally be substituted: biceps

10. System
a set number of repeated alternations of theses and arses of which there are three major categories:
a. those employing only one of the four kinds of arses, such the D arsis in dactylic or anapaestic meters.
b. those employing two of the four kinds of arses in regular alternation such as the iambo-trochaic meters, B C *alternating*; cretic or bacchaic rhythms, B A alternating; or ionic rhythms, D A *alternating*.[2]

---

[1] This alphabetical classification of the four types of arses was developed by Professor Howard Porter, but as far as I know, it has not been discussed anywhere but in the classroom. The chief advantage of his typology is that it enables one to analyze the repeated patterns of the alternations of short and long syllables within the linguistic frame in a clear terminology which is valid for all metrical systems, the simplest, such as iambic-trochaic, to the most complex, such as those found in Pindar. Moreover, his systematization obviates the non-linguistic terms of foot and metron inherited from the ancient grammarians whose "'ear' for classical Greek had already been lost," as Seth Schein expresses it in his dissertation presented to the Faculty of Philosophy at Columbia University, *The Iambic Trimeter in Aeschylus and Sophocles*, 1967, 11. Other scholars in the second third of the twentieth century, also aware that the "foot" is not a structural element of Greek metrics, have attempted to substitute the concept of *metra*. Such *metra*, however, have no more relationship to the semantic and syntactic frames of the language than do "feet," for they pay no attention to groups of syllables separated by "expected" breaks as the structural unit. For the position of O. Schröder, P. Maas, A. M. Dale, and D. Page in this development, see Schein, *ibid.*, 14-15, 132 n. 7. Interestingly enough, Porter's classification provides the solution for Maas' complaint against the existing bad stereotyped systems of metrics *op. cit.* (supra 1 n. 1) 6. It also satisfies the requirements for the justification of a new analysis of Greek meter given by A. M. Dale in "The Metrical Units of Greek Lyric Verse II," *CQ* 45, n.s. 1, 1951, 20: ". . . The only way to test each attempt at systematization is to try its capacity to bring the phenomena into an ordered whole and occasionally to give a better explanation than hitherto of puzzling factors by setting them in a new relation to others." Dale's three papers on Greek Lyric Verse have been made easily accessible by their incorporation into a volume of collected works: *The Collected Papers of A. M. Dale*, ed. T. B. L. Webster (Cambridge 1969), 41-97.

[2] Both a and b occasionally use another kind of arsis, frequently the c arsis, as a colometric period or end of a frame.

c. those employing two or more kinds of arses not in regular alternation, such as glyconic, $C\ D\ B$; phalaecean, $C\ D\ B\ B\ C$; or anacreontic, $D\ B\ B\ C$.[1]

11. Open colon

begins and ends *in arsi*, e.g.,

$C\ B\ C\ \times\ -\ \smile\ -\ \times$

$D\ B\ B\ C\ \smile\smile\ -\ \smile\ -\ \smile\ -\ \times$

12. Closed colon

begins and ends *in thesi*, e.g.,

$B\ C\ -\ \smile\ -\ \times\ -$

$D\ D\ -\ \smile\smile\ -\ \smile\smile\ -$

$B\ C\ B\ -\ \smile\ -\ \times\ -\ \smile\ -$ (lecythion)

$C\ D\ B\ -\ \times\ -\ \smile\smile\ -\ \smile\ -$

$D\ B\ -\ \smile\smile\ -\ \smile\ -$

13. Rising colon

begins *in arsi* and ends *in thesi*, e.g.,

$D\ A\ D\ A\ \smile\smile\ -\ -\ \smile\smile\ -\ -$ (ionic dimeter)

14. Falling colon

begins *in thesi* and ends *in arsi*, e.g.,

$D\ C\ -\ \smile\smile\ -\ \times$ (adonic)

$B\ B\ C\ -\ \smile\ -\ \smile\ -\ \times$ (ithyphallic) [2]

15. Ictus

an intensive stress generally on the fixed long syllabic pulse, or thesis, serving to emphasize the metrical and numerical alternation of short and long syllables.

16. Accent

term applied herein almost exclusively to the intensive stress on a Latin word, regulated by the law that such an accent cannot go farther forward than the antepenult of a word, and must fall on the penult of a word if that syllable contains a long vowel or diphthong.[3]

---

[1] Greek choral lyric frequently uses b and c combined in types of responsion.

[2] It is also possible to consider this colon in some types of verse as a *B B A closed*. See note p. 36 n. 2, 38 n. 1.

[3] L. R. Palmer, *The Latin Language* (London 1966⁵) 211 (henceforth Palmer *LL*) gives the following definition: "Accent is the prominence given by various means to one syllable of a word over others of the same word or utterance. Such prominence may be achieved by pronouncing at a higher pitch (the pitch or musical accent) or by a stronger expulsion of breath (the stress or expiratory accent)." See also W. S. Allen, *Vox Latina* (Cambridge 1965) 83 on the "Penultimate Law." (*VL*)

17. Break

   any place in a metrical line where a word-end occurs; term
   used interchangeably with word-end and word limit to avoid
   the inhibiting concepts of caesura and diaeresis.

18. Word-syllable pattern

   recurring patterns made by repeating words of a set number
   of syllables in a certain order, e.g., 3 2, a trisyllable followed
   by a disyllable, a common initial pattern in Catullus' sapphics and iambics, less frequent in phalaeceans; 1 3, a monosyllable followed by a trisyllable, frequent in phalaeceans,
   less common in other meters.

19. Position or numbering

   the numbering of each syllable as it occurs in sequential
   order in a line of a particular meter, e.g., the syllables of
   iambic trimeter being numbered from 1 to 12, those of
   sapphic or phalaecean hendecasyllable, 1 to 11; diagram
   given at the beginning of each chapter.

20. Localization [1]

   a name for the phenomenon that certain word shapes tend to
   appear in one place in a line rather than another, though
   "outer metrically" [2] either place is suitable, e.g., a cretic
   word _ ∪ _ is found in Catullus' iambic trimeter more
   frequently in the 8-10 position than in the 6-8.

II. Method

One of the chief requisites of a study of the metrics of Catullus
is the understanding of his positions in the history of the meters,
particularly with regard to any predecessors who may have experimented with Greek colometric patterns in Latin, and thus established the foundations. By this is not meant the customary
approach concerning literary influence of earlier upon later ages,
generally devoted to thematic affinities and aesthetic apprecia-

---

[1] This is a term used by E. O'Neill, Jr., "Word Accents and Final Syllables
in Latin Verse," *TAPA* 71, 1940 (*WAFS*) 349-350.
[2] This is also O'Neill's phrasing *ibid*. 336, n. 3. By "outer metric," he
means "the quantitative pattern of a verse-form," or the pattern of long and
short syllables required for a particular meter. "Inner metric consists of
the principles which govern the composition of words into verses, within
the limitations of the outer-metrical syllabic patterns of a particular verse
form." In other words, the term "outer metrical" denotes the numerically
regulated organization of syllables in respect to their quantity, not their
incorporation into words.

tion,[1] but something much less subjective: the actual study of word-shapes in a metrical line, irrespective of meaning. For words, even if linguists do not consider them separate phonetic entities,[2] are one of the manifestations of form in a metrical line, particularly if the vowel quantities of the syllables in a word are less important than the number of syllables in a word; or to put it more clearly, in a language where the stress on a syllable is more important acoustically than whether it contains a long or a short vowel, such as English vs. ancient Greek. In this sense, analyzing word-shapes in classical Greek verse can be uncontroversial, since it is accepted that Greek word accents are not stress but tonal accents.[2] First, the "expected" [4] colometric patterns are discovered, being those which occur most frequently. The second step in this type of analysis is to ascertain the next most frequent patterns, and so on, until one arrives at the rare and unexpected. When the expected is tabulated against the unexpected, certain criteria concerning the relationship of metrical form to content appear.[5] And this illustrates the chief obstacle to translation of poetry. What disappears in the translation is not just the metrical rhythm of alternating long and short syllables, and whatever phonetic properties they may have had in the original language, but the semantic realities of the syntactic frames as expressed in the metrical patterns.

What complicates this type of analysis for Latin poetry is that the reasons, however elusive, behind localization of word types,

---

[1] For this type of literary criticism with regard to Catullus, see the following:
R. Avallone, *Catullo e i suoi modelli romani* (Salerno 1944) (*C &MR*).
H. Bardon, "Catulle et ses modèles poetiques de la langue latine," *Latomus* 16, 1957, 614-621.
J. Bayet, "Catulle, la Grèce et Rome, l'influence grecque sur la poésie latine de Catulle à Ovide," *Fondation Hardt* 2, 1956, 3-39.
V. Errante, *La Poesia di Catullo* 2 (Milan 1945).
G. Lafaye, *Catulle et ses modèles* (Paris 1894).
J. Svennung, "Catulls Bildersprache 1," *UppsÅrsskr*, 1945[1], no. 3.
A. L. Wheeler, *Catullus and the Traditions of Ancient Poetry* (Berkeley 1964[2]).
[2] See discussion in Porter, *op. cit.* (supra 1 n. 1) 6, 8.
[3] See the well-documented discussion in W. S. Allen, *Vox Graeca, The Pronunciation of Classical Greek* (Cambridge 1968) 106-124, especially 106-119, and Porter, *op. cit.* (supra 1 n. 1) 25, 26 n. 1.
[4] See supra "Propositions," definition 4.
[5] For lucid analysis and illustration of the relationship between form and content, see Schein, *op. cit.* (supra 3 n. 1) 59, 76-77, 86, and Porter, *op. cit.* (supra 1 n. 1) 25, 38, 43, 49.

are related not only to aesthetic content and patterns of long and short syllables, but also to a third, and highly controversial element, Latin word accent. It is doubtful whether there is any area in the extensive field covered by the word φιλολογία which has received as comprehensive and exhaustive coverage as the subject of Latin word accent.[1] Moreover, there are few subjects which place the critic in such an uncomfortable position. He must state his opinions concerning a language for which there is no access to phonological reality,[2] as if he were a native speaker, in order to substantiate his theories. Yet, since he is not a native speaker, he is inevitably biased by the phonological reality of his own language.[3] Fully aware of this, I have assumed, on the basis of the vast amounts of linguistic evidence amassed by such philologists as Lindsay, Abbott, Sturtevant, Kent, Fraenkel, O'Neill, Knight, Meillet, and Palmer,[4] not to mention the host of lesser known scholars who

---

[1] "All statements pertinent to the reading or reciting of verse have in fact been subjected to the most exquisite of philological tortures and have so far failed to give clear and distinct answers," as K. M. Abbott has said, "Ictus, Accent, and Statistics in Latin Dramatic Verse," *TAPA* 75, 1944, 130. For an analysis of the problem in understanding the seeming contradictory evidence and terminology of the Roman grammarians, see the same author, "The Grammarians and the Latin Accent," *Classical Studies in Honor of William A. Oldfather* (Urbana 1943) 13-19. (*The Grammarians*). It is interesting to note that the subject of Latin accent was one of the preoccupations of Thomas Jefferson, before he became President. See L. Lehman, *Quantitative Implications of the Pyrrhic Stress*, University of Virginia Dissertation, 1924, 15-19.

[2] This is a phrase of Professor Porter's from one of his lectures. For a recent review of the controversy over the recitation of Latin poetry, see D. Norberg, "La Recitation du vers latin," *NPhM* 66, 1965, 496-508; bibliography 496, n. 1.

[3] A comment of N. E. Collinge is apt: ". . . lack of phonetic training causes inexact apprehension of sound," in "Phonetic Information in Dead Languages," *Proc. Fifth Internatl. Congr. Phonetic Sciences*, 1964, 235.

[4] The following is a chronological list of the major works of the above mentioned scholars related to the problem of the Latin accent.
W. M. Lindsay, *The Latin Language* (Oxford 1894) (*L.L.*).
——, *Early Latin Verse* (Oxford 1922) (*ELV*).
E. H. Sturtevant, "Notes on the Character of Greek and Latin Accent,"
  TAPA 42, 1911, 45-52.
——, "The Character of the Latin Accent," *TAPA* 52, 1921, 5-15.
——, "Syllabification and Syllabic Quantity in Greek and Latin," *TAPA*
  53, 1922, 35-51.
——, "The Ictus of Classical Verse," *AJP* 44, 1923, 319-338.
——, "Harmony and Clash of Accent and Ictus in the Latin Hexameter,"
  TAPA 54, 1923, 51-73.

have studied and had opinions on the subject, that Latin was a language where syllabic accent was indicated by intensity of emphasis. This was not necessarily louder or higher, but the same type of stress noticeable in English when a speaker in a normal tone of voice differentiates between the syllables of a word like "intention." Having taken this stand I have tried to avoid controversy in the realm of linguistics. For although I admire the linguist's ability to abstract the utter abstraction to the point where he not only hesitates in defining the term "syllable," but even doubts its phonetic existence,[1] it seems to me that it is simpler to use the

——, "The Doctrine of Caesura, A Philological Ghost," *AJP* 45, 1924, 329-350.
——, "Accent and Ictus in the Latin Elegiac Distich," *TAPA* 55, 1924, 73-89.
——, *The Pronunciation of Latin and Greek: the sounds and accents* (Philadelphia 1940[2]).
R. Kent, "The Alleged Conflict of Accents in Latin Verse," *TAPA* 51, 1920, 19-29.
——, "The Educated Roman and His Accent", *TAPA* 53, 1922, 63-72.
F. F. Abbott, "The Accent in Vulgar and Formal Latin," *CP* 2, 1907, 444-460.
E. Fraenkel, *Iktus und Akzent im lateinischen Sprechvers* (Berlin 1928).
E. O'Neill, *op. cit.* (supra 5 n. 1).
W. F. J. Knight, *Accentual Symmetry in Vergil* (Oxford 1950[2]).
A. Meillet, *Les Origines indo-européennes des mètres grecs* (Paris 1923) (*Les Origines*).
——, "La Place de l'accent latin," *MSL* 20, 1918, 165-171.
——, *Esquisse d'une histoire de la langue latine* (Paris 1966[7]).
Palmer, *LL* (supra 4 n. 3).
In addition to these there is a good bibliography on ictus and accent in P. W. Harsh, "Early Latin Meter and Prosody," *Lustrum* 3, 1958, 226-233. There is also a very good bibliography in Abbott, *The Grammarians* (supra 7 n. 1) 1. He refers to the important French article by L. Laurand, "L'Accent grec et latin, remarques et bibliographie choisie," *RevPhil* s. 3 12, 1938, 133-148.
[1] Lotz *op. cit.* (supra 2 n. 3) 128. "We have not talked of syllable, usually supposed to be the pillar of metre. Whether what is meant by syllable be a functional combinatory unit (as recently proposed) or a phonic sound unit limited by two lessenings of force, or two minimums of sonotory or of the air current, the term can hardly be operated with, not in linguistics either. Where, on the other hand, only a maximum is meant with an actual function in the phonic structure of linguistic elements, the ends of expression are fully served by the term 'sonant' as defined above. (Obscure definition on page 127.) Neither can it be proved that, in verse systems where stress is also relevant, the distribution of force should coincide with syllabic division. Also where, besides sonants, even consonants have a metric function, as in classical Greek verse and its imitations, Latin and Hungarian, it is not syllable, but a phonic unit reaching from sonant to sonant—i.e., the connection of a sonant with the following series of consonants—that makes the relevant unit of metre, which does not in any way coincide with syllable.

word "syllable" in reference to Greek and Latin metrics, rather than confuse the reader with three or four terms which may be phonologically more accurate, but are too cumbersome to handle easily in discussion. Once a text exists of a known language, even if we cannot know how the native spoke it, there are sufficient formal elements available for valid, objective appraisal, such as word-group patterns, length of words, number of words, word order within the metrical frame, and less objectively, the meaning of the text. When these formal elements are studied in juxtaposition with the awareness that Latin words require some kind of accent of intensity, one can point out where metrical ictus and word accent coincide, and where they do not. It is not necessary to make a value judgment. If the statistical count is high enough, it makes its own point. Controversely, if not high, the point is also clear. An error of some metricians up to the present has been that they have taken *a priori* a point of view without being content to look at the texts for what the texts themselves would reveal.

This objective approach, that is discovering from examination, rather than examining to discover, I have tried to follow in looking at the lines of Catullus' *polymetra*, a term I use to include all his meters except the dactylic hexameter and pentameter.[1] Together with his practice, that of the three Latin poets attempting the same meters who preceded him, Laevius, Matius, and Varro,[2] and that of his close inner group,[3] Bibaculus, Calvus, Cinna,

---

E.g.:

arm-av-ir-umqu-ec-an-otr-oi-aequ-ipr-im-us-ab-or-is

It follows that 'syllable' in metrics is entirely irrelevant." A more recent highly learned discussion of the same problem which manages to produce a definition of "syllable" is that by E. Hangen, "The Syllable in Linguistic Description," *For Roman Jakobson* (The Hague 1956) 213-221. His definition, after discussing some basic problems (215-216) is: "the smallest unit of recurrent phonemic sequences." (216).

[1] Some aspects of Catullus' handling of hexameter and pentameter, mostly with respect to observance of caesura and coincidence of ictus and accent, have been given a cursory treatment. See Sturtevant, "Accent and Ictus in the Latin Elegiac Distich" (supra 7-8 n. 4); D. A. West, "The Metre of Catullus' Elegiacs," *CQ* 51, 1957, 98-102; M. Zicàri, "Some Metrical and Prosodical Features of Catullus' Poetry," *Phoenix* 18, 1964, 193-205; G. Siefert, Jr., "Meter and Case in the Latin Elegiac Pentameter," University of Pennsylvania Dissertation, *Language* suppl. 49, 1952, 58-70; J. Hellegouarc'h, *Le Monosyllabe dans l'hexamètre latin* (Paris 1964).

[2] For dates and biographical information, see infra 40 n. 1.

[3] A great deal has been written about the Catullan circle, most of it speculation. The subject seems particularly attractive to the Italian scholars.

Cornificius, and Ticidas, has been examined. Inevitably the results
are not always the same for each meter. Some meters reveal more
conscious patterning than others, and in the case of the sapphic
hendecasyllable, as there are no extant Latin or Alexandrian
predecessors, the treatment is somewhat different. The basic
starting point of inquiry, however, is the same for every meter:
how did these Latin poets use the established patterns of Greek
colometry, particularly with reference to the positions of word-
shapes within the colon.

This entails first of all a brief discussion of the normative Greek
patterns for each meter. Then the Latin patterns of Catullus and
those of his predecessors and contemporaries are examined. The
critic must always keep in mind that the patterns which seem to
emerge from such fragmentary evidence as that afforded by his
predecessors and contemporaries, are only indicative of a trend,
and cannot be used as conclusive statistical evidence. Furthermore,
since words are not purely abstract explosions of breath, but carry
meaning, vocabulary similarities are interrelated with metrical
similarities in the comparison of poet with poet. This vocabulary
comparison has often led to the well-trodden path of discussing
literary influence, borrowed ideas, and conscious imitations of
subject matter, such as: since Mimnermus wrote of love and death
in elegiacs and had his Nanno, Catullus, who wrote of love and
death in elegiacs and had his Lesbia, must have imitated or been
influenced by Mimnermus. This kind of criticism, especially preva-
lent among French and Italian scholars [1] has little value, since it
does nothing to enhance one's understanding of either poet's
individual art in the blend of form and meaning. It has been avoided

---

Relevant books or articles which I have been able to locate are: L. Alfonsi,
Poetae Novi (Como 1945); A. Gandiglio, *Cantores Euphorionis* (Bologne
1904); A. Rostagni, "Partenio di Nicea, Elvio Cinna, e poetae novi," *AttiTor*
68, 1932-33, 497-545; *Storia della letteratura latina* I (Torino 1949) 337-351,
354-355; A. Traglia, *Poetae Novi* (Rome 1962) 1-24. The best source for
information concerning ancient testimony is in C. Neudling, "A Prosopography to Catullus," *IowaSCP* 12 (Oxford 1951). Basic bibliographical
information is also obtainable in Schanz-Hosius, *Geschichte der Römische
Literatur* I (Munich 1927[4]) 308-311 (*Geschichte* I). For Ticidas, who is not
included in Neudling because Catullus does not mention him by name,
see *RE* 6A[1], 844-846.

[1] M. Coulon, *La Poésie priapique dans l'antiquité et au Moyen Âge* (Paris
1932) is a good example of this, as well as the French and Italian authors
mentioned supra 6 n. 1.

in this book except where similarity in metrical usage highlighted a similarity of subject. Thus semantic and syntactic parallels have been indicated where they occur with a minimal attempt to explain the reasons. The main point of study has been to show that the Greek colometric patterns were absorbed by the Latin poets, yet the division of these cola into separate words was often different.[1] No one can know exactly what role, if any, Latin word accent played in this. Possibly because of word accent, there is a certain order of words with respect to the number of syllables in the word, which satisfies the aesthetic criteria of a poet. These criteria are admittedly subjective on his part, but nevertheless include an awareness of the rhythmical cadence of words, an awareness which he possesses to a greater extent than the non-poet. The poet's word-order will depend on several "physic factors" [2] such as the point he wishes to emphasize, his sensitivity to the relevancy of word-accent, as well as the choice of meter. Yet, in spite of the fact that these aspects of choice are subjective and to a degree even unconscious on the part of the poet, by studying a sufficient amount of his text, one can begin to detect which patterns the poet prefers and sometimes hypothesize.[3] The role of word accent is illustrative of this point. It often seems to function more in some meters than in others, such as the generally accepted tendency for coincidence of word accent and metrical ictus in the *D D D C open* second colon of the hexameter line, or the strong tendency to accent the second long syllable (position 4) in iambic trimeters, or the changes in accent pattern in the galliambics. Even in poems of the same

---

[1] Hellegouarc'h, *op. cit.* (supra 9 n. 1) 299 makes this observation: "Elle (cette étude) nous a permis en effet de constater, notamment à propos de l'emploi des prépositions, que les poètes latins donnent à l'ordre des mots dans le vers une importance primordiale. C'est pour avoir méconnu ce fait que certains ont voulu ignorer l'existence de la césure ou la considérer comme indépendante du sens de la phrase, alors qu'une lecture attentive des textes nous enseigne que c'est justement la répartition des mots par groupes sémantiquement associés dans le cadre des césures fondamentales qui explique toute la construction des vers latins."

[2] Lotz, *op. cit.* (supra 2 n. 3) 146.

[3] Cf. J. Marouzeau, *L'Ordre des mots dans la phrase latine* III: *Les Articulations de l'énoncé* (Paris 1949) 178-189, 196-197. He discusses primarily Vergilian, Lucretian, and Ovidian techniques with regard to placing words syntactically related in symmetrical apposition within the same line, and avoidance of, or effort to obtain, enjambement. Significantly, he does not mention Catullus; for this type of conscious grouping, though it does exist, is much less noticeable in his phrasing which is closer to Greek in its epexegetical organization.

meter, the function of word accent is not the same. Therefore, its role cannot be abstracted from the text and turned into a general law. Tendencies can be discovered; norms observed; and coincidence of ictus and accent tabulated. But the results of these objective phenomena must inevitably depend on the bias of the critic.

In the case of this study, where I have felt that metrical ictus and word accent had a function, such as in sapphic hendecasyllable or iambic trimeter, I have so stated, always aware that this is an opinion based upon my own understanding (derived from study of Catullus and many articles on the subject) [1] of what Latin stress accent is. However, in general I have tried not to emphasize ideas about ictus and accent since Latin as Catullus spoke it is a language for which there is no access to phonological reality.[2] But the most important contribution of this study is not primarily the "why," which can have various interpretations, phonic, linguic, psychic, as well as metric,[3] but the "fact," of word localization in Catullus' *polymetra* as an important part of the formal organization of his poetry; and to show that this localization is a function, not of the laws of the metrically permissible, the metrical avoidance, or the metrical violation, but of the colometric patterns as established in the Greek norms [4] as far as the syntactic requirements of Latin, such as the preferred final position for the verb,[5] permit. It is my own opinion that the chief value of amassing such statistics lies in achieving greater awareness of the inextricable intertwining of content, both aesthetic and thematic, and form, which incorporates both syllabic patterns of longs and shorts, and word patterns. To emphasize the one at the expense of the other is to ignore the poet.

---

[1] In addition to those listed supra 7-8 n. 4, see R. C. Tanner, "The Arval Hymn and Early Latin Verse," *CQ* 55, ns. 11, 1961, 209-212; E. Pulgram, "Accent and Ictus in Spoken and Written Latin," *ZVS* 71, 1953, 218-237; W. Beare, "The Meaning of Ictus as Applied to Latin Verse," *Hermathena* 81, 1953, 29-40, and "The Origin of Rhythmic Latin Verse," *Hermathena* 87, 1956, 3-20 (*Origin*); J. Enk, "The Latin Accent," *Mnemosyne* s. 4 6, 1953, 93-109; H. Drexler, "Quantität und Wortakzent," *Maia* 12, 1960, 167-189; E. Vandvik, "Rhythmus und Metrum, Akzent und Iktus," *Symb-Oslo* Supplbnd. 8, 1937; E. D. Kollman, "Remarks on the structure of the Latin Hexameter," *Glotta* 46, 1968, 293-316.

[2] See supra 7 n. 2.

[3] Lotz' terminology *op. cit.* (supra 2 n. 3) 120-125, 146.

[4] See Lotz, *ibid.*, 126 and Porter, *loc. cit.* (supra 2 n. 2).

[5] See Marouzeau, *op. cit.* (supra 11 n. 3) 137-175, 190-196.

In conclusion, a word should be said about the order of the chapters. In most books on Greek and Latin meter, the chapters begin with the simple iambo-trochaic systems and proceed to the complex combinations of systems requiring different types of arses in irregular alternation.[1] I have chosen, on the contrary, to begin with the complex, for two reasons. The first of these is that the system "c" meters [2] far outweigh the other two types in the *polymetra* of Catullus. The second is that his role in the transmission of these group "c" meters (most frequently given the name Aeolic or logaoedic) has not been given its due importance. His treatment of the sapphic hendecasyllable is discussed first because this meter had the most interesting development of any meter in the history of Latin literature, excepting the dactylic hexameter and pentameter. Two meters, the septenarius and asclepiadean major, have been relegated to the appendix since only one poem in each of these meters exists, 17 and 30. The number of lines, twenty-six and twelve respectively, is too small to provide statistical significance.

PROSODIC FEATURES

Because of the difficulty in being objective about distinguishing between individual words and word groups,[3] all words have been tabulated as separate entities, including monosyllabic prepositions, and thus generally part of the following word-group, or conjunctions. Enclitics -*que* and -*ne* have been considered part of the word to which they are attached. As for cases of elision,[4] a subject open to the greatest controversy, word-end is counted after the vowel or consonant(s) preceding the elided syllable, as: *Lesbi*(a) *atqu*(e) *amemus* forming the word-syllable pattern 2 1 3.

---

[1] See definition 10 page 3.

[2] *Ibid.*

[3] For the problems involved in distinguishing sense pauses, and different points of view between editors and metricians, see Porter, *op. cit.* (supra 1 n. 1) 22. A metrician is "prone to impose his feeling for the metrical structure on the normal phrasing of the line," while the conventions of punctuation" vary with different editors and do not always represent a "true phrase or clause division." On the other hand, Vandvik, *op. cit.* (supra 17 n. 1) 54-161, feels very strongly about the existence of word-groups and identifiable sense-pauses which, clearly to him, relate to "Gruppenakzente" and "Satzakzent" (73, 107). See also infra 25 n. 2, 28 n. 2, 30 n. 3 and 4.

[4] See discussion infra 31 n. 3, 109 n. 2. I have followed the method explained by Zinn (infra 17-18 n. 2) 38-39.

SAPPHIC HENDECASYLLABLE

$$\left.\begin{array}{ccccc|c|cccccc}
1 & 2 & 3 & 4 & 5 & 6 & 7 & 8 & 9 & 10 & 11 \\
\_ & \cup & \_ & \times & \_ & \cup & \cup & \_ & \cup & \_ & \times
\end{array}\right\| 3$$

$$\_\;\cup\;\cup\;\_\;\times \;\Big|\; 1$$

The sapphic hendecasyllable [1] is one of the more familiar of the so-called "logaoedic" or "Aeolic" meters or, to put it in general terminology, those meters which employ two or more different kinds of arses not in regular alternation. In its normative form it can be described as a *B C closed* colon followed by a *D B C open*. The first of these cola is the standard initial trochaic colon found frequently in Pindar's dactylo-epitrites as well as in trochaic tetrameters. The second occurs only in the sapphic hendecasyllable as a colometric unit. A sapphic stanza consists of three such lines followed by a colon of five syllables, the *D C falling*, or adonic tag,[2] which is one of the commonest colometric closes to the hexameter line as well as a generally favored ending for a sequence of metrical cola.[3] Although the adonic tag is written as a separate fourth line, it is often syntactically and metrically inseparable from the preceding *D B C open* colon, through synapheia or hypermeter.[4] The stanza could well be written as one of three lines, two short and equal, and a third, five syllables longer than the preceding two. From the time of Horace on, however, the adonic became more and more a self-contained semantic unit, so that the tragedian Seneca, and later Boethius, could omit it altogether,

---

[1] The name comes from Hephaistion, *Ench.* 14.1 (Consbr. 43).

[2] This name is apparently derived from three Greek words frequently used to fill the colon, according to the earliest allusion to the name in Sacerdos. "De adonio dimetro sapphico dactylico. Adonium dimetrum dactylicum catalecticum a Sappho inventum, unde etiam sapphicum nuncupatur, monoschematistum *est*: semper enim dactylo et spondeo percutitur, ὦ τὸν ᾿Αδωνιν." Keil, *Gr. Lat.* 6. 516.

[3] Porter, *op. cit.* (supra 1 n. 1) 13, n. 27.

[4] Synapheia is the term used to signify the fastening together of two lines of verse into one by avoiding a metrical pause between them, such as hiatus, final anceps, or word-end. Hypermeter is the practice of eliding the final syllable of one line of verse into the first syllable of the next line.

and medieval writers could use it as a separate meter.[1] In Greek treatment the normal colometric structure of the eleven-syllable line is frequently varied by having a break after 4, or more commonly after 6, a practice much more rare in the Latin adaptations of the meter for reasons which will be discussed later. Still, the foregoing description of the sapphic stanza has the advantage, in addition to that of simplicity and ability to incorporate all examples, of rendering attempts of both ancient [2] and modern [3] metricians to apply to the meter the traditional notion of "the foot" unnecessary. Furthermore, the traditional "foot" and "metron" terminology are particularly unsuitable in isosyllabic meters where $-\neq \cup \cup$.[4] The analysis in terms of arses thus obviates the three common conflicting theories, the choriambic nucleus theory,[5] the basically trochaic theory,[6] and the brilliantly complex cretic-and-anceps theory of A. M. Dale and D. Page, derived from P. Maas.[7]

---

[1] Such as the Irish Columban c. 600 A.D., F. J. E. Raby, *A History of Christian Latin Poetry* (Oxford 1953) 139, or the Norman Dudo born c. 970 A.D., F. J. E. Raby, *A History of Secular Latin Poetry in the Middle Ages* (Oxford 1934) 358. (From now on the two books will be abbreviated respectively as *CLP* and *SLP*.)

[2] For the four major ancient theories, choriambic, ionic, hemistiche, and dactylo-trochaic and their exponents, see A. Kolář, "De Romanorum metris Aeoliis, praecipue Horatianis," *LF* 62, 1935, 439.

[3] For a general survey of modern theories and theorists, see M. Lenchantin de Gubernatis, "I Metri eolici della lirica latina," *Athenaeum* 12, 1934, 239-243, and Kolář, *op. cit.*, 430-438. In addition, there is the important work of A. Meillet, *Les Origines*. In a brief article written two years earlier he makes an important point: "Les désaccords entre les métriciens et leurs discussions vaines proviennent en grande partie de l'erreur initiale qui consiste à vouloir découper en pieds des vers rythmés d'une manière trop souple pour se prêter à ces divisions." "Métrique éolienne et métrique védique," *BSL* 22, 1921, 17.

[4] This is most succinctly expressed by Meillet, *Les Origines*, 16-17, where he discusses the impossibility of the concept of "feet" in poetry in which a long and a short syllable are equal, such as in Vedic and Aeolian poetry.

[5] This is first expounded by Hephaistion 14 (Consbr. 43), followed in modern times by Wilamowitz, *GV* 104; Koster, *Traité* 241; L. Nougaret, *Traité de métrique latine classique* (Paris 1963) 98; D. S. Raven, *LM* 133; and supra n. 3.

[6] Diomedes first mentions this theory: see Kolář, *loc. cit.* (supra n. 2). Chief modern exponents are R. Westphal and P. Masqueray in Lenchantin de Gubernatis, *op. cit.* (supra n. 3) 241 n. 8; and F. Crusius, *Römische Metrik* (Munich 1959⁴) 106. O. Schröder is a dualist, holding to theory two for Latin, according to Lenchantin de Gubernatis, *ibid.* 242, on Schröder and others.

[7] A. M. Dale, "The Metrical Units III," *CQ* 45, n.s. 1, 1951, 119-129; D. Page, *Sappho and Alcaeus* (Oxford 1955) 318; Maas, *op. cit.* (supra 1 n. 4).

The sapphic hendecasyllable [1] first appeared, as far as literary evidence shows, on the island of Lesbos in the seventh century B.C. in the poetry of Sappho (whence its name) and Alkaios. It then suffered a literary eclipse of six centuries until revived by the Roman poet Catullus. It is strange that the Alexandrians, who as a rule tried their hands at so many meters, failed to leave behind any indication that they attempted the sapphic. Perhaps the Lesbian poets were too far outside the creative current of mainland lyric development. Whatever the reason, it appears that Catullus had no Latin or Alexandrian predecessors whose handling of the meter he could observe, and this may, to a large extent, be reflected in the so-called "lack of polish" of his sapphics of which critics who prefer the Horatian norm are wont to accuse him.[2] Horace, on the other hand, had Catullus' technique to study and absorb.[3] Furthermore, Catullus' great achievement is often said to lie in the area of his short hendecasyllabic and iambic poems,[4]

Th. G. Rosenmeyer, M. Ostwald, and J. W. Halporn, *The Metres of Greek and Latin Poetry* (London 1963) 29, hold to a combination of theory one and theory three. (Henceforth *MGLP*).

[1] Hephaistion also gives it the name ἐπιχοριαμβικόν (supra 14 n. 1).

[2] According to N. A. Bonavia-Hunt, Catullus' eleventh poem "exhibits a crude metrical structure, . . . (its) lines . . . are unmelodious and lack Horace's rhythmical polish and elegance," in *Horace the Minstrel, a Study of His Sapphic and Alcaic Lines* (London 1954) 9. In no case, however, do I mean to suggest that Horace's sapphics are better than those of Catullus. I have tried only to indicate the differences between the regularized Latin and the free Greek patterns.

[3] There has been endless discussion about how much Horace used Catullus, and what he meant in *Carm* 3.30 by "dicar . . . princeps Aeolium carmen ad Italos deduxisse modos." For various interpretations, see E. Sturtevant, "Horace and the Sapphic Stanza," *TAPA* 70, 1939, 295-296; C. W. Mendell, "Catullan Echoes in the Odes of Horace," *CP* 30, 1935, 295-297; J. Ferguson, "Catullus and Horace," *AJP* 77, 1956, 1-10; Bonavia-Hunt, *ibid.* (supra n. 2), who takes the interesting position of agreeing with Horace's claim in regard to the alcaic meter, but disagreeing with the claim for the sapphic. See also E. Fraenkel's comments on the passage in *Horace* (Oxford 1963²) 304-306, and S. Commager, *The Odes of Horace* (New Haven 1966³) 158 n. 81.

[4] Bonavia-Hunt, *ibid.* (supra n. 1): "It is in his use of the Greek iambic and phalecian metres that Catullus distinguished himself as a lyric poet . . ." See also K. Quinn's more detailed discussion of Catullus' genius with regard to style and construction for the shorter poems in "Docte Catulle," *Critical Essays on Roman Literature, Elegy and Lyric*, ed. J. P. Sullivan (Harvard University 1962) 32-41 (henceforth *Docte Catulle*). Unfortunately, he does not discuss Catullus' metrical technique which would strengthen his points even more. There is also H. A. J. Munro's statement: ". . . Catullus seems to have decided that the Sapphic was not suited to the genius of the Latin language, or at all events not to his own genius, and to have abandoned

for which he had both Alexandrian and earlier Latin models, and thus more background material with which to experiment. The only other example of the sapphic hendecasyllable which has survived in Greek is by an otherwise unknown Melinno, who wrote an encomium of Rome in five stanzas at the end of the first century B.C. or beginning of the first century A.D.[1]

The fact that Catullus had only seventh century predecessors in the sapphic hendecasyllable necessitates a slightly different treatment of this meter from that of Catullus' other meters discussed in this paper. Since there can be no comparison with earlier Latin poets, Catullus' position as an intermediary in the transfer of the sapphic from Greek into Latin is most significant. His role in this respect is seldom mentioned, while that of Horace is emphasized, principally, no doubt, because Catullus wrote only thirty lines in the meter as against Horace's 615. It is a moot point whether one can produce significant statistics from as small a sample as thirty lines. It is important to keep in mind, however, the innate difficulty of transcribing the Aeolic meters which were relatively free from regularization of ancipitia and word-end, into the poetry of a language which sought for regularization and was highly accentual. The struggle to develop a formalized structure for the Aeolic rhythms from the linguistic and phonemic material of Latin was Horace's task, and its achievement his chief contribution.[2] The

---

it altogether in favor of the phalaecian hendecasyllable which he made his own once and forever." *Criticisms and Elucidations of Catullus* (Cambridge 1878) 241.

[1] Preserved in Stobaeus *Flor.* 7.12 ed. O. Hense (Berlin 1894) 312. For the date, assumed from subject matter and metrical technique, see F. Welcker, *Kleine Schriften* (Bonn 1845) 160-168. Additional reasons for the date are given by H. Usener, *Beiläufige Bemerkungen, Kleine Schriften 3* (Stuttgart 1965²) 175. See also R. Heinze, *Die Lyrischen Verse des Horaz* (reprint Amsterdam 1959) 65.

[2] A complete bibliography on the various scholarly interpretations of Horace's contribution to the sapphic hendecasyllable is impossible here. A thorough list of modern authors who have something to say on the subject can be found in K. Numberger, *Inhalt und Metrum in der Lyrik des Horaz* (Inaugural Dissertation University of Munich, Faculty of Philosophy 1959) ix-xii. Additional articles not mentioned by him but which pertain to Horace and the Sapphic meter are J. C. Greenough, "Accentual Rhythm in Latin," *HSCP* 4, 1893, 105-115; D. Prakken, "Feminine Caesuras in Horatian Sapphic Stanzas," *CP* 49, 1954, 102-103; O. Seel & E. Pöhlman, "Quantität und Wortakzent im horazischen Sapphiker," *Philologus* 103, 1959, 237-280; E. A. Sonnenschein, "The Latin Sapphic," *CR* 17, 1903, 252-256; Sturtevant *op. cit.* (supra 16 n. 3); A. W. Verrall, "The Latin

patterns he fixed were religiously copied in the centuries after him by Seneca, Statius, Ausonius, Boethius, Prudentius, Ambrose, Paulus Diaconus, and other medieval poets and hymn writers.[1]

The chief concern in transcribing the sapphic hendecasyllable into Latin seems to have been to establish a permanent caesura, and to determine whether there was a definite metrical stress in the Greek which should be imitated.[2] Because of the trochaic nature of the initial *B C closed* colon, if the regular break after 5 was observed, correspondence of ictus and accent of word accent with the long syllables, would be easy to achieve.[3] In this respect, the fact that a monosyllable at 5 occurs only once in Catullus, 51.2, is significant. But unless the first word of the *D B C open* colon were

---

Sapphic," *CR* 17, 1903, 339-343; L. P. Wilkinson, "Accentual Rhythm in Horatian Sapphics," *CR* 54, 1940, 131-133; also Bonavia-Hunt, *op. cit.* (supra 16 n. 2) 16-24. Of particular importance are the tables and statistics given by L. J. Richardson, "On Certain Sound Properties of the Sapphic Strophe as Employed by Horace," *TAPA* 33, 1902, 38-44. The title is a bit misleading but the statistics are to the point and thorough. Special emphasis should be placed on E. Zinn's dissertation, mentioned by Numberger (supra) xii, *Der Wortakzent in den Lyrischen Versen des Horaz*: Abhandlung I (Maximilians University of Munich 1940). (Henceforth Zinn I).

[1] For reference to other hymn writers, see Greenough *op. cit.* (supra 17 n. 3) 109; L. P. Wilkinson, *GLA* 108; T. B. Rudmose-Brown, "Some Medieval Latin Metres, Their Ancestry and Progeny," *Hermathena* 53, 1939, 35 n. 1; Raby, *CLP* 129, 162, 188, 242, 329. For other poems after the fifth century in the sapphic meter, see *ibid.* 176, 301; Raby, *SLP* I, 149, 245, 302. For a brief history of the meter in general, and especially for modern language imitations, see G. H. Needler, *The Lone Shieling, Origin and Authorship of the Blackwood "Canadian Boat Song"* (Toronto 1941) 14-47. The various poems just referred to are only a sampling of the vast quantity written in the sapphic meter during the Middle Ages (see indices in *PLAC*, infra 34 n. 2, 68 n. 7). I am a little puzzled that Philip August Becker, the famous medieval metrician, could write: "Die sapphische strophe nicht ununterbrochen fortlebte; sie machte eine richtige Eklipse durch, und es ist nicht einmal sicher ob der schwache Versuch bei Venantius Fortunatus sie in die karolingische Zeit hinüberrettete, oder ob sie nicht durch Paulus Diaconus von Montecassino kam." See his article, "Die Anfänge der romanischen Verskunst," *ZFS* 56, 1932, 269.

[2] See list of authors supra 15 n. 3, 16 n. 2 and , 17 n. 2.

[3] "Ictus and accent fall into unison in Latin Trochaics with no perceptible effort," in Lindsay, *ELV* 283. "By accent Latin is still more trochaic than by quantity," in W. B. Sedgwick, "The Trochaic Tetrameter and the Versus Popularis in Latin," *G&R* 1, 1931-1933, 98. "It has long been recognized that in popular usage the quantitative octonarius catalectic—the *versus quadratus* or trochaic septenarius—shows an extremely close coincidence between its ictus and the penultimate word accent," in Tanner, *op. cit.* (supra 12 n. 1) 212.

a quadrisyllable, conflict of ictus and accent at 6 occurred. This presented no problem in Greek where word accent played little, if any, role; and although word-breaks tended to fall at certain places in the line more than others, these preferred word-ends were in origin related to the meaning of a phrase or line, rather than the accent of individual words. The interesting fact about fixing the break in the Latin sapphic after 5 is that it did not preserve trochaic correspondence of word accent on the theses, but actually forced two arses to bear the word accent, 4, since cretic words were not used in the 3-5 position, and 6, which is the first half of the D arsis. The first of these in the Greek sapphic was an anceps, but regularly from the time of Horace on it was long. In spite of the fact that there existed a general tendency for an anceps to become long,[1] these ancipitia did not normally receive a word accent which then later became a metrical one. Such was the result in the sapphic, however, of making the break after 5 the rule. Moreover, this regularized break after 5, coupled with the inhibition of a cretic word at 3-5, seems the chief reason behind the 4 anceps becoming permanently long, in Latin:[2] 4 consistently received the word-accent. And as the following tables will show, by the time of the Middle Ages this word accent was felt as a metrical accent regardless of whether it had been in the time of Catullus and Horace, or not. Significantly, the three cases of a short 4 in Catullus occur either in lines where the break is after 6, 11.13, 15, or where there is no mid-line break at all, as in 11.6. In other words, Catullus never permits a word accent to fall on a short 4, or in terms of word-localization, an iamb to fill the 4-5 space, which can be found in Sappho and Alkaios. The accenting of 6, a short syllable and half of an arsis was even more unusual, but this became the pattern. Catullus, as will be shown, was a middleman in the

---

[1] Note the anceps at 5 in iambic trimeter and choliambics, or final syllable of the hexameter. All of these, however, occur at colometric ends. (See infra 87, 160 n. 3.)

[2] Some scholars avoid making an issue of the reasons for the fourth syllable becoming permanently long by saying that it was just a regularization of an existing tendency. Cf. Heinze, *op. cit.* (supra 17 n. 1) 71, who also suggests it was to avoid a strong trochaic beginning: see also Wilkinson, *GLA* 107, Ferguson, *op. cit.* (supra 16 n. 3) 7, where he also suggests that it added "weight which is characteristic of Latin rather than Greek." Verrall, *op. cit.* (supra 17 n. 2) 340, relates it to musical terms, though I am afraid only he knows what he means by talking of a change from the 3 time of Greek rhythm to the 2 time of Latin.

process of metrical systematization, being oriented toward the freedom of the Greek, while Horace disciplined the form into Roman rigidity. The final result of Horatian regularization was a line with a fixed break after 5 and four stress accents, three of which were the rule, 1, 4, and 10, and the fourth generally on 6, but sometimes on 8; occasionally there were three accents in the second colon, on both 6 and 8,[1] as well as 10. Of all these accents, only 1 and 10 are theses in the Greek description of the meter; but that 4 and 6 were felt to have dominant stress accents in the line the many examples of medieval "stress sapphics,"[2] as distinct from quantitative sapphics, clearly reveal. The poets in modern languages and even those who have written Latin sapphics in modern times, who, in imitating the meter, have failed to observe these accent patterns,[3] have written metrically incorrect stanzas.[4]

The purpose of the tables which follow is to show Catullus' position in the long history of the sapphic hendecasyllable with regard not only to metrical ictus, but also to that feature particularly significant in the Latin language, word-group patterns. Six poets are cited to illustrate the gamut of metrical development from complete freedom to complete regularization: Sappho, Alkaios, Catullus, Melinno, Horace, and Paulus Diaconus. Thirty lines have been chosen from Sappho and Alkaios, since that is the total number of Catullus' sapphics, although there are considerably more

---

[1] Rudmose-Brown, *op. cit.* (supra 18 n. 1) 36, has explained the phenomena in more general terms by saying that every line accents 4 and 10, and the median is either 6 or 8. He does not mention the nearly universal accent at 1.

[2] For examples of stress sapphics, see Crusius, *op. cit.* (supra 15 n. 6) 132; Rudmose-Brown, *loc. cit.* (supra n. 1); Greenough, *loc. cit.* (supra 17 n. 2); Raby, *CLP* 329, *SLP* 302.

[3] A good example of this is my own Latin *Alma Mater*, written by W. T. Weathers, where the first line of stanzas one and three begin with two disyllables, likewise stanza one, line 3, thus producing an accented 3, which practically never occurs in the verse of Horace, Catullus, or subsequent poets. See *Randolph-Macon College Songs* no. 1. The music is even more at fault in stressing 1, 3, 5, 8 and 10 throughout, for the composer, Frank A. Taber, assumes that musical stress must coincide with the long syllables of the metrical pattern. ". . . a stressed syllable where there is a long struck by the ictus in the Latin metre . . . gives an entirely different accentual rhythm, and in no way reproduces the effect of the Latin metre," as Rudmose-Brown says *op. cit.* (supra 18 n. 1) 57.

[4] Rudmose-Brown gives some examples of French and Italian Sapphics which are faulty in this respect *ibid.* 56-57.

than thirty lines of sapphics from both poets, especially from Sappho.[1] However, the text of Alkaios' poems in the sapphic strophe presents many difficulties, notably with line-ends, as to correct readings, so that it is difficult to find even thirty lines which have not been restored in some degree. Nevertheless, it must be borne in mind that the statistics thus resulting from only a portion of a work cannot be absolute; they will reveal only a relative trend. The statistics for Horace have been compiled from those of Prakken, Richardson, Seel & Pöhlman, and Zinn (supra 17 n. 2) based on a total of 615 lines. There are only five stanzas by Melinno, too few to be absolute, but at least revealing. All thirteen stanzas of the eighth century poem traditionally credited to Diaconus are included.[2] This poem has been chosen as an example of the extreme degree of stylization and uniformity possible in quantitative Latin sapphics. A similar regularity exists also in Seneca,[3] Statius,[4] Ausonius,[5] and Boethius.[6]

The following table shows predominant accent patterns in the three Latin authors.

---

[1] *PLF*: Sappho A. 1.1-24; 31.1-15; Alkaios 34.1-12; 42.9-12; 45.1-8; 69.1-8; 308.1-4; 362.1-4. For emendations and supplements in the fragments of Alkaios respectively, see *PLF* 265, 278, 286, 226, 253, 311.

[2] The text for this poem is most readily available in *The Oxford Book of Medieval Latin Poetry*, ed. F. J. E. Raby (Oxford 1959) no. 66, 87-89. However, I have used a different final stanza, that of S. A. Hurlbut, *A Series of Mediaeval Latin Hymns*, St. Alban's Press (Washington 1936) Part V 8, because of the uncertainty concerning the text. See *PLAC* 1, 83-84, which gives fourteen stanzas by including both versions. However, the last stanza is different from that in *The Oxford Book*. Actually, the authorship is uncertain, but not the eighth century date. The poem is famous, not because of its rigid adherence to the Horatian norm, but because Guido of Arezzo (c. 990-1050) is said to have taken the names for the notes of the scale from syllable 1 and 6 of the first three lines of stanza one. See Needler, *op. cit.* (supra 18 n. 1) 12, and H. R. Bitterman, "The Organ in the Early Middle Ages," *Speculum* 4, 1929, 397-398 n. 1. Regardless of the credibility, the story points out the importance of the stress accent on 1 and 6.

[3] See Raven, *LM*, 144-145 and 179 for list of Seneca's sapphics.

[4] *Silv.* 4.7.

[5] 2.1, 5.7 and 8. Ausonius has one line in the last stanza of 2.1 which alludes directly to Sappho and Lesbos, with a break after 6 instead of 5:
Lesbiae depelle modum quietis (2.1.23).

[6] Boethius wrote some stichic sapphics, 2.6 and 4.7; one adonic, 4.7.35; and some sapphics alternating with other meters, 2.3, 3.10. This last is particularly interesting because it is a mixture of two types of hendecasyllable, the sapphic and the phalaecean. (See infra 48-49 for discussion.)

	CATULLUS	HORACE [1]	DIACONUS
1 4 6 10	22%	32%	54%
1 4 8 10	22%	17%	13% [2]
1 5 7 10	17%	4%	
1 5 8 10	7%	2%	

These patterns are for the whole lines, but even when the pattern for the whole line is not regular, the accenting of the arsis at 4 is significant:

$$59\% \qquad 92\%\ ^{3} \qquad 100\%$$

Generally speaking a break after 5 automatically places the word-accent on 4, unless there is a cretic at 3-5 which never occurs in Latin or 5 is filled by a monosyllable and preceded by a word of two or more syllables, a phenomenon so rare in Latin that in 615 sapphics of Horace it is found only once, and this monosyllable is elided with the preceding word.[4] The figures just given also show the percentage of lines composed of the two normative cola, the *B C closed* and *D B C open*. The tendency for regularization can be seen immediately when these percentages are compared with those of the Greek poets: Sappho 46%, Alkaios 59%, Melinno 66-2/3%. The high degree of regularity in Melinno compared with Sappho is one of the reasons for dating her after Catullus. The remaining lines in Horace [5] all have a break after the sixth syllable. This is not true of Catullus or the Greek poets who employ breaks at other positions besides those after 5 and 6.

[1] Because of the length of time involved in scanning all of Horace's sapphic verses, I have based the statistics for accent patterns of lines with a break after 5 on Richardson's table *op. cit.* (supra 17 n. 2) 40, and those with a break after 6 on Zinn II 24-25 (infra 23 n. 3).

[2] The remaining 33% of Diaconus' lines begin with a monosyllable, with an accent pattern of either 2 4 6 10, or 2 4 8 10. This last occurs twice in the thirty lines of Catullus, and twenty-three times in Horace; 2 4 6 10 occurs thirty-two times in Horace. (See Richardson, *loc. cit.*, supra n. 1.).

[3] This figure is based on the statistics of Seel & Pöhlman, *op. cit.*, 275, and Prakken, *op. cit.* (supra 17 n. 2) 102. Cf. Richardson, *op. cit.* (supra 17 n. 2) 38.

[4] *Carm* 3.27.39. Zinn I, (supra 17 n. 2), 48, thinks that the normal 4 accent occurs anyway because of "Synaloephe." One cannot say, however, that in all cases of two continguous monosyllables, 4 and 5, that 4 will always receive the accent. Cf.*Carm* 1.12.23 *nec te*, 31 *quod si*; Diaconus 51: *supplices ac nos veniam precamur*. Of the three consecutive monosyllables in Catullus' 51.2, on the other hand, *fas* is in the strongly accented position as well as being the dominant word from the aspect of meaning. (See infra 25 for discussion of the accentuation of monosyllables.)

[5] 11% of the forty-five studied lines, 8% of the total corpus of Horatian sapphics (fifty-two lines according to Seel & Pöhlman, *op. cit.* supra 17 n. 2, 275).

After	SAPPHO	ALKAIOS	CATULLUS	MELINNO
3	3%		7%	7%
4	20%	20%	7%	7%

The two lines in Catullus with a break after 3 and the two lines with the break after 4 occur in poem 11, including the much-tortured eleventh line of that poem.[1] That Horace should regularly employ a break after either 5 or 6 does not require that Catullus be placed under the same obligation. His models are the Lesbian poets of the seventh century who show no such inclination for regularity or word breaks as does Horace. Aware of the normative colometric organization, they constantly play against it, creating a tension between syntactic and stanzaic structure. But since Latin lacks the colometric and epexegetical coherence of Greek, Catullus' sapphics being an attempt at a close imitation of the Greek, may seem cut up and patternless.[2] It was Horace who discovered a potential for a pattern in the sapphic which was a function of the accentual nature of the Latin language. This pattern consists of organizing the eleven syllables of the sapphic line into a specific number of words, ideally four, and seldom more than six.[3]

---

[1] Some scholars would prefer to emend lines with these unusual breaks. See Fordyce, 127; F. A. Todd, "Catullus 11," *CR* 55, 1941, 70, who bases his reasons on a rather categorical statement that the Latin sapphic "always has a caesura" (71). By caesura he means a break only after 5 or 6, and in order to make this possible, cites examples of where a break between compound words equals a caesura. He also gives a summary of earlier attempts to emend the line as does Hudson-Williams, "Catullus 11, 9-12," *CQ* 46, 1952, 186. The most thorough discussion, evincing as much logic as any of the others, and showing that the problem of emendation is, to a great extent, a subjective matter, is by G. Giri, *De Locis qui sunt aut habentur corrupti in Catulli Carminibus* (Augustae Taurinorum 1894) 85-89. Also reasonable is J. Garcia's explanation that Catullus was imitating Greek practice, cf. "La Cesura en el verso 11 del carmen 11 di Catullo," *Emerita* 9, 1941, 160-162.

[2] Compare not only the close approximation of thought in Catullus' translation of Sappho 31.1 in poem 51.1, but also the almost identical word patterns:

Sappho	$-\cup$	$-$	$\times$	$-\cup$	$\cup-$	$\cup-\times$
Catullus	$-\cup$	$-$	$\times$	$-\cup$	$\cup-$	$\cup-\times$

A whole line composed of the same word-syllable pattern is not found in Horace at all, although the half-line, up to the break after 6, occurs once: 4.11.29.

[3] For every possible combination of word-syllable patterns in Horace, see E. Zinn II, *Die Lyrischen Verse des Horaz nach Wortgrenzen und Akzent geordnet, op. cit.* (supra 17-18 n. 2) 7-28 (henceforth Zinn II), for the eleven-syllable line, 29-32 for the adonic.

And it was this patterning of words that lead to the dominant 1 4 6 10 accents so prominent in all examples of the sapphic meter after the time of Horace.[1]

The following tables make clear the rigorous word-syllable schemes adopted by Horace and perfectly copied by Diaconus. The tables also show how little Catullus employs this type of schematization. In fact, there is barely any more evidence of interest in word patterning or localization in his lines than there is in those of Alkaios.

Typical Syllable Patterns for Four-Word Lines

				SAPPHO	ALKAIOS	CATULLUS	MELINNO	HORACE	DIACONUS
3	2	3	3			3%		7%[2]	26%
2	3	3	3	3%	10%[3]	3%	7%	6%	18%
3	2	4	2		3%	3%		8%	8%
2	3	2	4					2%	3%
2	3	4	2			3%		5%	3%
3	2	2	4					4%	
3	3	2	3			7%	7%	2%	

Percentage of Total Number of Lines of Four Words

				SAPPHO	ALKAIOS	CATULLUS	MELINNO	HORACE	DIACONUS
				7%	23%	36%	20%	34%	59%

The increase in percentages does not show an increase in patterning for any of the first four poets because each example is found only once. With special reference to Catullus, eleven out of thirty lines are composed of four words, but only six of these eleven are patterns found in Horace, while three of them involve a monosyllable and a word of four or more syllables as well as no mid-line break, features not found in Horace, but existing in the Greek poets.

---

[1] With reference to the accentual nature of the line it is interesting to note Rudmose-Brown's comment *op. cit.* (supra 18 n. 1) 33: "The great popularity of the Sapphic in the Middle Ages was perhaps due to the fact that it was the only classical quantitative metre which also had a quite definite accentual rhythm. Whether written correctly as to quantity or without regard to quantity, the effect on the congregation would be the same." This would only be true, however, if words of the proper number of syllables are used according to Horace's patterns. No medieval Latin sapphic ever looked like the pattern given above 23 n. 2.

[2] The figures for Horace are based on Richardson's tables for the total 615 lines. See *loc. cit.* (supra 22 n. 1).

[3] 10% may seem high, but it means that this pattern occurs three times; 3% means only once. In general, Horatian patterning is double that of the earlier poets, and the jump in percentage in Diaconus is considerably greater.

If the lines are studied in terms of the four types of cola resulting from the breaks either after 5 or after 6 the syllable patterns of the words in these shorter cola appear even more regularized than in whole lines. The following patterns are most frequent in the *B C closed* colon:

			SAPPHO	ALKAIOS	CATULLUS	MELINNO	HORACE	DIACONUS
3	2		17%	7%	13%		31% [1]	36%
2	3		7%	22%	13%	7%	21%	26%
1	2	2	3%		7%	7%	15%	28%
2	1	2		3%	13%	20%	14%	3%

These are not the only possible combinations of syllables for the *B C closed* colon, but the contrast between the high total of percentages in Horace and Diaconus, 81% and 93% respectively, and the considerably lower percentage in Catullus, 46%, would indicate that Horace definitely preferred certain arrangements of words as against Catullus' considerably more varied word-patterning. The third scheme, 1 2 2, is interesting because it places a word accent on the short second syllable, and raises the question of how strong an accent an initial monosyllable was felt to have.[2] I do not propose any categorical answer, but in this connection it is interesting to note that by the eighth century A.D., the first syllable of the line, whether monosyllable or not, was strong enough to be used as a mnemonic device for learning the names of the scale.[3] Also in connection with word patterns and the third scheme, Catullus, although employing an initial monosyllable nine times in thirty lines (four of which are elided disyllables), only twice follows the monosyllable with two disyllables, whereas in a poem as regularized as that of Diaconus, of the twelve initial monosyllables eleven are followed by two disyllables, and one by a quadrisyllable.

---

[1] The figures for Horace are based on the total number of lines, and the table found in Seel & Pöhlman, *op. cit.* (supra 17 n. 2) 272-273.

[2] A monosyllable occurs at 1 more frequently than at any other position in either the Greek or Latin poets: Sappho 11/49; Alkaios 8/36; Catullus 9/32; Melinno 5/15; Horace 11/33 (in the sample of forty-five lines); Diaconus 12/18. See J. Hellegouarc'h, *op. cit.* (supra 9 n. 1) 25-42, where he discusses the semantic and linguistic functions of the initial monosyllable, but not its accentual function. No doubt statistics in this regard are hampered by the subjective concept of "phrase accent" which the problem of monosyllabic accent involves. See O'Neill, *WAFS*, 339 n. 10.

[3] The pattern in Diaconus' first line is 1 2 2 4 2: *Ut* queant laxis *re*sonare fibris. See supra 21 n. 2.

For the normal second colon of the line, the *D B C open*, the typical patterns are:

	SAPPHO	ALKAIOS	CATULLUS	MELINNO	HORACE	DIACONUS
3 3	10%	13%	13%	33%	26%	58%
4 2	10%	10%	23%	7%	21%	23%
2 4	3%				9%	7%
2 1 3	3%	7%	3%	7%	12%	5%
2 2 2	7%	3%		7%	11%[1]	

When it comes to lines with the break after 6, commonly called the "feminine caesura," there is almost no repetition of word-pattern in the Greek poets, and practically none in Catullus either.[2] The number of lines and the percentage of lines in the five poets having the break after 6 is:

SAPPHO	ALKAIOS	CATULLUS	MELINNO	HORACE
7 23%	4 13%	8 26%	3 20%	52 8%

Here are the commonest word-syllable patterns for the lines with the break after 6. It is important to keep in mind, however, the small percentage of the total that these lines represent.[3]

	SAPPHO	ALKAIOS	CATULLUS	MELINNO	HORACE
3 3		3%	7%	7%	4%
2 1 3	3%			3%	2%
1 2 3		3%	10%	7%	1%
2 4	3%[4]	3%	3%	7%	1%

For the second part of the line, the most common arrangements are:

	SAPPHO	ALKAIOS	CATULLUS	MELINNO	HORACE
2 3	7%		20%	7%	5%
3 2	7%	7%		13%	2%
2 1 2	3%	3%			8%
1 1 3	3%	3%	3%[5]		

---

[1] A final colon composed of three disyllables is completely "trochaic" in accent, yet Wilkinson, *GLA*, 133, suggests that Horace's preference for certain word arrangements at the beginning of a line was to avoid an opening "sing-song" trochaic effect, such as existed in the popular trochaics. I cannot see that there is anything less "sing-song" in effect about a closing trochaic rhythm than in an opening, or why to end with a trochaic rhythm would be less reminiscent of the popular songs.

[2] No line with such a break occurs in Diaconus; therefore, he is omitted from the next three tables.

[3] It must also be borne in mind that these statistics for Sappho and Alkaios are only representative, not absolute.

[4] Sappho twice has an interesting opening pattern never found in Latin, 2 2 2, perfect trochees. Alkaios' fourth pattern is 3 1 2: it occurs once in Sappho.

[5] An even clearer picture of the preference for word-group patterns in the

This table is interesting because it shows the variety existing in the Greek poets in contrast to the greater uniformity in the Latin.[1] It also shows the Latin preference for three-syllable words.

Thus far the discussion has been concerned with the eleven-syllable line. There remain a few points to be made about the concluding colon, the five-syllable adonic, or *D C falling*. The following are the most frequent word patterns:

			SAPPHO	ALKAIOS	CATULLUS	MELINNO	HORACE	DIACONUS
3	2		22%	10%	56%	20%	53%	69%
2	3		22%	10%	22%	60%	32%	23%
I	2	2	11%	10%	11%		6%	8%

Two other patterns favored by the Lesbian poets and occurring very rarely in Horace, but not found in Catullus at all, are: an adonic composed of one pentasyllabic word, and the pattern 1 4. The first of these has a frequency of 40% in Alkaios, and .2% in Horace. The second is found in Sappho 33%, and once in Horace.[2] It is clear from the above table that in Latin a definite preference exists for the 3 2 adonic. Interestingly enough, this is also true of the adonic closing of the Latin hexameter, in contrast to the Greek preference for a 2 3 clausula.[3] Moreover, the preference for 3 2 rather than 2 3, which exists also in the *B C closed* colon,

lines with the break after 6 is obtainable by basing the percentages not on the total number of lines, but only on the number of lines with the "feminine caesura," as follows:

First half:

			SAPPHO	ALKAIOS	CATULLUS	MELINNO	HORACE	DIACONUS
3	3				25%	25%	33-1/3%	46%
2	I	3		11%		13%		21%
I	2	3			25%	38%	33-1/3%	15%
2	4			11%	25%	13%	33%	15%

Second half:

			SAPPHO	ALKAIOS	CATULLUS	MELINNO	HORACE	DIACONUS
2	3		22%		25%	75%	33%	59%
3	2		22%		50%		67%	23%
2	I	2	11%					10%
I	I	3	11%		25%	13%		

[1] There are other varieties found in Sappho: 4 1, 2 2 1. 4 1 occurs once in Catullus. Horace uses 2 4 seven times, and 2 1 1 2 once.

[2] See Seel & Pöhlman, *op. cit.* (supra 17 n. 2) 276 for all Horatian patterns.

[3] The relevant statistics for this ending of the Greek hexameter are found in Porter, *op. cit.* (supra 1 n. 1) 54. Percentages are not given, but total numbers, the frequency pattern being 2 3, 3 2, and 5. As for the Latin practice, O'Neill, *WAFS*, 336-341, indicates that the order of frequency in Latin hexameters in general were 3 2, 2 3, 2 1 2. "The vast majority of hexameters are so constructed that their last two feet contain one or another of the following arrangements of words." (336.)

would indicate that the focus of metrical patterning lay more on the relationship of three-syllable words to two-syllable words, and not on location of word accent and metrical ictus.[1] For ictus and accent coincide in either case. The third aspect of the adonic, which has already been alluded to (supra 14), is its tendency to become a separate line, not only in the sense of rounding off the thought epigrammatically,[2] but metrically. This tendency is already apparent in the poems of Alkaios. In the stanzas studied for this discussion, there is not a single example of either a hypermetric verse elided with the closing adonic, or even a word divided between line three and line four of a stanza. This is no proof that Alkaios did not make use of synapheia, only that in ten adonics taken from his fragments there is no example of it. In the fragments of Sappho, on the contrary, although there are no hypermetric lines, there are four examples of words divided between line three and line four. One would expect that Catullus, who is so much freer than later Latin poets in his word patterns for the sapphic, and who in several lines copies Sappho's patterns closely, would certainly have examples of these run-over lines. In ten stanzas there are two examples of hypermetric lines, one elided with the adonic, 11.19, and one between lines two and three, 11.22, and one example of word division with the adonic, 11.11. Strangely enough, the poem that purports to be the translation of Sappho, 51, contains no example of either. This percentage, 3 out of 40 (actually 39, as one adonic is missing), 7%, is considerably higher than that of Horace, nine out of 820, 1%.[3] However, although hypermetric lines and synapheia are infrequent in the Latin sapphics, both Catullus and Horace closely follow the Greek practice of enjambement between line 3 and the adonic, in generally permitting no break of thought or punctuation.[4]

---

[1] O'Neill, *ibid.* 337, "The positions of the word-accents are obviously identical . . ."

[2] Wilkinson, *GLA*, 106, discusses this aspect.

[3] There are five examples of synapheia with the adonic, two of which are elided, and four examples of synapheia between lines 2 and 3, of which three are elided. Cf. Zinn II 5-6.

[4] This is completely true of Catullus. Sense pauses are found after line three in Horace: 1.2.31, 51; 2.16.31; 4.2.59, for example. However, it must be remembered that punctuation is generally made by the editor for the benefit of the reader, so no hard and fast rule is possible. See Porter, *op. cit.* (supra 1 n. 1) 22. Sense pause after line 3 also occurs in Sappho 1.3, Alkaios 42.11, and in Diaconus 3, 35, 51.

One may well ask, since the arrangement of words is clearly so precise in Horace and even more so in Diaconus, whether there is any relationship between the ends of words and sense pauses [1] in their sapphics, or in the less patterned stanzas of Catullus, Alkaios, and Sappho. The following table shows the number and percentage of sense pauses in the six poets.

After	SAPPHO		ALKAIOS		CATULLUS		MELINNO		HORACE [2]		DIACONUS	
1									4	.7%	1	2%
2	1	3%	1	3%	2	7%			24	4%		
3	1	3%	1	3%	3	10%	1	7%	34	7%		
4	3	10%	2	7%	2	7%			3	.5%		
5	3	10%	1	3%	8	26%			83	13%		
6	2	7%	2	7%	2	7%			3	.5%		
7	4	13%			1	3%			23	4%		
8	3	10%	1	3%	1	3%			17	3%		
9	2	7%							11	2%		
10	1	3%							1	.2%		
11	9	32%	5	17%	13	37%	5	33%	150	23%	17	44%
At End of												
Adonic	6	60%	7	70%	9	90%	5	100%	194	95%	13	100%

The first point which is obvious is that the Latin poets regarded the whole stanza as a separate unit much more than is apparent in Sappho or Alkaios.[3] Melinno seems to have imitated this Latin practice, thus providing another reason for dating her after Catullus. Moreover, there are almost no sense pauses within the lines in Melinno and Diaconus, and very few in Alkaios,[4] although more than 50% of the lines of the Greek authors have the word break after 5,[5] and every line in Diaconus has a word-end at 5. Furthermore, in Melinno and Diaconus there is a tendency to compose in terms of couplets, for the greatest number of sense pauses occur at the

---

[1] See infra 30 n. 4 on the difficulty of using the "sense pauses" as a clearcut phenomenon which can be statistically analyzed.

[2] The figures for Horace, covering 615 hendecasyllabic lines and 205 adonics, are based on the tables in Richardson, *op. cit.* (supra 17 n. 2) 42.

[3] "Since the sapphic is the classic hymn metre, the stanzas are frequently self-contained and end with a full stop or a colon." Bonavia-Hunt, *op. cit.* (supra 16 n. 2) 21. The reasoning is backwards, however. It was the increasing tendency toward making the stanza a "self-contained" unit that is one of the reasons for its becoming the classic hymn meter. Another is its unvarying accentual pattern easily imitated by choosing the correct word-syllable patterns. (Supra 22, 24.)

[4] Eight out of thirty lines in contrast to twenty out of thirty in Sappho, nineteen out of thirty in Catullus, for example.

[5] See supra 22, 23.

ends of lines 2 and 4. This is the reason why the total number of
sense pauses in these authors is so small. Thus the sense pauses
at 5 steadily decrease (with respect to the chronological sequence
of the poets) while the word-end at 5 steadily increases; for example,
Horace shows 92% word-end at 5, but only 13% sense pause; Catullus 59% word-end at 5, 26% sense pause. A second, more important, point relates particularly to Catullus' use of the meter. The
correlation of sense pause and word-end within the line is greater
than in any of the other poets. 44% coincide at 5, for instance,
while only 21% in Sappho and 11% in Alkaios coincide there.[1]
Or again, the word break after 4 which occurs six times in both
Alkaios and Sappho, only twice in Alkaios, and three times in
Sappho, marks a sense pause. However, in both cases in Catullus
it is marked not only by a sense pause, but by an important monosyllable.[2] The percentage of coincidence at 6 in Catullus, however,
is less than that in Alkaios, although more than found in Sappho.[3]
In general then, although fixed word patterns became established
in the practice of Horace and later poets, they were less related
to syntactic patterns than in the practice of Catullus, and to a
similar extent, that of Sappho.[4]

The discussion of Cutullus' handling of the sapphic meter should
not be left without a brief mention of his use of elision. Although
I am not convinced that tabulations of elisions reveal anything

---

[1] According to Richardson's table, *op. cit.* (supra 17 n. 2) 42, only 13 %
coincide at 5 in Horace.

[2] 11.11 *Rhen(um)*, 11.23 *flos*. (Compare this with two lines of Sappho, for
instance, which contain only three words, where the first word-end is after
4 but no syntactic end: 1. 1 of the pattern 4 3 4, 1. 15 of the pattern 4 4 3.)
In both cases Catullus seems to use this rarer break for purposes of semantic
emphasis. A word-end at 4 occurs thirty times in Horace. (See Zinn II, 7 F
& H; 25 F.)

[3] 2/9 in Sappho, 2/4 in Alkaios, 2/8 in Catullus, 3/74 in Horace. However,
the percentage of coincidence of sense pause with word-end at 7 is greatest in
Sappho, 44 %, in contrast to Catullus' 25 %. There is a word-end at 7 five
times in Alkaios, but no sense pause. In Horace a word-end occurs at 7 224
times, a sense pause only twenty-three times. See Richardson, *op. cit.*
(supra 17 n. 2) 39 & 42.

[4] In the rest of this study, the subject of sense pauses and elisions will not
be discussed in detail. The extreme patterning of the sapphic hendecasyllable
is not anywhere nearly so evident in the other meters which employ different
kinds of arses not in regular alternation, and sense pauses are quite often
the subjective interpretation of an editor. The role of elision has been thoroughly treated and carefully documented in Soubiran's comprehensive
tome mentioned infra 31 n. 3.

of a crucial metrical significance, elided syllables mark a particular kind of word-end about which there is some disagreement. Therefore, a brief table follows, showing the number of occurrences on each syllable.[1]

Elided Syllables	1	2	3	4	5	6	7	8	9	10	11	Total
Catullus	2	4	4	1				1	1			13
Horace [2]	3	5	23	3	6	4	3	13	11	4	11	86

Whatever one's opinion about the effect or purpose of elision,[3] it is clear that Catullus uses it a great deal more than Horace. The percentages are: Catullus 43%, Horace 14%. After Horace, elision practically disappears, and is non-existent in Diaconus, for instance. The number of elisions at 11 in Horace is interesting for it also shows occurrences of monosyllables in that position. This figure, when added to the number of pure monosyllables at 11, gives a total of eighteen, compared with four in Catullus. The contrast in percentages here is great (3% for Horace and 13% for Catullus), but though the percentage in both is not high, it is clear that monosyllabic endings were permitted.[4] Moreover, the percentage

---

[1] Forms elided with the verb "to be" are omitted.

[2] The figures for Horace are those of Richardson, *ibid.* (supra 30 n. 3) with the exception of the first syllable under which I have included the three examples of synapheia from the preceding line.

[3] For two interesting articles on this subject, see A. G. Harkness, "The Relation of Accent to Elision in Latin Verse Not Including the Drama," *TAPA* 36, 1905, 82, and by the same author, "The Final Monosyllable in Latin Prose and Poetry," *AJP* 31, 1910, 154. That the subject to a large extent is one involving opinion rather than fact, the following quotation from the latter article will show: "Elision in general denotes rapidity of expression combined with emotions; the elision under discussion (Cat. 73.6) denotes rather deliberation combined with emphasis. The elision at the end of the line, especially in the case of the double elision of *atque*, welds two lines into one and instead of two light lines we have the effect of one long line." (167) The fullest, most up-to-date treatment of the subject of elision in Latin poetry of all periods can be found in J. Soubiran, *L'Elision dans la poésie latine* (Paris 1966).

[4] Metricians often make sweeping statements about final monosyllables. "Now distaste for monosyllabic endings was more or less universal in both Greek and Latin verse." O'Neill, *WAFS*, 338. Harkness, in the second of the two articles mentioned in the preceding note, *loc. cit.*, implies that Horace uses monosyllabic conjunctions and prepositions at the end of a line with elision to "add impressiveness to the thought and to give a bold sweep to the verse." See also Hellegouarc'h, *op. cit.* (supra 9 n. 1) 50-69. "Virgile et ses successeurs n'ont pas totalement évité le monosyllabe final, mais ils ont cherché à tirer de cette disposition des effets stylistiques. Au contraire,

of monosyllabic endings in Alkaios and Sappho is the same as
in Catullus.

In conclusion, it must be admitted that all aspects of Catullus'
treatment of the sapphic stanza have not been discussed. Vocabulary and subject matter, which I deal with in other meters,
have been omitted here because of the absence of Latin predecessors. In addition, the phenomenon of word-localization, that is,
the localizing of words of specific metrical types, has little significance in the sapphic meter with the exception of the inhibition
of the cretic at 3-5 and the iamb at 4-5 in Catullus, because of the
strict quantitative requirements of syllables where resolution does
not exist, and even ancipitia disappear after Catullus, except in
the final syllable. For example, in the Greek scheme, iambic words
could be used at positions 2-3, 4-5, 7-8, or 9-10. However, the
only place where word localization is clear is the 4-5 iamb, found
only once in Sappho, even though the 4 anceps is short seven
times in Alkaios, twice in Melinno, and three times in Catullus.
On the other hand, the 7-8 iamb in Latin is virtually a function
of the break after 6, since a monosyllable at 6 is extremely rare.[1]
Trochaic words are also limited by the strict "outer-metrical
schema."[2] Hypothetically they could be used at 1-2, 3-4, 5-6, 8-9,
or 10-11, and in Sappho a trochaic word shape actually does occur
at least once in each of these positions. However, a 3-4 trochee is
not found in any other Greek author, nor is a disyllable found in
that position at all in Latin. Such a word shape would prevent
the 4 accent, and require either a monosyllable at 5, the colometric
end, which is virtually non-existent in Latin unless preceded by
a companion monosyllable at 4, or it would require a trochee at
5-6, a rarity occurring only once in all Horace,[3] and once in Catullus.
This is in the first line of poem 51 which is as close an approximation

---

les Satiriques ont multiplié les emplois du monosyllabe, moins par affecta-
tion, que pour donner à leurs oeuvres le ton vif et familier qui convenait au
sujet." (69)
    [1] The frequency in Catullus and Horace is 3.3% and 3.5% respectively.
However, the sole occurrence in Catullus is not followed by a 7-8 iamb, and
only six of the twenty-two instances in Horace are. (See Zinn II, 15, 24.)
In Sappho and Alkaios the percentage of monosyllables at 6 is 10%, or three
examples in each. Two in Sappho and one in Alkaios are followed by the
7-8 iamb. A monosyllable occurs twice in Melinno at 6, one followed by the
7-8 iamb.
    [2] O'Neill, WAFS, 345.
    [3] See tables in Seel & Pöhlman, op. cit. (supra 17 n. 2) 275.

of the first line of Sappho's poem 31, in meaning and word shape, as a translator could achieve. Clearly, because of the schematic requirement of long and short syllables and colometric breaks, three-syllable words have even less possibility for various positions. A cretic word, $- \cup -$, has three possible locations, 1-3, 3-5, or 8-10. It is found in all authors only at 1-3. 3-5 does not exist in Latin because 4 is always long, except for the three times in Catullus where it is either an initial syllable or incorporated into a word of more than three syllables. 8-10 occurs only once in Horace, and not at all in Catullus; the reason, however, is not so clear. One is tempted to say it is because of dislike for final monosyllables, but as has already been shown,[1] monosyllables are permitted at line-ends. Thus the location of words of particular metrical shape are severely restricted by the metrical scheme of the sapphic hendeca-syllable.

What this section has attempted to show, however, is that there did develop in the sapphic hendecasyllable a preference for a certain sequence of words of a particular number of syllables, and that the insistence on this preference is the chief contribution of Horace in the development toward the stereotyped form exem-plified by Diaconus.[2] The four most common patterns became: 3 2 3 3, 2 3 3 3, 3 2 4 2 and 1 2 2 3 3. Furthermore, because of the dominant feature of word-accent in Latin, the word-group patterns had sufficient phonetic reality to result in "stress sapphics" of an accentual pattern that differed completely from the thesis-arsis pattern of the original Greek models. Finally, this accentual phenomenon occurred as a result of certain preferred arrangements of words, not vice versa, which Horace discovered in the usage of Sappho, Alkaios, and Catullus.

---

[1] See supra 31-32.

[2] Richardson, *op. cit.* (supra 17 n. 2) 40, expresses this in an interesting way. He says that out of 1,024 possible positions of wordbreaks, a number he arrives at from the formula $F = 2^{n-1}$, where n equals the number of syllables, Horace uses only eighty-nine, "confining himself generally to 18." Richardson explains how he gets the formula in another article on Horatian metrics, "Horace's Alcaic Strophe," *CPCP* 1, 1907, 175.

PHALAECEAN HENDECASYLLABLE

I	2	3	4	5	6	7	8	9	10	11
X	X	–	⏑	⏑	–	⏑	–	⏑	–	X

The phalaecean hendecasyllable, so named after an Alexandrian poet, Phalaikos, whose extant poems consist of a mere twenty-three lines in the Greek Anthology,[1] of which only eight are stichic hendecasyllables, was an extraordinarily popular meter for light verse among the ancient Greeks and Romans. The evidence for this lies not so much in the number of lines in the meter which have come down to us,[2] as in the many authors who used the meter,[3]

---

[1] His actual date and native city are unknown, although it is generally accepted that he lived in the latter part of the fourth century B.C. Cf. Wilamowitz, *HD* 134, and *RE* 19[2], 1614. The poems are *AP* 13.5, 6, 27. 13.6 is the hendecasyllabic poem.

[2] I do not suggest that I have located all the extant hendecasyllables in Greek or Latin. The problem of finding all Greek hendecasyllables is complicated by the differences of opinion between scholars as to the correct line division in the lyrics of the tragedians as well as those of Pindar. However, I have supplemented the meager selection of W. Meyer, "Caesur im Hendeca-syllabus," *SBMünch*, 1889, II 210, with a few more lines, principally from tragedy and fragments from Sappho. This brings his total of eighty-one Greek hendecasyllables to 113. The Delphic paean to Dionysos (infra 66 n. 5) possibly contains eighty-four phalaecean hendecasyllables. However, the lines are too mutilated to use the emendations for statistical purposes. T. Cutt, in his careful study, *Meter and Diction in Catullus' Hendecasyllabics* (Chicago University Dissertation 1936) 25-26 has given a total of 5,429 Latin hendecasyllables. To these should be added twenty-two from the circle of Catullan friends (infra 41, supra 10) as well as 177 lines from the Latin Anthology edited by F. Bücheler, A. Reise, and E. Lommatzsch (Amsterdam reprint 1964), henceforth *AL*. This number includes nos. 336 and 337 from the codices, overlooked by Cutt, as well as 155 lines from the epigraphical collection, *AL* 2[2] 1504-1518, 1553, and 2[3], 2141-2142. This brings the Latin grand total to 5,664, not counting those from the Carolingian Renaissance, for which see indices in *PLAC* 1, 2, 3[22], 4[3]; Rudmose-Brown, *op. cit.* (supra 18 n. 1) 40-42; and M. Kawczynski, *L'Origine et l'histoire des rythmes* (Paris 1889) 125.

[3] Of the early Greek lyricists we can assume Sappho, Alkman, and Anakreon on the basis of extant fragments and references by the Latin grammarians. The dramatists who used the meter are Sophokles, Euripides, Aristophanes, and Kratinos the comedian. The philosopher Herakleides Pontikos is credited by Suidas with possibly having used the meter (11.70). The list of fourth and third century Alexandrians is even longer: Kallimachos, Theo-

its frequent employment for inscriptions,[1] and the continuous endeavor of the metricians to analyze its origin. It was an unsolvable puzzle which apparently both Greek and Latin grammarians worked at with no satisfactory result.[2] The uncertainty of what label to give the meter; ionic, dactylo-trochaic, antispastic, logaoedic, or choriambic is, of course, the result of misguided desire to impose upon a meter which is isosyllabic the convenience of the traditional terminology of "foot" and "metron". However, in spite of the invaluable work of Meillet [3] in showing the Vedic and folk origins of isosyllabic meters, the futile discussion still continues.[4] Yet, as Cutt has shown in the dissertation already

kritos, Phalaikos, Diophanes Myrina, Phlakkos, Antipater of Thessalonika, Alphaios of Mytilene, and Parmenon. There are also two lines of uncertain date, but probably first century B.C., in the Oxyrhynchus fragment on meters. *P OXY* 2. 220. For a list of Latin poets, see Cutt *loc. cit.* (supra 34 n. 2) n. 2, to which should be added Laevius, and the Catullan group, Bibaculus, Calvus, Cornificius.

[1] Examples of its use in Greek inscriptions are found in G. Kaibel, *Epigrammata Graeca ex Lapidibus Conlecta* (Hildesheim reprint 1965) praef. 431a; 261b; 811. For Latin examples, see *AL* (supra 34 n. 2). These epitaphs date from the time of Hadrian or later.

[2] One of the earliest references to the derivation controversy occurs in a fragment from one of Varro's *Menippean Satires*, fr. 230, where he decides the meter is a form of ionic trimeter. It is interesting that the papyrus fragment on meters (supra), which is dated the end of the first century B.C. or first century A.D. is also concerned with the derivation of the phalaecean, calling it a catalectic trimeter. This theory is in line with that of Hephaistion, *Ench.* 10.3 (Consbr. 33) who calls it a catalectic antispastic trimeter. Chronologically, Hephaistion is preceded by Caesius Bassus, in whose work, *De Metris*, the fragment of Varro just mentioned is found (Keil, *Gr. Lat.* 6. 261). Bassus, of the first century A.D., offers two opposing solutions, that it is a sotadean or an ionic a minore, although he shows seven different ways of looking at the meter. Diomedes, of the fourth century A.D., associates the meter with the first half of the hexameter line and the first half of an iambic line (Keil, *Gr. Lat.* 1. 509). Marius Victorinus, also of the fourth century, called the meter a union of heroic hexameter and trochaic (Keil, *Gr. Lat.* 6. 121.13). Terentianus Maurus, late second century, holds with the ionic a minore theory (Keil, *Gr. Lat.* 6. 409.2846). These are only a few examples of various metrical theories. In the index of Keil, *Gr. Lat.* 6 there are twenty-seven entries under the words *phalaecium metrum*, convincing evidence of the metricians' preoccupation with the problem, "quo nascitur hendecasyllabus phalaecius".

[3] *Les Origines* and "Metrique éolienné" (supra 15 n. 3).

[4] Wilamowitz, for example, advanced the ionic theory in "De Versu Phalaeceo," *Mélanges Henri Weil* (Paris 1898) 459, only to retract it in favor of the antispastic notion two decades later in *GV* 149. The ionic theory is also discussed by K. Münscher, "Metrische Beiträge," *Hermes* 56, 1921, 73-77. A. Kolář analyzes the phalaecean under the chapter on mixed meters, calling it an acatalectic pentapody. See *De re metrica poetarum Graecorum*

cited, the origin of the meter or "theory of the rhythm" [1] is irrelevant to the study of the combinations of words which are sought
to fill the rhythmical pattern. It is precisely in cases of such controversy that the alphabetical system of describing the syllabic
quantities between theses is so valuable. In these terms the phalaecean hendecasyllable can be described as a whole line, *C D B B C
falling*.[2] If we look at the positions of the most frequent word-
breaks in Latin, the line can be divided into two different patterns:
the break after 5 results in a *C D falling* colon followed by a *B B C
falling*, or *ithyphallic* colon, best known as the second part of the
Horatian "archilochean" line which begins with four dactyls.
If the chief break occurs after 6, the colometric patterns are *C D
closed*, followed by a *B B C open*, the pure iambic form of the
common opening iambic colon, the *C B C open*.

One of the most interesting features of the phalaecean meter
is the lack of regularization in both Greek and Latin with respect
to word-breaks, word-patterns and accent patterns. Concerning
the first of these, Meyer's controversial statement made in 1889
about the meter needs reassessment: "Im Allgemeinen muss man
also zugestehen, dass diese griechischen Hendekasyllaben keine
bestimmte Caesur kennen und dass hier nur der Zufall regiert." [3]
In the first place, the value of this statement hinges upon what is
meant by "Caesur" and "bestimmte," even if the last part of the
sentence is disregarded as being unreasonable. That Greek poets
were less concerned in every meter with particular positions for
word ends than Latin poets is a fairly safe statement; but this
does not mean that accident was the governing principle. If "Cae-

---

et Romanorum (Prague 1947) 224-226. Koster, *Traité* 238 calls it a glyconic
plus an iambic catalectic syzygy. This description is close to that in *MGLP*
(supra 15-16 n. 7) 88, where it is described as a combination of a glyconic and
a bacchaic. Raven in *Greek Metre* (Faber & Faber 1962) 70-72 analyzes it
as a choriambic nucleus with additions, similar to the ancient *adiectio* and
detractio theory. D. Page, following the lead of A. M. Dale, considers the two
syllabae ancipites at the beginning of the line the "base," and the rest of the
line consists of additions. (See supra 15 n. 7.) The applicable pages in Dale's
article are 124-128. See also the comments of F. della Corte, "Varrone
metricista," *Fondation Hardt* 9, 1962, 143-148 where he discusses Varro's
ionic a minore theory, and Heinze, *op. cit.* (supra 17 n. 2) 9-13.

[1] *Op. cit.* (supra 34 n. 2) 3.

[2] The line can also be considered as a *C D B B A closed*, particularly in
the case of choral lyric, if the next colon begins *in arsi*.

[3] Meyer *op. cit.* (supra 34 n. 2) 210.

sur" means a *mid-line* "Ruhepunkt für die Zunge,"[1] then Meyer is right, for there is no observable regular *mid-line* break in the extant lines of Greek hendecasyllable. However, elsewhere in the article Meyer uses the word "Einschnitt," as an equivalent for "Caesur," as well as word-ends which occur anywhere, so that his argument has no great value. In the second place, the ninety-five pre-Catullan Greek examples of the meter chosen for evaluation definitely show preferences for word-ends at certain positions rather than others. This is particularly true of the Alexandrian period where breaks after 3 and 7, or 2 and 7, are most common, as will be subsequently shown.

If one looks at the sixth and fifth century Greek fragments, one finds no evidence that the meter was used stichically, other than an allusion by the Latin grammarian of the first century A.D., Caesius Bassus, to lines written in the phalaecean hende-casyllable by Sappho "et continuati et dispersi."[2] Thanks to the Berlin papyrus, discovered in 1880,[3] six legible lines of hendeca-syllables exist from two poems which were written in strophes composed of choriambs, glyconics, and hendecasyllables.[4] Inter-estingly enough, all six lines have a word-end after 3, but there is no preferred position for a word-end in the rest of the line. Of the two other early lyricists who probably used the meter, Alkman and Anakreon, there are no certain examples because of the disagree-ment among scholars as to line division.[5] However, from fifth century drama there are a few isolated specimens of the meter, generally found interspersed among glyconics and pherecrateans, or choriambs. Six lines have been chosen from both Sophokles [6] and Euripides,[7] nine lines from Aristophanes,[8] and finally the two-line

---

[1] *Ibid.* 211.　　　　　　　　　　　　　　[2] Keil, *Gr. Lat.* 6.258.16.

[3] For more detail, see F. Blass, "Die Berliner Fragmente der Sappho," *Hermes* 37, 1902, 456.

[4] *PLF* 95.11; 96.5, 8, 11, 14, 17. It is clear from the strophic pattern that lines 20, 23, 26, 29 and 32 in fragment 96 must also have been hendecasylla-bles, but only a few words can be discerned because of the bad condition of the papyrus.

[5] If we follow Bergk's lineation, we would have one fragment from Alkman, 66.2, and two from Anakreon, 38 and 39.2. However, Page insists upon making the last word of each of these fragments into another line: Alkman 38, Anakreon 58 and 52. Cf. Bergk, *PLG* 58, 266; and Page, *PMG* 45, 201, 199, respectively.

[6] *Aj.* 634, 645; *Ph.* 1140, 1145, 1163, 1168.

[7] *Supp.* 962, 970; 900-901, 911-912.

[8] *Av.* 1411, 1415; *Eccles.* 938-939, 942-943; *Vesp.* 1226-1227, 1248.

fragment from Kratinos quoted by Hephaistion as an example of the meter.[1] In these twenty-three examples from drama, a word limit at 5 or 6 is the most frequent,[2] whereas a word-end at 7, the Alexandrian preference, occurs only three times. At the beginning of the line only Sophokles' verses show any consistent patterning in that all six have a word-end at 2.

It is clear from the above brief discussion that there is no distinct word-patterning in the early Greek use of the meter, although the total of twenty-nine lines is not large enough to justify a conclusion. The picture, on the other hand, changes after the remnants, equally small and scattered, from the Alexandrian period are examined. The uniformity in the practice of Kallimachos, Theokritos, and Phalaikos is striking.[3] This is most evident in the preference for word-ends at either 2 and 7, or 3 and 7, whereas a word break after 5 is rare, and one after 6 even more so. Of the three instances of a word-end at 5 in Theokritos *Epigram* 22, for example, all have a break after 7 as well. In the other two epigrams where he uses the meter, 17 (where phalaecean hendecasyllables are alternated with trimeter) and 20 (which alternates hendecasyllables with a long line composed of dactyls and trochees) comprising a total of five lines, a break after 5 occurs twice and a break after 6 three times. Only one line, however, has no word limit at 7. Similarly, in the eight lines by Kallimachos,[4] only one has no word-

[1] Fr. 321 (Consbr. 33.3, 4). There are many more examples of the *C D B B C falling* sequence in Greek drama and in the lyrics of Pindar. However, as these rarely occur stichically, a different type of analysis is required, particularly because word ends do not always occur at the end of the sequence. For this reason there is disagreement as to the correct place of line end. (See also p. 64 n. 5.) Moreover, it is difficult to locate all examples of the pattern in the drama without scanning every chorus since different scholars use different names for the meter, such as O. Schröder calling it a combination of a glyconic and bacchius, cf. *Aristophanis Cantica* (Leipzig 1930) 18, *Vesp.* 1227; 19, *Vesp.* 1247; while Jebb uses the general term of logaoedic hexapody in the introductions to his commentaries on Sophokles, and not all editions agree on line division.

[2] There is a break after 5 in eleven of the total twenty-three lines, and a break after 6 fourteen times. However, a monosyllable, generally the definite article, occurs at 6 in six of the fourteen instances, making the break after 5 the more important.

[3] The Alexandrian period is the only one to leave examples of the stichic use of the meter: Theokritos *Epigr.* 22; Phalaikos *AP* 13.6; Phlakkos *AP* 6.193; Antipater *AP* 7.390; Alphaios *AP* 9.110.

[4] Pf. frags. 222, 226, 395, and *Epigr.* 38.2, 4; 40.2, 4, 6.

end at 7. Nine of the thirteen lines by Theokritos [1] have a break
after 2, while seven of the eight lines by Kallimachos have a word-
end at 3, and four have a word-end at 2.[2] Kallimachos also uses a
single four-syllable word to fill the 3-7 space four times. As for
Phalaikos, all eight lines of his epigram (see 34 n. 1) have a word
limit after 7, and three have a four-syllable word in the 3-7 space.
There is not a single instance of a break after 6, and only one
after 5. The six stichic lines of Phlakkos,[3] on the other hand,
show less regularization, with a break after 5 twice, after 6 three
times, and a prominent break after 7 twice.[4] Antipater [5] has a
break after 6 three times, after 5 twice, and after 7 once.

A third group of poems where hendecasyllables in Greek are
found are the *skolia*,[6] or drinking songs. These are of a somewhat
indeterminate date, but their old tradition and preference for a
break after 6 would indicate a pre-Alexandrian composition.[7] In
the collection there are ten poems whose first two lines consist of
phalaecean hendecasyllables, making a total of twenty lines.[8]

---

[1] *Epigr.* 17.2, 4, 6; 20.1, 3; 22.1-8.
[2] In three of the seven examples of a break after 3, position 3 is filled by
a monosyllable giving the place of greater importance to the break after 2.
[3] *AP* 6.193.
[4] A prominent or significant break at 7 means no word-end at 5 or 6. See
infra 43-45.
[5] *AP* 7.390.
[6] Page in *PMG* calls them *Carmina Convivialia*.
[7] For a general commentary, see R. Reitzenstein, *Epigram und Skolion*
(Giessen 1893) 13-44. Unfortunately, he does not discuss the meter except to
mention Aeolic and Ionic influences. The fact that four of these skolia, *PMG*
10-13, celebrate the heroes of the Peisistratean era, Harmodios and Aristo-
geiton, he considers an indication of the antiquity of the γένος. Corroborating
this are Aristophanes' allusions to "the Harmodios" as if it were the title of
a well-known folk-ditty. (See notes on the texts of the *Wasps* 226 and the
Ecclesiazusae 938 by B. Rogers, *The Wasps of Aristophanes* (London 1915)
191-193, and *The Ecclesiazusae* (London 1917) 144. The use of a meter with
D and C arses not in regular alternation is also evidence for early folk-verse.
Reitzenstein implies this *op. cit.* 43-44, particularly when he says: "Kurze
Lieder in aiolischem Rhythmus sind nach dem Paian in Athen in älterer Zeit
allein gesungen worden und nahmen darum am Reichsten den religiösen
Stoff in sich auf. Schon während der Kämpfe gegen die Peisistratiden bestand
diese Art in Athen heimisch gewordenen 'Volksliedes' und zeigt den Einfluss
der mächtigen Poesie der Insel-Griechen auf das geistige Leben des noch
unentwickelten Athen." His argument would have much greater weight
had he gone into the subject of metrical usage in more detail. See infra 65-67
for comments on the antiquity of the paean and the eight-syllable glyconic.
[8] *PMG, Carmina Convivialia*: 1-7, 10-11, 13. I have not included in my

In twelve lines the principal break is after 6, while the second most common word-end at 3 occurs eleven times. Mid-line breaks at 5 occurs in four lines, three of which are followed by a monosyllable.

The conclusion from the preceding is that Meyer's statement needs qualification. Although there is less regimented patterning of positions for word-ends in Greek hendecasyllables than in Latin, as will be seen shortly, definite preferences do exist. A prominent word-end at 5 is the most common in fifth century drama, while the chief break in the *skolia* is after 6. On the other hand, the Alexandrian poets, Kallimachos, Theokritos, and Phalaikos, seem to have experimented with word limits at 7. Actually, in the total number of lines the break after 5 has a frequency of only 22% as the dominant word-end. This will be referred to later in connection with the Latin practice. At the beginning of the line a break after 2 or 3 is the most common, and one after 4 the most infrequent.

The earliest extant examples of the meter in Latin, those of Laevius and Varro, predate Catullus by barely more than one or two decades.[1] Moreover, the two lines from Laevius [2] cannot with certainty be ascribed to him, so that only Varro can be said to

discussion the seventeen lines from Kaibel's inscriptions, 261b, praef. 431a, and 811, or the Oxyrhynchus fragment, because they are all post-Catullan. 811 is interesting, however, in that it shows a decided preference for the break after 5 which would indicate Latin influence. The first line of the *P OXY* fragment has a trisyllable in the 5-7 position.

[1] The exact dates for the three chief predecessors of Catullus who experimented with *polymetra*, Laevius, Matius, and Varro, cannot be determined. The consensus is that the *floruit* for the first two is 104-100 B.C. See F. Leo, "Die Römische Poesie in der Sullanischen Zeit", *Ausgewählte Kleine Schriften* I (Rome 1960) 249-282; H. Bardon, *La Littérature latine inconnue* I (Paris 1952) 161-163, 189-195; Schanz-Hosius, *Geschichte der Römischen Literatur* I (Munich 1927⁴) 267-269. Leo suggests a span of thirty years, 100-70 B.C., for the Sullan Age, although Sulla does not become a number-one man in Roman politics until 88 B.C. Varro's long life, however, 116-27 B.C., covered both the Sullan and Ciceronian ages. Unfortunately, the evidence for dating the *Menippean Satires* is inconclusive, although traditionally given as 80-67. C. Cichorius, *Römische Studien* (Stuttgart 1961²) 207-227 works out a logical dating, from his point of view. F. della Corte, probably the most important living scholar working with Varro and the satires, thinks they were written over a much longer period of time. See particularly "Varrone e Levio di fronte alla metrica tradizionale della scena latina," *AttiTor* 70, 1935, 375-384, *Varronis Menippearum Fragmenta* (private lithograph Torino 1953) 131-132, 139 n. 6 and 9. (*VMF*), and *Varrone: il terzo gran lume romano* (Florence 1970).

[2] Morel, *FPL* 62, fr. 32.

have written hendecasyllables before Catullus. Seven sure lines exist [1] and two additional fragments are possible depending upon variant readings.[2] Twenty-two lines remain from those written by Catullus' contemporaries, Bibaculus, Calvus, Cinna, and Cornificius. For the sake of convenience, all the fragmentary lines of Laevius, Varro, and Catullus' contemporaries will be given below.[3]

Laevius

Hac qua Sol vagus igneas habenas	M 32
immittit propius iugatque terrae	

Varro

gravis quem peperit Iovi puellum	d C. 19 [4] Ἄλλος οὗτος
	Ἡρακλῆς
nautae remivagam movent celocem	B 49 *Bimarcus*
et pullos peperit fritinnientis	B 565 *Virgula*
	Divina
quos non lacte novo levata pascat	B 566
sed pancarpineo cibo coacto	B 567
libamenta legens caduca victus	
ad quos cum volucris venit putillos	B 568
usque ad limina nidi amica vilis	

Bibaculus

Si quis forte mei domum Catonis,	M 1
depictas minio assulas et illos	
custodes videt hortulis Priapos,	
miratur, quibus ille disciplinis	
tantam sit sapientiam assecutus,	
quem tres cauliculi, selibra farris,	
racemi duo tegula sub una	
ad summam prope nutriant senectam.	
Catonis modo, Galle, Tusculanum	M 2
tota creditor urbe venditabat,	
Mirati sumus unicum magistrum,	
summum grammaticum, optimum poetam	
omnes solvere posse quaestiones,	
unum deficere expedire nomen.	
En cor Zenodoti, en iecur Cratetis!	

---

[1] Bücheler, fr. 565-568.

[2] F. della Corte in "Rileggendo 'Le Menippee'," *GIF* 1, 1948, 70, changes Bücheler's reading of fr. 19 so that the line becomes a phalaecean instead of an example of ionic a minore. Fragment 101 can be a hendecasyllable if a missing initial syllable is assumed.

[3] For information on Catullus' circle, see supra 9 n. 3.

[4] This is F. della Corte's rendition of Bücheler fr. 19: "gravidaque mater peperit Iovi puellum," *VMF* 6, and supra n. 2.

Cato grammaticus, Latina Siren   M 17
qui solus legit ac facit poetas.

Calvus

    et talos Curius pereruditus   M   1

    durum rus fugit et laboriosum   M   2

Cinna

    At nunc me Genumana per salicta   M   9

    bigis raeda rapit citata nanis.

Cornificius

    deducta mihi voce garrienti   M   1

In the observations which follow concerning the Latin hendecasyllable, these lines will be used for illustration, along with the
527 [1] lines of Catullus, and the 2,070 lines of Martial.[2] To the period
between Catullus and Martial belong the eight lines of Maecenas,
the 294 lines of the *Priapea*,[3] and the forty-three lines of Petronius.

---

[1] Since I have used throughout the statistics of Cutt which are based on
527 hendecasyllabic lines of Catullus, as he discounts the fifteen decasyllabic
lines and ten lines which are identical, my percentages are based on 527. To
be thoroughly accurate, 537 should be used, but using the smaller total makes
no difference with the significant figure.

[2] The percentages I have arrived at for Martial are based on the accurate
study of C. Giarratano, *De M. Val. Martialis Re Metrica* (Naples 1908).
However, he did not make any analysis of word types in the line. Therefore,
in the parts of the discussion dealing with number of words in a line and
word-patterning, the percentages and evidence are drawn from the 212 lines
of the first book of the epigrams only.

[3] Very little has been done on the collection of poems known as the *Priapea*
for their own sake. Most of the scholarly attention has been devoted to
ascertaining who was the author. The only work that passes as a commentary
on the collection is that by F. Bücheler, "Vindiciae Libri Priapeorum,"
Kleine Schriften I (Berlin 1915) 328-362. There is, of course, the general
article in *RE* 22[2], 1908-1913, and that of Schanz-Hosius, *Geschichte* 2, 1935[4],
274-275. Two works of particular interest discuss whether to ascribe the
Priapea to Ovid or not, and thus cover some of the rudimentary metrical
aspects such as caesura and elision, as well as vocabulary: R. F. Thomason,
The "Priapea" and Ovid: A Study of the Language of the Poems (Nashville
1931), and R. S. Radford, "The Priapea and the Vergilian Appendix,"
TAPA 52, 1921, 148-177. H. Fairclough, "The Poems of the Appendix
Vergiliana," *TAPA* 53, 1922, 1-34 discusses vocabulary similarities of the
three so-called Vergilian *Priapea* on the authority of T. Birt, *Jugendverse
und Heimatpoesie Vergils* (Teubner 1910), which is still the standard work on
the subject of both the *Priapea* and the *Catalepton*, although in general it
touches on the former only in connection with possible Vergilian authorship
of the three *Priapea* at the beginning of the *Catalepton*. For the most recent
reference to the corpus and tradition of the *Priapea*, see Appendix B 521-522
in J. W. Zarker, "Catullus 18-20," *TAPA* 93, 1962, 502-522. See 505 for
comments on Radford and Thomason.

Statistics taken from these lines may be used occasionally to emphasize important points, but the focus is on the norms and tendencies in the practice of the Catullan group, contrasted with that of Varro, and the resultant similarity in the lines of Martial. Of course, the wholesale lifting by Martial of lines from Catullus, whether for paraphrase or parody, is so ubiquitous that some might think the statistics of small value. However, this is not a treatise to attack Martial's originality, but rather to indicate the imitations of word patterns. As an example of late Latin usage, lines from the *De Geometria* of a ninth century codex will be mentioned.[1]

In observing the most common word-breaks in the Latin handling of the meter, one discovers, in reality, very little more rigidity or patterning in the early experimenters with the rhythm than in the Greek examples,[2] with the possible exception of Varro. The midline break is more or less equally divided between 5 and 6 in all the poets except Varro and Bibaculus. Of Varro's eight phalaeceans, only one has a word-end at 5, and this occurs because of elision in an emendation where the manuscript is corrupt (568.2). In contrast, Bibaculus prefers the word-limit at 5 in thirteen out of seventeen lines. Catullus has a slightly higher number of lines with the break after 5, 293, than that after 6, 215.[3] The difference in Martial is somewhat greater, with preference for 6: 786 breaking after 5, 1093 breaking after 6. Of the thirty lines from the late Latin example, eighteen have the mid-line break at 6 while only five have the break at 5. However, all poets except Varro, Laevius, Calvus, and Cornificius (the lines of these last three are too few to make conclusions of value), also have examples of the significant [4] Alexandrian break after 7.[5]

---

[1] *PLAC* 4[1], 259.

[2] This is where I question Meyer's predetermined conclusions. If examples in all the authors with more than thirty lines reveal permissible word limits at 3, 4, 5, 6, 7, and 8, even though the predominance is at 5 or 6, one is hardly justified in calling those after 5 and 6 regular, and everything else irregular. E. Leutsch in "Zu Catullus," *Philologus* 10, 1855, 742 seems willing to accept any break as a caesura, even one after 4, which would indicate that the search for a "bestimmte Caesur" was somewhat hopeless.

[3] Meyer, *op. cit.* (supra 34 n. 2) 219 gives a few statistics about the *Priapea* which would indicate a preference for word-end at 6.

[4] The term "significant" means that there is no word-limit at 5 or 6.

[5] According to Meyer's figures *loc. cit.* (supra n. 3) a break after 7 in the *Priapea* has a frequency of 2%.

Percentages of the Most Frequent Word-Limits

Break After	LAEV.	VARRO	BIBAC.	CALVUS	CINNA	CORNIF.	CAT.	MARTIAL	*De geometria*
	(2)	(8)	(17)	(2)	(2)	(1)	(527)	(2070)	(30)
5	50	13	76	50		100	55	38	17
6	50	87	18	50	50		41	53	59
7			6		50		3	7	10

The table makes it clear that only Bibaculus and Catullus preferred the word-end at 5 over that at 6, and that the limit at 7, undeniably less frequent, cannot be disregarded or condemned as "unregelmässig."[1] Moreover, if the reason for the interest in the position of the caesura is to draw conclusions concerning the importance of the Latin word-accent in the meter, as Meyer indicates further on in a second but related article,[2] certainly the admission of a break after 4 or after 7 is significant. Neither of these result in conflict of ictus and accent, so their rarity must have some other reason, especially when a principal break after 7 is quite common in Alexandrian hendecasyllables.[3] Rather than emphasize the caesura or lack of caesura in Latin hendecasyllables, it is more valuable to observe word patterns and positions in a line to see if the unusual variations are for a special effect. For instance, of the forty-seven examples in Catullus of a word-end after 4, only six [4] have a trisyllable in the 5-7 position, yet all six have particular

---

[1] This is a favorite word with Meyer, *ibid.*

[2] "Über die weibliche Caesur des klassischen lateinischen Hexameters und über lateinische Caesuren überhaupt," *SBMünch* 1889, II, 234-245. He suggests that the Roman poets tried to achieve a different ictus-accent relationship before the mid-line caesura from that at the end of the line. He fails to make it clear, however, what this difference actually was, unless disharmony and harmony. Furthermore, he contradicts himself by saying that the Roman poets were not at all interested in word accent, and that coincidence or conflict of word and verse accent was purely mechanical and not intended (242).

[3] See supra 38.

[4] There are actually seven examples. However, two lines are exactly identical, 41.4 and 43.5, so Cutt treats them as one line for statistical purposes. The others are 41.1 *puella*, 41.4 *amica*, 41.7 *puella*, 49.2 *fuere*, 50.14 *labore*, 58a.10 *amice*. This last is something of a puzzle in that the editors separate it off by a comma from the preceding word *mihi* which is not only elided with it, but seems closely connected with it grammatically. It is the only Catullan example of a 5-7 word preceded by a monosyllable, in contrast to eight examples in the Greek fragments, and should perhaps be considered as a sample of a central four-syllable word in the 4-7 position, of which there are also very few examples in Catullus (cf. infra 45-46).

significance in the interpretation of the poem, such as heightening the irony, balancing thought and sound, or emphasizing the defects of the chief personages in the poem.[1] This feature of Catullan technique is all the more interesting when compared with either the Greek remnants or either Latin examples. Of the 113 Greek hendecasyllables, there are only three examples of an isolated (that is, not preceded by a monosyllable) trisyllable in the 5-7 position.[2] There is no example in Catullus' Latin predecessors or contemporaries. In the thirty instances in Martial,[3] which give the same percentage of frequency as in Catullus, 1%, there is little indication that the poet considered the central position emphatic, other than the six examples of using a proper name in that place. Thus, one is led to the conclusion that Catullus in his phalaeceans made use of trisyllabic words in the rare central position for special effect as he did in other meters.[4]

A central four-syllable word in the 4-7 position in Catullus is equally rare, occurring only seven times,[5] although its frequency in other writers of hendecasyllables is considerably higher:

ALEXANDRIANS	BIBACULUS	CINNA [6]	CATULLUS	MARTIAL [7]
22%	6%	50%	1%	5%

---

[1] See Cutt's discussion *op. cit.* (supra 34 n. 2) 20. He relates the phenomenon to his thesis that one of the requirements of hendecasyllabic meter is the undivided pyrrhic. He considers *labore*, 50.14, a "more open violation of the rule", *ibid.* 18-19. It seems to me, however, that there is a definite play on the interpretation of the word of which the reader is meant to be aware because of its central position similar to the "special purpose" Cutt discusses on page 20. There is a hint of heroics as well as a suggestion of a certain type of activity, not purely mental, in which Catullus and Calvus might have indulged that would have resulted in *defessa membra*, as well as the excuse mentioned by the poet of having passed a sleepless night.

[2] Phalaikos *AP* 13.6.4; Theokritos *Epigr.* 22.8; Kaibel, praef. 431a. 5.

[3] See Giarratano *op. cit.* (supra 42 n. 2) 53 under "Formam E." 1.52.8 and 14.52.2 are incorrect.

[4] Words in the 5-7 position in Catullus' iambics are also rare, but are generally used for particular emphasis when they occur. See infra 94 n. 2, 98, 111.

[5] 6.10, 9.9, 15.19, 32.11, 36.14, 41.6, 57.2. All but 36.14 are examples of trisyllables and an enclitic *-que* or *-ve*.

[6] It must be remembered that there are only two lines of hendecasyllables from Cinna, so the percentage can hardly be of value. The four-syllable word itself seems to be a rare adjective formed from an uncertain proper noun. (Cf. Morel 89.)

[7] In this connection it is interesting to note the percentage in the *Priapea*, 6%, comparable to Bibaculus and Martial, and thus higher than Catullus.

Actually, in Catullus' hendecasyllables, the use of four-syllable words in general is not great. The most frequent is the choriambic word-shape in position 3-6, occurring seventy-one times, or 13%.[1] More significant for the rhythm of the meter is the distribution of three-syllable words. Dactylic and anapaestic words are, of course, limited by the nature of the meter to the 3-5 and 4-6 position respectively.[2] Cretic words, although there is a possibility of positioning at 1-3, 6-8, and 8-10, are almost entirely found only at 6-8, the reasons being that 2 is much more frequently long than short,[3] and final monosyllables are rare. However, trisyllables of the shape $\cup - \cup$ have four possible positions, 2-4, 5-7, 7-9, 9-11, yet 2-4 never occurs, and 5-7 only rarely.[4] The following table indicates the various poets' preferences for 7-9 and 9-11.

	LAEV.	VARRO	BIBAC.	CALVUS	CINNA	CORNIF.	CAT.	MARTIAL [5]	De Geo- metria
5-7							1%	1%	3%
7-9	50%	38%	12%		50%		13%	16%	37%
9-11		25%	24%		50%		20%	22%	17%

One further fact relating to trisyllabic words is that anapaestic and dactylic words are less frequent than pyrrhic words in filling the two short syllables of the "pyrrhic sequence," as Cutt calls it.[6] The following table shows the distribution of two- and three-syllable word-shapes in the undivided pyrrhic sequence.[7]

	LAEV.	VARRO	BIBAC.	CALVUS	CINNA	CORNIF.	CAT.	MARTIAL	De Geo- metria
3-5		13%	29%				19%	22%	10%
4-5	50%		48%	50%		100%	30%	28%	10%
4-6	50%	38%		50%			21%	23%	40%

[1] See Cutt, *op. cit.* (supra 34 n. 2) 10. This percentage is similar to that of his contemporary, Bibaculus, of 12%, and that of his predecessor, Varro, 13%. A sample percentage taken from the 212 lines of Martial's first book reveals only 5%. The percentage is low among the Alexandrians, 4%, high in the *skolia*, 20%, while that of fifth century drama is the same as Catullus, 13%. Highest of all is the percentage in the Greek inscriptions, 29%.

[2] A dactylic word could be used in the 1-3 position, but the meter would require that the final syllable be lengthened. Interestingly enough, there is only one instance of this in Catullus, 38.8.

[3] According to Cutt's statistics, a short 2 occurs thirty-one times (7-11).

[4] See preceding discussion 44-45, and diagram, graph infra 151, 152.

[5] The statistics for Martial in the rest of this chapter are based on the 212 lines from Book 1.

[6] See Cutt, *ibid.*, 15.

[7] See discussion of four-syllable words on 45-46, tables 62, Cutt 10, 32-33.

The preceding statistics are interesting because they show that the distribution of words in the central position in the line bears no relationship to word and verse accent, if one assumes that verse accent must be on the long syllables. However, the infrequency of 4-7 or 5-7 words in Latin hendecasyllables could be related to verse accent if one assumes that certain syllables, regardless of quantity, were preferred for accentuation. The pyrrhic, choriambic, and anapaestic combinations result in an accented 4, which is also the preferred accented syllable in iambic trimeter, choliambics, and sapphics.[1] Dactylic words, and words of more than three syllables covering positions 2-5 or 1-5, or disyllabic words from 3-4, result in an accented 3. It is clear, however, if one compares the following table of accent localization with that of accent localization in the sapphic hendecasyllable, that there is much less regularization in the phalaecean hendecasyllable.

Accented	LAEV.	VARRO	BIBAC.	CALVUS	CINNA	CORNIF.	CAT.	MARTIAL	De Geometria
3		25%	35%		50%		29%	35%	20%
4	100%	63%	58%	100%		100%	64%	58%	67%
10	100%	100%	100%	100%	100%	100%	98%	99%	100%

The question might be raised as to why the percentage of accented 3 is higher in Martial than in Catullus, considering the fact that the percentage of word-ends at 6 is higher, and that of pyrrhic words is virtually equal: Catullus 29%, Martial 28%. The reason lies in a particular aspect of Catullan versification: the use of initial monosyllables.[2] Moreover, the percentage of monosyllables is higher in general in Catullus than in Martial, particularly at 2 and 3.

Monosyllable at	VARRO	BIBACULUS	CATULLUS	MARTIAL	De Geometria
1	63%	29%	50%	48%	33%
2	25%	18%	29%	20%	
3	25%	6%	21%	14%	3%

---

[1] See pages 91, 110, and 22 respectively.
[2] On initial monosyllables, see 25 n. 2, 75-77, 115 n. 1, 128. Leutsch *loc. cit.* (supra 43 n. 2) suggests that the use of initial monosyllables in the line was to strengthen the effect of the masculine caesura of the dactyl, a proof to him that the hendecasyllabic line was composed of five feet, the second of which was a dactyl. Thus, a break after 3 is essential to avoid coincidence of word and verse foot. However, according to the tables of Cutt relevant to this point, coincidence in the "first foot" occurs in Catullus with a frequency of 30%, *op. cit.* (supra 34 n. 2) 8, and in the dactylic "second foot" 19%, *ibid.* 9—percentages which seem a little high to justify the verb "avoid."

A corollary of this is the increase in four-syllable 2-5 words and dactylic words in Martial: Catullus 3%, Martial 5%; 2-5 words, 19% to 22% increase of dactylic words.[1]

A second interesting comparison of phalaecean hendecasyllables with sapphic, showing less regularization in the former, is the trend toward lines composed of only four words.[2] Here the percentages for the fragmentary predecessors and contemporaries of Catullus are probably unreliably high, since the lines were chosen by later encyclopedists and grammarians as illustrations of the unusual.

Percentage of Four-Word Lines

								De
LAEV.	VARRO	BIBAC.	CALVUS	CINNA	CORNIF.	CAT.	MAR.	Geometria
50%	50%	59%	100%		100%	24%	25%	59%

By comparing these percentages with those of four-word lines in sapphics, one can see that systematization in phalaeceans had a much slower development than that of sapphics. In order to be more accurate, however, one should not overlook the role of Boethius, whether he influenced later poets or not. The total number of lines he wrote in phalaecean hendecasyllables is not high, 37, and only eighteen are stichic.[3] The percentage of four-word lines is 10% more than in Martial. The most interesting observation of his treatment of the meter, however, is in the location of accented syllables. The poem where these accents have the most significance is 3.10, where phalaeceans are alternated with sapphics. If one becomes disassociated from the notion of the Greek rhythmic pattern of thesis and arsis and looks at the distribution of the Latin words in the lines, one realizes that phalaeceans and sapphics can be written with identical accent patterns by stressing the accents of the words. This fact is of small concern to poets familiar with vowel quantities, but for Latin poets of the Middle Ages who were not always accurate with quantities, it was extremely important to devise some system of word patterning which would distinguish between the two types of eleven-syllable line. As is shown in the chapter on sapphics, a line composed of four words whose

---

[1] See table p. 62.
[2] Compare with similar tables for the sapphic meter p. 24.
[3] 1.4, 3.4, 3.10, 4.4. 27% of the phalaecean hendecasyllables of the *Priapea* are four-word lines.

syllabic lengths are 3 2 3 3, will result in the ideal sapphic accents of 1, 4, 6 and 10.[1] The same syllabic grouping in the phalaecean meter will result in 2, 4, 6 and 10 being accented, except where 2 is short in a cretic wordshape, which is virtually non-existent, except in Catullus. If, however, a word limit at 6 is regularly observed, as it came to be in phalaeceans, an accented 6 is impossible. Thus, the later Latin phalaecean hendecasyllables have an accent pattern of 2, 4, 7 or 8, and 10.[2] That these accents became important is evident in the poem of Boethius mentioned above.[3] In the eighteen lines alternating phalaeceans and sapphics, only two vary from these accent patterns; namely, lines 7 and 8. The first of these, quantitatively a phalaecean, has an accented 6 (a set sapphic accent by this time in literary development), because there is a word limit at 5 followed by a three-syllable word. Line 8, a sapphic line, has an accented 8, which though found in sapphics, has a lower frequency than that of the accented 6.[4] Clearly, however, such a regularization did not take place with the phalaecean hendecasyllables to the extreme degree shown in the sapphic meter.

Another proof of lack of regularization can be seen in the fact that even the lines composed of four words, and this percentage is low, show almost no patterns that are repeated enough times to give significant percentages. Those which are most common in Catullus are less common in Martial, and vice versa.

Syllabic Patterns of Four-Word Lines
Percentages Based on Number of Four-Word Lines

				VAR. (4)	LAEV. (1)	BIBAC. (10)	CORNIF. (1)	CAT. (131)	MAR. (53)	*De Geometria*
2	4	2	3	25%				15%	6%	6%
2	3	3	3			10%		9%	17%	
3	3	2	3		100%			11%	8%	22%
3	3	3	2					7%	4%	16%
3	2	2	4			20%	100%	4%	6%	

---

[1] See tables in the sapphic section p. 22, 24.
[2] See Rudmose-Brown's discussion on Carolingian phalaeceans, *op. cit.* (supra 18 n. 1) 41-43 and 55.
[3] In connection with sapphics and phalaeceans being used in the same poem, epigram 1504, *AL* 2², 407, provides a singular example. Three lines are in sapphics, 6, 10 and 23; the remaining forty-nine are in phalaeceans. The composer may or may not have been very skillful; most of the poem is made up of a series of centos fom Catullus and Horace. But he did not observe the regular sapphic accents in his three lines of 4, 6 and 10, and every possible variety occurs in the phalaecean lines, including a great many "divided pyrrhics" (see supra 45 n. 1).   [4] See table p. 22.

These are the five highest percentages. Other combinations of syllable patterns are even lower. There is, of course, no value in the percentages of Laevius and Cornificius. They are included only to show the frequency of these patterns in Catullus, Martial, and the *De Geometria*. Virtually no similarity or trend of word-patterning in this meter can be observed, unlike the patterning in the sapphic hendecasyllable.[1]

A final factor which should be briefly mentioned in connection with phalaecean hendecasyllables, for it ties in with Meyer's "bestimmte Caesur" or lack thereof, as well as differentiation from more regularized sapphic hendecasyllables, is the number of lines composed of only three words. Admittedly the number is not high, but considering the fact that there are only two certain lines in all of Horace's sapphics[2] composed of only three words, and no examples in Catullus' sapphics or those of later Latin poets, the twenty-five lines in Catullus' phalaeceans and ten lines in Martial's first book are important. That the phalaecean hendecasyllabic line was never quite so definitively divided into two almost equal halves,[3] as was done for the sapphic hendecasyllable by the "master craftsman" Horace, would seem evident from the tables and statistics already given. Perhaps had Martial spent more effort in establishing Roman form out of Greek chaos, the end result of the phalaecean meter might have been more similar to that of the sapphic. Unfortunately for Meyer, Leutsch, and others who have spent valuable years in chasing caesuras, Martial was not Horace. Other than making syllables 1 and 2 consistently long, a practice not always followed by later composers in the meter,[4] he does not appear to

---

[1] Note the steady increase in percentages of sapphic four-word lines from Catullus, to Horace, to Diaconus (p. 24).

[2] 2.10.5, 4.2.9. 4.6.14 may be read as two words or a compound.

[3] Meyer seems to imply that there was something wrong with a line which had a break after *only* 4 *or* 7, *op. cit.* (supra 34 n. 2) 212. However, he is inaccurate because there is no line in hendecasyllables that is composed of only two words except the last line of Sidonius Apollinaris' poem 23. Therefore, the word *only* is wrong. Lines with the less common word-end at 4 either have one at 6 or at 7 as was discussed on 44-45, or occasionally at 8. Those with word limits at 7 when not preceded by breaks after 5 or 6, have word-ends at 3 or 4. Dominant breaks at 3 and 7, 4 and 7, or 4 and 8, have the effect of making the line tripartite. A line divided into three more or less equal sections would seem to be just as good as one divided into two more or less equal sections, unless one has a preconceived opinion on the subject.

[4] For example, Ausonius, as Münscher mentions, *op. cit.* (supra 35 n. 3) 74.

have observed any more systematization than Catullus. Hendecasyllables were certainly not considered lines divided into two
equal halves by the Greek poets of the Alexandrian period, nor
apparently by the earliest poet who used them, Sappho. And even
though the dramatic fragments of the fifth century and the *skolia*
show considerably higher instances of this bipartite division, it is
far from being universal. Moreover, when a line such as Sophokles'
Ph. 1140 has a word-end at 2, 3, 4, 5, 6 and 9, who can be sure
he knows the position of the chief break? Meyer would say that
this shows that Greek hendecasyllables had no "bestimmte Caesur."
The same type of argument could be used for the Latin. The result
is that *bestimmte* turns out to be less of a certainty and more of
an opinion.[1] Terms like "rule" and "violation" can only be accepted
by overweighting one aspect of the evidence.[2]

To return to the three-word line, it has a certain usefulness based
on the needs of the Latin language as well as that of variety.
It offers the opportunity of including long proper names and abstract
feminine nouns ending in *io*, polysyllabic adverbs and compara-
tives, and genitive plurals.[3] Yet even though most of the three-word
lines are so patterned that a break after 5 or one after 6 exists, the
very fact that there are only three words has the effect of making
the line tripartite.[4] It is interesting to note that though the percentage of these three-word lines in Catullus and Martial is only 5%
and 4% respectively, such a minimum frequency was considered
enough authority by Sidonius Apollinaris in the fifth century

---

[1] If the only lines from Catullus that existed were 3.13, 6.9 and 13.5,
whose word limits respectively occur at 1, 3, 5, 6, 8; 4, 6, 7, 8, 9; and 1, 2, 3,
4, 5, 8, one could assume that the "bestimmte Caesur" was at 8, with the
break after 4, 5 or 6, as the "ersatz" or "hilfs-Caesur." See Meyer, *loc. cit.*
(supra 50 n. 3) 212.

[2] *Ibid.* 213.

[3] See Cutt's discussion on the use of polysyllabic words at line
ends, *op. cit.* (supra 34 n. 2) 43-54. I do not mean to suggest that
polysyllables occur only in three-word lines, of course. Words of more
than four syllables are found in 11% of Catullus' lines, while three-word
lines only in 5%.

[4] Of the thirteen combinations found, 3 5 3, 3 4 4, 4 3 4, 2 5 4, 2 6 3,
3 3 5, 5 2 4, 5 4 2, 2 4 5, 6 2 3, 2 3 6, 1 4 6, 5 3 3, the first five prevent
a central 5 or 6 break. 3 5 3 is the most common in Martial, while 3 4 4
and 2 6 3 is most common in Sidonius Apollinaris who has a 7% frequency
of three-word lines. Catullus uses no pattern more than three times, but he
uses those combinations which result in a break after 5 or 6 much more
than those which do not, 18:7.

A.D. to be used thirty-nine times in 510 lines.[1] In addition, more than half of these thirty-nine lines, twenty-one to be exact, have word arrangements which obviate a break after 5 or 6. To further emphasize the point, according to Meyer's figures, 13% of Sidonius' lines have no "regelmässig Caesur,"[2] a significantly higher percentage than the 4% of Catullus or the 9% of Martial.[3] The point which must be realized, then, is that tripartite lines, as well as the more common bipartite lines, are perfectly permissible.

To conclude this section, then, the statistics show that the hendecasyllabic meter, whether Greek or Latin, was relatively unsystematized. Perhaps it was this very freedom from regulation which caused it to be employed in poems of banter, ridicule, and personal feelings. This, unfortunately, is a matter of opinion to a large extent. What scholars would like the evidence to do is to explain the origin of the meter, or at least what Catullus thought the origin was; or if neither of these, to figure out who were his models.[4] If one is honest, one must confess that there is not sufficient evidence. From the fragments of predecessors and contemporaries which can be used for comparison, it seems clear that Sappho was not a model. Furthermore, the Alexandrians with their greater use of word limits at 3 and 7, had less influence than scholars would like to assume.[5] Catullus' word patterns resemble those of fifth century drama and the drinking songs. In fact, the best hypothesis to fabricate out of the insufficient evidence is that these *skolia* were his models. Here, metrical analysis might support the theory, but subject matter does not seem to. Moreover, there are examples of resolutions in the hendecasyllables of the *skolia* which are not found in Catullus.[6] Another conjecture is disqualified. If, on the

---

[1] *Carm.* 23.3, 14, 22, 26, 27, 29, 41, 58, 62, 68, 94, 138, 151, 157, 164, 211, 239, 246, 255, 257, 280, 295, 301, 314, 317, 319, 330, 356, 366, 413, 427, 432, 440, 460, 474, 479, 480, 483, 508.

[2] *Op. cit.* (supra 34 n. 2) 224. I don't believe this justifies Meyer's use of the word "willkürlich," however.

[3] Cf. tables supra p. 44. The break after 5 and 6 total 96% Catullus, and 91% in Martial.

[4] Lafaye is one of the few metricians who realizes the impossibility of this, although even he implies its desirability. *Op. cit.* (supra 6 n. 1) 98-99.

[5] Leutsch, *op. cit.* (supra 43 n. 2) 740: ". . . so hat Catull mit richtigem takte auch hier an Kallimachos sich angeschlossen, der wohl zuerst so wie bei Catull wir es finden die einzelnen füsse des verses eng verbunden, den vers durch cäsuren gekräftigt und dadurch dem character der stichischen composition gemäss behandelt zu haben scheint."

[6] *PMG* 890 (no. 7), 893 (no. 10), 896 (no. 13).

other hand, one ceases insisting on the universality of Latin regimentation in all meters, and acknowledges the possibility of "aiolische Freiheit" [1] operating in Latin as well as in Greek, the difficulties concerning caesura or diaeresis, iambic, trochaic, or spondaic beginnings, and even divided pyrrhics disappear. It has been made clear that within this "aiolische Freiheit" certain word-syllable patterns are repeated with considerably greater frequency. To decide who was a model for Catullus, on the other hand, is not possible. The variety of his patterning would indicate that he knew the meter as used by Greek poets of all periods, and that this usage had been completely absorbed. There is little evidence that he was concerned with the derivation of the meter,[2] or that he was aware of the ideas of his older contemporary Varro who called the meter an ionic a minore trimeter.[3] The aspect of Varro's technique which is completely different from the rest of Greek and Latin usage is the omnipresent word limit at 6, and never filling the pyrrhic sequence with a two-syllable word. Also, the first two syllables of the line are always long. It could be argued that on the basis of only eight or nine lines surviving in the meter, the evidence is not sufficient. However, when there is as high a percentage as 25% in the rare use of the divided pyrrhic as against Catullus' 9% or Bibaculus' 5%, and no examples of a pyrrhic word as against Catullus' 30% and Bibaculus' 48%,[4] the absence is noticeable. The determining factor, no doubt, is Varro's insistence on a word limit at 6. A pyrrhic at 4-5 compels a monosyllable at 6, if the word-end at 6 is to be preserved, making the break after

---

[1] A term borrowed from Münscher, *loc. cit.* (supra 50 n. 4).

[2] Here one runs into the problem of interpreting the evidence. Della Corte, "Varrone metricista" (supra 35-36, n. 4) 146, says that Catullus' use of one long syllable to fill the normal two shorts of the pyrrhic 4-5 is proof that he believed in the dactylo-trochaic scansion of the meter. Kroll, however, in his commentary on Catullus (96), suggests that it is a mistake to seek any particular reason behind Catullus' handling of the meter other than experimentation

[3] Keil, *Gr. Lat* 6. 261.18. Here, again, two scholars differ on interpretation. Della Corte, *loc. cit.* (supra n. 2) says Varro believed in this ionic a minore derivation because in Greek usage the seventh syllable could be long or short. Heinze, *op.cit.* (supra 17 n. 1) 10-12, on the other hand, believes that nothing should be inferred from this brief reference to a statement of Varro's by the grammarian Caesius Bassus because it is out of context. And there is no way of knowing the context. Probably it is a reference to Varro's having learned to use meters wherein one foot may contain four syllables.

[4] See tables supra 46.

5 more important than after 6. The only line where a monosyllable at 6 occurs in Varro is an interpolated line, fr. 568.2. Moreover, it becomes a monosyllable only through elision.[1] Thus the absence of pyrrhic words is a corollary of the preferred break after 6. How this relates to the ionic a minore statement is not clear.[2] Catullus and his circle were certainly disciples of "aiolische Freiheit" with no indication of being influenced by Varro.

Before leaving the subject of Catullus' treatment of phalaecean hendecasyllables, a brief look at vocabulary is in order. Cutt's dissertation has proved conclusively that Catullus chose certain types of words to fill metrical positions in the lines more frequently than others,[3] and that certain stylistic effects, particularly l-sounds at the end of a line,[4] are highlighted by Catullus' choice of words. Assuming the validity of his conclusions, one would like to see if they can be applied to his predecessors or contemporaries. One can hardly expect to find much from thirty-two fragments, practically all of which are extant only because they illustrate some rare grammatical form or obscure word. The situation is further complicated by the uncertain readings of many of the lines containing words which could be compared.[5] This is particularly the case with the Varronian fragments. For instance, it is tempting to compare Varro's use of the diminutive *puellum* in fr. 19 in the 9-11 position with the seventeen occurrences in Catullus of the more common diminutive *puella*.[6] However, differences of opinion between scholars as to the correct reading for the line, and therefore on the actual meter of the line, stand in the way.[7] Similarly, one would

---

[1] The various readings are:
a. Lindsay Nonius Marcellus M 336. 10:   usque ad limina † nitida vilis
b. Scaliger & Riese, *VSM* (infra 123 n. 1): usque ad limina nidica esca vilis
c. Muller Nonius Marcellus M 336.10: usque ad limina niduli esca vilis
d. Bücheler, *Varronis Menippeae* 568.2: usque ad limina nidi amica vilis

[2] The break after 6 is not the normal position in a trimeter line, but after 5. In the examples of what Koster, *Traité* 203 calls ionic a minore trimeter from Anakreon, not one has a word-end at 6. One might well be justified in thinking that Varro's evidence is contradictory.

[3] *Op. cit.* (supra 34 n. 2) chapters IV and V.

[4] *Ibid.* 34-43.

[5] The only aspect of the two lines attributed to Laevius which can be compared is that line 1 begins with three monosyllables, a Catullan practice in 7% of the lines.

[6] See Cutt, *op. cit.* (supra 34 n. 2) 34-35.

[7] Lachmann inserted the word *alvo* after *mater* to make it an ionic line. See *In T. Lucretii Cari de Rerum Natura libros Commentarius* (Berlin 1882)

like to see a parallel to the multiplicity of Catullan l-sounds and the use of diminutives at the end of the line in Varro's *putillos*, fr. 568.1. Here again, the manuscripts' readings and the scholars emendations do not agree.[1] A third possibility, and interesting from the suggestiveness implied by Catullus' use of it,[2] is *amica*. It is found in the 7-9 position of the same fragment of Varro's *Virgula Divina* already discussed, fr. 568. In fact, the satire *Virgula Divina* contains six of the possible eight or nine lines of Varro's hendecasyllables. But the word *amica* is an invention by Bücheler, thus negating the value of comparison.

If, however, Varro does not offer any conclusive examples of similarity of diction to that of Catullus, his contemporaries do. This is particularly true of Bibaculus, probably because he has the largest number of extant lines. Compare the first words of fragment 1 with Catullus' poem 14.24:

Bibaculus	si quis forte mei domum Catonis
Catullus	si qui forte mearum ineptiarum

The fourth word is particularly interesting because it is an unusual example of the divided pyrrhic where the 5-6 space is filled by a pronominal form. There are only two other instances of it in Catullus, 50.16 and 58.3, *tibi* and *suos*. It would be convenient if one could make a nice hypothesis about the type of disyllabic words in general used to fill the 5-6 space and then see if the fragments offered corroborative evidence. This is what Cutt has attempted to do,[3] but his categories are so broad, forms of the verb "to be," sentence enclitics, proclitic pronominals, verbs closely joined with infinitives, words involving elision, a few words requiring special consideration, that the hypothesis seems to be one based more on opinion than on fact. In the fragments from predecessors and contemporaries there are four examples of a disyllable in the 5-6 position. Two of these are in Varro, fr. 566 *novo*, and fr. 567.2 *legens*. These certainly do not seem to fit into any of Cutt's catego-

---

276. Keil's edition of Priscian, *Gr. Lat.* 2. 232. 7, leaves a crux after *mater*. Della Corte calmly states that Lachmann's insertion was an error, deletes *mater* on the grounds of its being superfluous, and changes the ... *que* to *quem*. See supra 41 n. 4.

[1] The manuscripts give either *ut illos* or *apud illos*. Scaliger conjectured *pusillos* and Bücheler *putillos*.

[2] See infra 107 n. 1.

[3] *Op. cit.* (supra 34 n. 2) 15-23.

ries. Neither does the example from Cinna, fr. 9.2 *rapit*. Only the one just mentioned from Bibaculus seems comparable. There are ten examples in Catullus.[1] Of course, it is difficult to draw any conclusive evidence from such fragmentary material, but it seems more probable that it is the paucity of words of this type, because of the less frequently divided pyrrhic, which lends itself to devising attractive hypotheses rather than that the poet thought of particular categories to fill the position.[2] One factor that Cutt does not mention which could have significance is that a disyllable in the 5-6 position results in a word accent at 5, thus stressing the uncommon division even more than if followed by a trisyllable or quadrisyllable. Here, the tantalizing questions, are accent rules for enclitics different from the regular penultimate rule, and, to what extent does the Latin word accent change its place, may be involved.[3] Certainly, Martial's use of the dative pronominal forms with a long *i* is interesting. Whether it indicates deliberate archaism, imitation of Catullus, or a survival of an older form in the colloquial language of his day cannot be determined. In any case, Cutt's point about the greater infrequency of the divided pyrrhic in hendecasyllables than in other Aeolic meters is worth noticing as a distinguishing feature,[4] apparent in the usage of Laevius, Bibaculus, and Catullus, but not in the fragments of Varro.

There are other similarities of word and verse position between Bibaculus and Catullus.

	Position	Word	BIBACULUS	CATULLUS
1.	1-2	unus	(unum) fr. 2.6	(unum) 10.17, (unam) 45.21, (un(o) 45.23, (un(o) 57.7
2.	1-2	omnes	fr. 2.5	5.3, 45.4
3.	1-2	tantus	(tantam) fr. 1.5	(tanto) 49.6, 55.14
4.	4-5	quibus	fr. 1.4	10.12, 41.5

---

[1] *Ibid.* 16-18, 30.

[2] For the purposes of comparison, Martial in Book I has fifteen disyllables in the 5-6 position, five of which are filled with a pronominal form, three a verb closely associated with an infinitive, and two the verb "to be." But as Martial was a blatant imitator of Catullus, the fact that these illustrations support Cutt's hypothesis does not prove that Catullus knew about it.

[3] A few references on this subject are: Lindsay, *L.L.* 162-164; A. Ahlberg, *Studia de Accentu Latina* (Lundae 1905); Fraenkel, *op. cit.*, (supra 7 n. 4), 273-299; Zinn I 81-86; R. W. Tucker, "Accentuation before Enclitics in Latin," *TAPA* 96, 1965, 449; and Allen, *VL* 87-88.

[4] See Cutt, *op. cit.* (supra 34 n. 2) 15-16.

Position	Word	BIBACULUS	CATULLUS
5. 6-7	ille	fr. 1.4	(illa) 5.11, 42.7
6. 9-11	poeta	(poetam) fr. 2.4	(poetis) 14.5
		(poetas) fr. 17.2	(poetae) 14.23
			(poetam) 16.5
			(poetae) 36.6
			(poeta) 49.5, 6
7. 10-11	unus	(una) fr. 1.7	(una) 21.5, (unam) 58.2
8. 10-11	ille	(illos) fr. 1.2	6.9
			(illa) 47.4, 58.1
9. 8-11	venditare	(venditabat) fr. 2.2	(venditare) 33.8

Undoubtedly, there is nothing overly significant about most of these examples. However, 6 calls for a comment. Five of the six times the noun *poeta* occurs in the 9-11 position in Catullus, it is preceded by a trisyllable. Four times it is in close association with the word *pessimus*, the direct opposite of the trisyllable which precedes the word in Bibaculus, fr. 2.4. Compare:

summum grammaticum, optimum poetam	Bibaculus 2.4
saecli incommoda, pessimi poetae	Catullus 14.23
electissima pessimi poetae	36.6
agit pessimus omnium poeta	49.5
tanto pessimus omnium poeta [1]	6

The fifth example in Catullus, 14.5, is connected with *perdo*, the common verb of execration. The sixth, 16.5, is perhaps the most clever of all. Centrally located in a poem meant to shock, which begins with the verb *paedicabo*, is the *castus* and *pius poeta*.

> Nam castum esse decet pium poetam
> ipsum, versiculos nihil necessest;

The passage has often been taken as the *apologia pro vita sua* [2] without much regard for the context. This is not the place to give

---

[1] The two lines of 49 should also be taken in context with the irony of the last line of the poem: "quanto tu optimus omnium patronus."

[2] Pliny the Younger was the first literary critic to do so. See *Epistles* 4.14 and 5.3. Lafaye devotes several pages *op. cit.* (supra 6 n. 1) 106-113 to a discussion of the poet's privilege, and almost requirement, to write indecent verse. R. Hack, "The Law of the Hendecasyllable," *HSCP* 25, 1914, 107-115, deprecates Lafaye's remarks, but still makes the error of discussing the above passage out of context: ". . . Lafaye accepts Catullus' apology and proceeds to justify it by some curious statements about dual personality and the Roman definition of chastity. Catullus, according to this view, is not insincere in detaching himself from his work, and is quite within his rights in claiming the honorable title of 'pius poeta'" (110). "M. Lafaye takes these lines (16.3-5) as the solemn statement of a poet who aspires to be dignified in

a commentary on the poem, but only to call attention to the fact that here Catullus uses a favorable adjective with the noun *poeta* in contrast to the derogatory ones elsewhere and the obscenity in the rest of the poem. Therein lies the interest in comparison with the fragment of Bibaculus mentioned above, as well as the second's example in Bibaculus where the word also occurs with no critical implications:

qui solus legit ac facit poetas   M 17.2

The singular location of this noun at the end of the line,[1] the opposing adjectives used in connection with it, and the insinuations involved in the poems containing this noun are strong indications of repartee between the two poets.[2]

the more personal part of his dual personality; I regard them as the half-joking apologia of Catullus in reply to an accusation, which (as Robinson Ellis suggests) was not made very seriously" (113). He is referring to R. Ellis, *A Commentary on Catullus* (Oxford 1889) 59. See also Munro, *op. cit.* (supra 16 n. 4) 79. Commentators generally avoid discussing the poem in detail because of its obscenity; Fordyce omits it altogether. Nevertheless, it is an excellent example of what Quinn calls "subtle conscious craftsmanship" (*Docte Catulle* 44), and "cyclic effect" (*The Catullan Revolution*, Melbourne 1959, 58). I think it is clear that Catullus is casting gibes at the concept, revolutionary in his day, that anyone who picks up an instrument to write verse is automatically a poet. That this argument had top priority as a discussion topic is clear from the many references to it in Cicero, for example *Arch.* 7.18 where Ennius is the *sanctus poeta*; or the derogatory terms *malus poeta* 10.25, and in the *Pis.* 29.70 "ut Graeculum, ut adsentatorem, ut poetam." There are always going to be good poets and bad ones; Catullus is just placing himself among the former and Furius among the latter, and perhaps mocking Cicero's and Varro's outmoded concepts that poets must be ancient and dignified. (Cf. Varro, *Ling.* 5.88 where *poeta* seems to mean a type of general reference book, and the noun is an impersonal plural form.) For the position on poetry of Cicero and Catullus, see also D. F. S. Thomson, "Catullus and Cicero: Poetry and the Criticism of Poetry," *CW* 60, 1967, 225.

[1] There are actually five possible positions for this word in the line: 1-3, 2-4, 5-7, 7-9 and 9-11. The second possibility involves an initial short syllable at 2 in a trisyllable word which never occurs in Catullus. A trisyllable in this position only occurs six times, possibly related to the divided pyrrhic. (See Cutt's tables, *op. cit.* supra 34 n. 2, 9, and previous discussion about divided pyrrhics, supra 45 n. 1, 67). The 5-7 trisyllable occurs only six times also, but not filled by *poeta*. The most common positions for a trisyllable with a ∪ _ ∪ shape are 7-9 and 9-11. . . . *poeta noster* would be a perfectly good ending for a hendecasyllable line; but *poeta* is never found in the 7-9 position. Of the seven occurrences of the noun in Catullus, all are found in the hendecasyllables, and only one is not the final word of the line. Poem 35 begins with the noun, an example of the less common initial short syllable.

[2] I have gone into the relationship between these two poets at greater length in "M. Furius Bibaculus and Catullus," *CW* 62, no. 4 (1969) 112-114.

Two other contemporaries are left to be discussed in terms of vocabulary: Calvus and Cinna. Calvus is mentioned by Catullus a sufficient number of times to assume a close relationship,[1] particularly poem 50 discussing how the two worked together composing poetry. One would expect to see evidence of this in Calvus' fragments. Unfortunately, too little remains to reveal Calvus' side. Interestingly enough, however, both lines of his hendecasyllabic fragments end in a five-syllable word, an ending which occurs forty-two times in Catullus, and the preferred position for five-syllable words.[2] The second of Calvus' two lines is extraordinarily similar to two of Catullus. [3]

It is certainly very likely that Bibaculus was imitating a use of Catullus rather than the other way around. The significance, however, is the similarity. The use of the word *poeta* and its associated adjectives does bear some light, in my opinion, on the identification of the Furius in 16, 23 and 26. (The same name is found in 11, but the meter is sapphics.) No one seems to have discussed this fact in using the Bibaculus fragments to bolster the theory that Catullus' Furius is Suetonius' Furius Bibaculus. (See Suetonius *De Gram.* 11.) An article by L. Richardson, Jr., "Furi at Aureli, Comites Catulli," *CP* 58, 1963, 93-106, analyzes the relationship between Catullus and Furius, but does not take up the problem of whether this Furius was Furius Bibaculus, the poet. He alludes briefly to the *pius poeta*, without mentioning its position in the line, or the other poems in which the word *poeta* occurs: "For surely a phrase like *pium poetam* is not to be taken very seriously" (99). W. A. Heidel, in "Catullus and Furius Bibaculus," *CR* 15, 1901, 216, uses only the weak evidence of "the spirit of the poems" being similar to refute the august German authority, Otto Ribbeck. (Cf. O. Ribbeck, *Geschichte der Römischen Dichtung* I², Stuttgart, 1894, 346.) Neudling, *op. cit.* (supra 9-10 n. 3) 71-72 accepts the arguments of Heidel and uses a citation in Quintilian, 10.1.96, on invective in Bibaculus, Catullus, and Horace as further evidence. That both mention Cato is only an additional argument if one accepts the identification of Catullus' Cato, 56.1. as M. Valerius. If the pieces of evidence are laid out clearly, two poets use the same meter, two poets mention a prominent personage, two poets discuss poverty and villas up for sale, and two poets not only are concerned with the position of the poet in society, but use the noun in the same spot in the line, the weight of the evidence makes arguing against a connection very difficult. The references by one poet to the *nomen* of the other under such conditions of metrical and stylistic similarity go far toward indicating that Catullus' Furius and Suetonius' Furius Bibaculus are one and the same person. (The chronology of Bibaculus' life, as much of it as can be ascertained, is thoroughly discussed in Neudling, *ibid.* Birth and death dates may be uncertain, but he was clearly alive and writing in the Varronian era.)

[1] 50.1, 8; 14.2; 53.3; 96.2.
[2] See Cutt, *op. cit.* (supra 34 n. 2) 33.
[3] Compare Martial's obvious imitation of Catullus, 11.6.3: versu ludere non laborioso.

durum rus fugit et laboriosum	Calvus	M 2
doctis Iuppiter et laboriosis	Catullus	1.7
malest, me hercule, et laboriose		38.2

An adjective not too common,[1] used with the same implications of meaning and in the same place in the line,[2] preceded by the same monosyllable in two poets who are known to have been closely associated, is noteworthy.

Of similar interest is the noun *bigae* in Catullus 58a.4 and Cinna fr. 9.2. Here, however, the words do not occur in the same position in the line. Nevertheless, it is another example of a not overly common word being used by two poets who knew each other quite well.[3] Note that both contain the notion of swiftness in the same place in the line, 7-9:

| bigis raeda rapit citata nanis | Cinna | M 9.2 |
| non Rhesi niveae citaeque bigae | Catullus | 58a.4 |

Two points in concluding can be made about Catullus and his treatment of the phalaecean hendecasyllable. The first is that he is an apostle of "aiolische Freiheit." There is virtually no "ideal" pattern for a phalaecean line if one looks closely at Catullan practice. The following patterns are the most typical: [4]

$$\times \quad \times \quad - \mid \cup \cup \mid - \quad \cup \quad - \mid \cup \quad - \times$$
$$\times \quad \times \mid - \quad \cup \cup \mid - \quad \cup \mid - \quad \cup \quad - \times$$
$$\times \mid \times \mid - \mid \cup \cup \quad - \mid \cup \quad - \quad \cup \mid - \times$$

---

[1] Note the comment on the word in Fordyce 86.

[2] There would be only one other possible position for the adjective, of course, 5-8, which would result in the less common divided pyrrhic. As far as I know, there is no example of a five-syllable in this position in either Greek or Latin.

[3] Cf. 10.30, 95.1, 113.1, and Neudling, *op. cit.* (supra 9-10 n. 3) 79, 81-82.

[4] These examples do not show Catullus' use of the divided pyrrhic or five-syllable words. My experiment with the meter in English on the basis of Catullan patterns compared with Tennyson's *Milton, Hendecasyllabics* which stresses the long syllables, produces the following lines which only show one aspect, word-syllable patterning. It does not show word-sense patterning, which, as Quinn has so admirably pointed out, is the other remarkable feature in Catullus' poetry. Cf. *The Catullan Revolution*, 61, *Docte Catulle*, 32-47.

> If we then always valuing emotion,
> permit absolute anarchy to flourish,
> eagerly follow intricate idealism,

Although the evidence is scanty, Catullus' "aiolische Freiheit" which reflects an "intensive study of the masterpieces of ancient literature,"[1] contrasts with Varro's rigidity. The latter always has the first two syllables long and constantly observes a word limit at 6. The meager examples from Catullus' contemporaries indicate that they handled the meter as he did. The second point is that, instead of an interest in colometric frames, Catullus' hendecasyllables reveal an interest in aspects of individual words: the number of syllables in words,[2] and repetition of certain types of words in particular positions in the line;[3] and the acoustical value of vowel and consonant recurrence.[4] This second point has been less emphasized in this discussion than the first, since it has been so thoroughly covered in Cutt's dissertation.[5]

TABLES OF WORD LOCALIZATION FOR FRAGMENTS

	LAEVIUS	VARRO	BIBA-CULUS	CALVUS	CINNA	CORNI-FICIUS
	(2)	(8)	(17)	(2)	(2)	(1)
I. Monosyllables						
A. ⌣						
at 9			2 12%			
B. —						
at 1	1 50%	5 63%	4 24%	1 50%	1 50%	
at 2	1 50%	3 38%	3 18%	1 50%	1 50%	
at 3	1 50%	2 25%	1 6%	1 50%	1 50%	
at 6		1(?) 13%	2 12%	1 50%		
at 8						1 50%
II. Disyllables						
A. ⌣ —						
1-2				1 6%		
5-6		2 25%		1 6%		1 50%

English can only approximate the meter by locating words according to the number of syllables and the stressed syllable of the word as it is spoken in prose. The result is strikingly dactylic. Copying the last line of the above patterns breaks the dactylic rhythm, although "definite" is not an anapaestic word.

> time will come, definite, disastrous, sudden . . . .

Tennyson's poem, however, is rather poor as far as imitating the most significant points of word localization and polysyllables. In the twenty-one lines there is not a single accented 4, and divided pyrrhics occur in twelve lines ("magazines" in the 4-6 position in line 17 is undoubtedly considered by the poet to have an accented ultima). Also, the frequency of monosyllables in the first half of the line is way beyond that of any Greek or Latin author.

[1] Quinn, *Docte Catulle*, 47.   [2] See also Quinn, *ibid.*, 32, 42.
[3] Cutt, *op. cit.* (supra 34 n. 2) 40-55.   [4] *Ibid.* 55-57.
[5] Tables of word localization for the fragments follow. For Catullus, see Cutt, *op. cit.*, 7-12.

	LAEVIUS	VARRO	BIBA-CULUS	CALVUS	CINNA	CORNI-FICIUS
	(2)	(8)	(17)	(2)	(2)	(1)
7-8		4 50%	3 18%			
B. _ ∪ [1]						
3-4		1 13%	1 6%		1 50%	
6-7			4 24%			1 100%
10-11		3 38%	2 12%			
C. ∪ ∪	1 50%		8 48%	1 50%		1 100%
D. _ _						
1-2		2 25%	4 24%	1 50%	1 50%	
2-3		1 13%	2 12%	1 50%		
III. Trisyllables						
A. ∪ _ ∪ [2]						
7-9	1 50%	3 38%	2 12%		1 50%	
9-11		2 25%	5 29%		1 50%	
B. ∪ _ _						
9-11	1 50%	2 52%	2 12%			
1-3			1 6%			
C. _ ∪ _						
6-8	1 50%		4 24%			
D. _ ∪ ∪						
3-5		1 13%	5 29%			
E. ∪ ∪ _						
4-6	1 50%	3 38%		1 50%		
F. _ _ _						
1-3	1 50%		4 24%			1 100%
IV. Quadrisyllables						
A. _ ∪ ∪ _						
3-6		1 13%	2 12%			
B. ∪ ∪ _ ∪						
4-7			1 6%		1 50%	
C. _ ∪ _ ∪						
6-9			1 6%			
8-11			3 18%			
D. _ ∪ _ _						
8-11			2 12%			1 100%
E. _ _ _ ∪						
1-4		1 13%				
V. Five Syllables						
A. _ _ ∪ ∪ _						
2-6		1 13%				
B. ∪ _ ∪ _ ∪						
7-11		1 13%			2 100%	

[1] It is interesting that there is no example of this word-shape in the 8-9 position in the fragments, and only seventeen examples in Catullus, or 3%. Cutt connects this with the logaoedic pentameter theory of the meter, *op. cit.*, 26, 30 n. 2.

[2] For 5-7, see supra 44-45.

GLYCONIC AND PHERECRATEAN COLA

1 2 3 4 5 6 7 8
× × _ ◡ ◡ _ ◡ ×

1 2 3 4 5 6 7
× × _ ◡ ◡ _ ×

The eight-syllable Aeolic colon known as the glyconic,[1] and its catalectic twin, the seven-syllable pherecratean,[2] are two of the most common cola of monody and choral lyric poetry from its earliest beginnings to the time of the Roman tragedian, Seneca. Examples of the two cola, used either stichically and separately, in stanza combinations involving repetition of one and then the other, or joined together in one long line, can be found in both Greek and Latin poetry. The last mentioned combination acquired by some obscure reasoning the name priapean.[3] These few statements are probably the only uncontroversial ones, however, which can be made on the subject, and do not really analyze the nature

---

[1] For a reasonable discussion of the possibility of existence of a Glykon after whom the meter was named, see Bergk, *PLG*⁴ 3, 709, n. fr. 79a. The earliest reference to his name occurs in Hephaistion, *Ench.* 10.2(Consbr. 32) in the section under antispastic meters. "Δίμετρον δὲ ἀκατάληκτον τὸ καλούμενον Γλυκώνειον, αὐτοῦ Γλύκωνος εὑρόντος αὐτό.

> Κάπρος ἠνίχ' ὁ μαινόλης
> ὀδόντι σκυλακοκτόνῳ
> Κύπριδος θάλος ὤλεσεν."

[2] This meter seems to have been named after the comic poet, Pherekrates, a contemporary of Aristophanes, according to Hephaistion, *Ench.* 15.23 (Consbr. 55). The quote from Pherekrates would indicate that it was his own metrical experiment. "Καὶ τὸ ἐκ τῶν ἀντισπαστικῶν δὲ καταληκτικῶν διμέτρων δικατάληκτον, ὃ Φερεκράτης ἐνώσας σύμπτυκτον ἀνάπαιστον καλεῖ ἐν τῇ Κοριανοῖ·

> ἄνδρες πρόσχετε τὸν νοῦν ἐξευρήματι καινῷ
> συμπτύκτοις ἀναπαίστοις."

[3] The assumption, based on the commentary of Choiroboskos (Consbr. 241) on Hephaistion, *Ench.* 10.4, is that the combination of the two cola acquired the name priapean because an Alexandrian grammarian, Euphronios, used the combination to write dedicatory poems to a rather new divinity, Priapos. For a discussion of the origin of the god and comparatively late introduction into mythology in the Alexandrian period, see H. Herter, *De Priapo* (Giessen 1932) 1-25.

of the meter.[1] A vast amount of effort has been expended over the centuries in the attempt to diagnose its derivation, particularly whether it is anapaestic, iambo-trochaic, or choriambic in origin.[2] If it is indubitably a dimeter as Münscher has said,[3] how can it be connected with anapaests as Pherekrates implies? For although the fragment from Pherekrates quoted by Hephaistion [4] specifically refers to the seven-syllable colon, it seems hardly possible to consider the eight-syllable colon an entirely different meter. Or is the comic poet making a mocking allusion to some unknown controversy of his time? And most important of all, what does he mean the audience to understand by the word συμπτύκτοις? Even the word καινῷ is open to debate since the seven-syllable colon is found in Sappho, Korinna, Anakreon, Pindar, Aischylos, Sophokles, Euripides, and Aristophanes,[5] to mention only the most

---

[1] In this chapter, I only discuss the pure glyconic and pherecratean forms as found in Catullus, i.e., where the D arsis occurs as the second arsis. I omit those varieties where the D arsis falls as the first or the third, which Hephaistion includes under the heading, Polyschematic, (16. 1-3, (Consbr. 56-57), or those which lack a first syllable, generally termed "acephalous." See *MGLP*, (supra 15-16 n. 7), 50. The necessity for calling all these forms glyconic arose from the failure of ancient grammarians to understand that the number of syllables is the dominant feature of Aeolic rhythms, and that there is no fixed location for the D arsis. For discussion of the possibilities of responsion between the pure glyconic and other forms of eight-syllable cola, see Münscher, *op. cit.* (supra 35 n. 3) 69-70, Wilamowitz, *GV* 256-263.

[2] For discussion of the pertinent passages from ancient metricists, Hephaistion, Aristides Quintilianus, Caesius Bassus, Terentianus Maurus, and Sacerdos, as well as references to various scholiasts on Pindar, see W. J. W. Koster, "De Glyconei et Pherecratei Origine," *Philologus* 80, 1925, 357, 362-365. In the same article (351 n. 1), Koster also gives the names of several 19th century German scholars who wrestled with the problem of derivation. See also the general discussion of the nature of the glyconic in Wilamowitz, *GV* 244-254. Other 20th century scholars are mentioned by J. A. Davison in "Double Scansion in Early Greek Lyric," *CQ* 28, 1934, 181-189, where he suggests the novel idea that Alkaios and Sappho had two different schemes for scanning glyconics, either a dimeter made up of a trochaic dipody followed by an iambic dipody, or a trimeter made up of a spondee and two dactyls. Münscher, *op. cit.* (supra 35 n. 3) 68-69, touches on the problem of choriambic, trochaic, and iambic scansion while tearing apart O. Schröder's concept of a "choriambischen Urdimetron" put forth by the latter in *Vorarbeiten zur griechischen Versgeschichte* (Leipzig 1908) 4 ff.

[3] *Ibid.* 68.

[4] Supra 63 n. 2: "And the dicatalectic line composed from two antispastic catalectic dimeters which Pherecrates having put together calls a 'folded-together' anapaest." J. C. Edmonds in his footnote on the passage in *The Fragments of Attic Comedy* (Leiden 1957) I 207, pictures a folded together anapaest like this: _ | _ _ | ∪ ∪ _ | _.

[5] It is almost impossible to locate every instance of the seven- or eight-

important poets. Perhaps the novelty lay in using this colon stichically, for there is no literary evidence of this practice before the time of Aristophanes. In the final wedding chorus of the *Birds*, the colon occurs in two stanzas three consecutive times.[1] But as two of each of these three lines consists of the Hymen jingle, Ὑμὴν ὦ Ὑμέναι' ὦ, the passages can hardly be said to be stichic examples of the pherecratean. However, the use of the colon in the wedding songs, as well as short hymns with religious context, is an indication of its early folk origin. A corroborating proof is the fact that both the glyconic and the pherecratean are indivisible units, formed of alternating B and D arses, based on syllable count.[2]

---

syllable colon in Greek. Moreover, although choral lyric undoubtedly echoes early colometric units, such as the eight-syllable glyconic and seven-syllable pherecratean, the complex structure of this type of lyric requires a freer type of analysis than that of the simple stichic forms of monody. The problem is further complicated by disagreement among scholars as to correct line division. For example, cola exist in Sophokles' choral lyrics which could be called priapean if they were placed together in one line, particularly where words run over into the next colon such as *OC* 672-673, 658-686; *OT* 1187-1188. A. M. Dale in *The Lyric Metres of Greek Drama* (Cambridge 1968²) 43 and 134 calls the combination of the eight- and seven-syllable line a "dicolon" and suggests it serves often as a clausula or period close. For a similar approach to this, see H. Pohlsander, *Metrical Studies in the Lyrics of Sophocles* (Leiden 1964) 164-165, and metrical index, 204-205, 213. The following are a few examples of the seven-syllable colon in Greek. Sappho *PLF* 111.1, 121.1; Korinna *PMG* 1 col. iii 16, 21, 36, 51; Anakreon *PMG* 3.3, 8; 12.3, 8; 13.4, 8; 15.4; 16.4; 17.4; 23; Pindar *O* 1.4, 15, 33, 44, 62, 73, 91, 102; 10.1, 19, 37, 55; Aischylos *Pers.* 271, 277, 556-557, 566-567, 639, 646; *Th.* 312, 314; *Supp.* 639, 640, 652, 653, 664, 665, 674, 675, 684, 685, 694, 695; Sophokles *El.* 1065, 1077; *OT* 1192, 1201; *Ph.* 172, 183; *Tr.* 530; Euripides *El.* 119, 124, 134; *Alc.* 966, 977; Aristophanes *Av.* 1735-1737, 1741-1743; *Eq.* 976, 980, 984, 988, 990, 994.

[1] *Av.* 1735-1737, 1741-1743.

[2] Some of the aspects of the meters of the Ṛgveda, assumed by most scholars to be the oldest surviving example of Indo-European poetry, even though changed from its original form, show a marked similarity to certain Greek meters, particularly those of system c (supra 4). On proofs of the extreme antiquity of Vedic verse, possibly as early as 4000 B. C., and no later than 1500 B.C., see N. N. Law, *Age of the Ṛgveda* (Calcutta 1965) introduction and page 15. Among the similarities are strict measurement by number of syllables, eight, eleven, or twelve; the indifference in the quantity of initial and final vowels; the indivisible eight-syllable line and its catalectic companion, the seven-syllable, by which I mean no predominant break; and the five-syllable colon, a feature of the eleven- and twelve-syllable meter, as well as existing in Vedic in a doublet form, comprising the decasyllable or pentad. See E. V. Arnold, *Vedic Metre* (Cambridge 1905) 10-19, and A. Bergaigne and V. Henry, *Manuel pour étudier le sanscrit védique* (Paris 1890) 41-44. The principle work on comparison of Greek and Vedic meters has been done by

The glyconic can thus be described simply as an eight-syllable colon of the form *C D B closed*, while the pherecratean is a seven-syllable *C D C falling* colon.[1] Occasionally, the initial thesis is short, as in the hymen cry, giving a syncopated effect perhaps, but not changing the basic pattern of the colon.[2] This only occurs twice in the extant fragments of Anakreon from whom the greatest number of lines formed of these two cola have come down.[3] However, a short second syllable, quite common in the other Greek poets though not as frequent as the long second syllable, is found only once in Anakreon.[4]

These factors are not particularly significant except in the light of Catullan practice and his possible models. It is interesting to note in this regard that there are almost no examples of the meter from the Alexandrian period, except for the two paeans inscribed on marble blocks discovered at Delphi, the one to Apollo by Aristonoos c. 230,[5] and the other to Dionysos by Philodamos c. 335,[6]

Meillet, *Les Origines*, 11, 31-42, 52-56, 77. Concerning the eight-syllable verse, he says (53): "Ce type se retrouve en pàli dès la date la plus ancienne." See also G. B. Pighi, "I Ritmi eolici nella metrica greca," ῍Ερανος, *Raccolta di Scritti in Onore del Casimiro Adami* (Verona 1941) 31, for a discussion of the correspondence of Vedic cola with Aeolic. He follows Meillet very closely. Münscher uses the term "urdimetron" to indicate the antiquity of the glyconic and its relative, the choriambic dimeter *op. cit.* (supra 35 n. 4) 69.

[1] This colon can also be considered a *C D A closed*, particularly in sequences where it occurs in Pindar and the following colon begins *in arsi*. See supra 36 n. 2 and infra n. 2.

[2] There are many examples of this in Pindar, such as *N* 2.1, 6, 11, 16, 21; *O* 1.1, 12, 30, 41, 59, 70, 88, 99. Some examples from the dramatists are Aischylos *Pers.* 636, 642; Sophokles *OC* 685; Euripides *Tr.* 310, 314, 331; Aristophanes *Av.* 1736, 1737, 1742, 1743, 1755. The examples from Euripides and Aristophanes illustrate the ritual hymen cry in the eight-syllable colon. It is possible that the initial short syllable is earlier in form than the initial long. It is not found in Latin with the possible exception of Catullus 34, 1-3. (See infra 82).

[3] *PMG* Anakreon 3-28. A short ι occurs in 16.1 and 24.

[4] *PMG* 25.

[5] This is the date given by A. Fairbanks in "A Study of the Greek Paean," *Cornell SCP* 12, 1900, 119. For thorough metrical analysis of the hymn, see O. Crusius, "Die Delphischen Hymnen," *Philologus* 53, 1894, Ergänzungsheft 24. There are six strophes of eight lines each. The fourth and the eighth line of each strophe is a pherecratean.

[6] This is the date given in *RE* 19² 2442. The poem consists of twelve strophes of thirteen lines each. Lines 6, 8, 9 and 12 of each strophe are glyconic in form, while 10 and 13 are pherecratean. Line 7 is hendecasyllabic, usually phalaecean in form. Unfortunately, neither of these two poems, or a third

and one line by Kallimachos.[1] One cannot overlook the probability of other literary paeans written in glyconics which could have influenced Catullus enough to be inspiration for poem 34,[2] for instance, but the fact remains that conclusions cannot be drawn from probabilities.

When one turns to Latin predecessors or contemporaries of Catullus who used the meter, the number is equally meager. The only two certain predecessors are Plautus and Varro, while from contemporaries there are only one-and-half lines from Ticidas, and one-and-a-half lines from Calvus.[3] Catullus' output in glyconics and pherecrateans, however, more than compensates for the paucity of predecessors at least in popularizing the meter in Latin.[4] Glyconics are found in Horace in combination with other *C D alternating* cola,[5] but never in stichic stanza form with the phere-

which Crusius (*ibid.*) writes out in glyconic lines, has been preserved in a sufficiently unmutilated form to permit statistical analysis of word-types or word-positions in the line. In fact, Fairbanks (*ibid.*) gives this last mentioned hymn, which was found with its musical notation, a completely different rendering from that of Crusius. A more recent interpretation of Philodamos' paean is that by R. Vallois, "Les Strophes mutilées du péan de Philodamos," *BCH* 55, 1931, 241-364. The text, giving a total of 156 lines, is on pages 357-362.

[1] Pf. fr. 401.

[2] O. Crusius, *ibid.* (supra 66 n. 5), 75: "Auf die Erwähnung der Olive allein beschränkt sich Catull in einem Hymnus, der sich an hellenistische Vorbilder anschliessen mag."

[3] The difficulties with Plautus will be discussed briefly later. See metrical index in W. M. Lindsay, *T. Macci Plauti Comoediae* (Oxford 1913) at end of volumes 1 and 2. Varro's two glyconic lines are fr. 437:

> per
> aeviternam hominum domum,
> tellurem propero gradum

Ticidas' fr. 1 and Calvus' fr. 4 probably come from wedding songs using both the eight-syllable and seven-syllable colon:
Ticidas:

> felix lectule talibus
> sole amoribus

Calvus:

> vaga candido
> nympha quod secet ungui

For Ticidas' relationship to the Catullan circle, see *RE* 6A[1], 544-546.

[4] He wrote a total of 230 glyconic cola and eighty-two pherecratean, including the four lines from fragment 1.

[5] 1.3, 5, 6, 13, 14, 15, 19, 21, 23, 24, 33, 36; 2.12; 3.7, 9, 10, 13, 15, 16, 19, 24, 25, 28; 4.1, 3, 5, 12, 13. See Zinn II, 107-119, for complete analysis.

cratean closing line, as in Catullus and Anakreon. Nor is the fifteen-syllable priapean line found in Horace, although three and one-half lines exist in this meter from his patron, Maecenas.[1] Controversy still rages over the authorship of the twenty-one lines in the fifteen-syllable priapean meter generally included in the *Catalepton* of Vergil, but also printed with the collection of poems called *Priapea*.[2] However, the fifteen-syllable line is not found after the Augustan age. Seneca experimented with stichic glyconics in the choruses of several of his plays,[3] but the meter was not used again until the fourth century A.D. in the poetry of Prudentius.[4] Stichic glyconics, and glyconics alternated with sapphics occur in Boethius, as well as pherecrateans with asclepiadeans or with iambic dimeter.[5] Interestingly enough, he never uses the seven-syllable colon in its traditional role of completing a glyconic sequence. His total output in the meter is considerable,[6] but his example does not seem to have been followed in the Middle Ages except for a brief revival by the scholars of the Carolingian renaissance.[7] In these verses

---

[1] Morel, *FPL* 102 fr. 4. See also P. Lunderstedt, "De Maecenatis Fragmentis," *Commentationes Philologae Ienensis* 91 (1911) 1-119.

[2] Vergil *Priapea* 3, or *Priapea* 85 in L Müller, *Catulli Tibulli Propertii Carmina* (Leipzig 1880) 118. Zarker *op. cit.* (supra 42 n. 3) 501-522 is a proponent of Catullan authorship. For a good bibliography on the controversy, see 506 n. 1. Some of his reasons are based on metrical analysis, but he does not go into word-position study which is certainly as significant as trochaic, iambic, or spondaic beginnings, or frequency and location of elision.

[3] *HF* 875-894; *Med.* 75-92; *Thy.* 336-403; *HO* 1031-1130; *Oed.* 882-914 (although 891 seems to be a *B C B closed* colon). The preceding lines are examples of stichic glyconics. However, the *C D B closed* colon and the *C D C falling* are found occasionally interspersed with other combinations of C-D arses, such as *Ag.* 589-595 or 626-637.

[4] *Perist.* 7, ninety-five stichic lines. *Praefatio* containing fifteen stanzas of three lines each: a glyconic, an asclepiadean, and a sixteen-syllable choriambic line. There also exists in the Latin Anthology a poem of thirty-three stanzas, each composed of three asclepiadeans and one glyconic, by a contemporary of Paulinus of Nola, who died c. 431. See *RE* 5[2] under Endelechius and *AL* 1[2] 334, 893.

[5] *Consol.* 1.6, 2.3, 8, 3.12, 4.3, 5.4 glyconics; 2.2, 4 alternating pherecrateans.

[6] 189 glyconics and twenty-one pherecrateans.

[7] For complete list, see the indices of *PLAC* 2, 719-721; 3[22], 815-816, 4[3], 1161-1162. These include Wandelbert (who also wrote on the origins of the asclepiadean, glyconic, phalaecean, pherecratean, and sapphic meters, *PLAC* 2, 570-571), *Conclusio PLAC* 2, 603 eight stanzas consisting of three lines each, a glyconic, asclepiadean, and alcaic; 285 stichic pherecrateans on the Creation of the World *PLAC* 2, 619; Walafrid Strabo, *PLAC* 2, 360, and Heiricius, *PLAC* 3[1], 474-476. By an unknown author in a ninth century codex there are twenty stichic glyconics to Carolus Calvus (*PLAC* 4[3], 1077). For additional stichic pherecrateans, see the eighty lines in *PLAC* 4[1], 243 II,

there is also no example of the glyconic stanza with a pherecratean close, although occasionally, as in the experiments of Heiricius, the two are combined as individual lines in stanzas containing other *C D* cola.[1]

After this brief summary of the history of the glyconic and pherecratean meter, it is worthwhile to look at the type of subject most frequently covered to see what light may be thrown on the inspiration of Catullus. The Latin poet chose his Greek meters with full awareness of their background and place in the history of poetry. This seems particularly evident in the glyconic and pherecratean. What is involved is more than just an imitation of the patterns or even subject matter of Sappho or Anakreon (and an accurate discussion of those of Sappho is impossible because of so little concrete evidence), but rather an awareness of traditional functions of these forms as cult, and thus choral and group, meters.[2] He recalls their traditional folk association with the children of Leto [3] and group singing of wedding songs [4] in his two stanzaic poems, 34 and 61. The two insignificant fragments of epithalamia from his contemporaries, Calvus and Ticidas, are probably tributes

and the twenty-two lines by Eugenius Vulgarius in *PLAC* 4[1], 414 III. Some lines by Boniface, *PLAC* 1, 18 III, could be construed as accentual glyconics.

[1] Supra 68 n.7 consists of eighty-four lines divided into twenty-one strophes. Each strophe is supposedly composed of an adonic, archilochean, pherecratean, and a glyconic. The lines give evidence of interest in making the word accent coincide with the long syllable. For example, not a single glyconic line ends with a disyllable.

[2] See Münscher, *op. cit.* (supra 35 n. 4) 71 where he calls the glyconic "ein altbeliebtes Kultmass," and mentions the two Delphic paeans (supra 66-67) in support of his theory.

[3] Anakreon *PMG* 3, Euripides *IT* 1089-1122 (where pure glyconics are interspersed with other eight-syllable cola, and *Ion* 184-190 where the chorus' admiration for the temple of Apollo grows out of Ion's opening paean. Other divinities may also be invoked, particularly Dionysos, in glyconics: Anakreon *PMG* 12, or the Delphic Paean of Philodamos (supra 66). The chorus in Euripides *Alc.* 962 ff. call upon necessity as a divinity.

[4] For a general discussion of wedding songs, see E. Mangelsdorff, *Das lyrische Hochzeitsgedicht bei den Griechen und Römern*, Diss. Giessen (Hamburg 1913) and Wilamowitz, *GV* 253 n. 2, 254 n. 1. There does not seem to be any work dealing with glyconics in wedding songs; however, many examples exist, and the ritual seven-syllable hymen cry is probably very early. See Sappho *PLF* 111.1. (Pindar 3.18, though not glyconics, mentions the marriage cry in a strophe containing *D B* cola), Euripides *Tr.* where mad Kassandra gives the cry 310, 314, 331, the take-off on wedding songs in Aristophanes *Av.* 1736-1737, 1742-1743. Examples in acephalous glyconics occur in Aristophanes *Pax* 1329-1337. See also Plautus *Casina* 800, 808, the earliest example of the hymen cry in Latin.

to Catullus' endeavor in this field.[1] Strangely enough, the tradition was not preserved by Horace who, with possibly two exceptions,[2] in general preferred the sapphic stanza for his attempts at the cult hymn.[3] In Seneca's tragedies the paean-type of joyful chorus using glyconics in the traditional association is found in the typical wedding-song praise of bride and groom in the *Medea*, 75-92, and in the paean [4] for Thebes in *Hercules Furens*, 875-894. However, the other examples of stichic glyconics [5] are of a general philosophizing nature. The same type of cautionary moral is found in Boethius' attempts at the meter,[6] a theme which occasionally appears in the glyconics of Greek tragedy,[7] but is not as dominant as the paean.

If, however, the relationship of Catullus' stanzaic glyconics to the meter's traditional role is clear, the position of the fifteen-syllable priapean line is not as obvious. In spite of the testimony of Choiroboskos that the meter was used by an Alexandrian to celebrate Priapus,[8] very few lines exist in the priapean meter which actually mention the divinity.[9] None exist in Greek, and the authorship of the longest Latin poem is uncertain.[10] On the other hand, Catullus 17 is also in this meter, and the question logically arises

---

[1] Supra 67 n. 3. Varro's two glyconic lines (supra 67 n. 3) do not seem to be related to any tradition.

[2] 1.21 is a poem to Latona which contains glyconics and pherecrateans. 3.38 is dedicated to Neptune, but it also mentions Diana.

[3] The principal example is the sapphic *Carmen Saeculare* which commences invoking Phoebus and Diana. Another cult-type hymn is the one to Mercury, 1.10, also in sapphics.

[4] Deriving a broad definition of the paean from Fairbanks, *op. cit.* (supra 66 n. 5) 39-53, I imply by the word, a hymn for part of a religious service or festival, generally attached to song and dance in connection with processions and with sacrifice, to express worship and obtain the god's blessing.

[5] Supra 68 n. 3.

[6] Supra 68 n. 5.

[7] Euripides *HF* 638-700 contains some glyconics and pherecrateans (669-672). The general purport of the chorus is the inability of mankind to distinguish between good and evil.

[8] Supra 68 n. 3.

[9] There are only twenty-five and one-half lines in the priapean meter specifically dedicated to Priapus, Cat. fr. 1 and 2, *Priapea* 85. The meters of the Latin *Priapea* are mostly elegiac, hendecasyllabic, and choliambic.

[10] Supra 68 n. 3. Of the many examples of poems in the Greek Anthology which mention Priapus, or are actual dedications to him, only one is not in elegiacs, 6.193, containing six lines of hendecasyllables. *AP* 6.21, 22, 33, 89, 102, 192, 193, 232, 254, 292; 9.338, 437; 10.2, 4-9, 14-16; 16.86, 236-243, 260, 261.

as to what connection there is between choral cult poetry and the use of the two combined cola in a poem which seems so completely unrelated to cult. The answer is really quite simple as soon as one realizes that poem 17 is phallic in insinuation, if not in dedication.[1] As phallic images are clearly an important aspect of the folk wedding song,[2] the poem can thus be considered a take-off on the typical priapic dedication, where the divinity boasts of his sexual potency, and allusions are made to figs, grapes, goats, cucumbers, nuts, etc.[3] This the choice of the meter, as well as vocabulary, makes abundantly clear.[4] It is impossible to know, of course, what connection the fifteen-syllable line as used by Catullus had with that used by the Greek tragedians, simply because line division is so uncertain.[5] Interestingly enough, the one place in Plautus where it is clearly found occurs in a wedding farce preceded (with a few lines of dialogue intervening) by a mock-ritual hymen refrain.[6]

---

[1] As was most sensibly pointed out by N. Rudd, "Colonia and Her Bridge: A Note on the Structure of Catullus 17," *TAPA* 90, 1959, 238-242, the point of the poem is not the location of Colonia nor the possibility of local scandal, but the ridiculous position of an impotent old man married to a sexy young girl. *Se sublevat* line 18, and *excitare* line 24, are meant to imply more than that the old man cannot get himself up!

[2] For an interesting reference and description, see Pliny *H.N.* 15.23.86. According to A. Rossbach, *Untersuchungen über die römische Ehe* (Stuttgart 1853) 340-344, the custom of singing phallic poems, or Fescennine verses, at weddings grew out of folk celebrations of marriages of agricultural divinities. The *locus classicus* relevant to the phallic aspect of the Latin epithalamia is, of course, Cat. 61.126-140.

[3] See particularly *AP* 6.102, 16.236-243, 260-261 for Greek, or *Priapea* 6, 20, 28, 51. The fondness for parody on folk themes can be seen in Aristophanes. See *Eq.* 973-996, which can be interpreted as a take-off on a popular glyconic-pherecratean tune. See note in B. Rogers, *The Knights of Aristophanes* (London 1910) 136. Compare *Pax* 1324 ff. where figs are the erotic symbol.

[4] Unfortunately, the fragment by Maecenas in this meter (supra 68 n. 1) is only an excerpt, making an evaluation of the metrical association impossible. The subject of the passage has been thoroughly analyzed by Lunderstedt, *op. cit.* (supra 68 n. 1) 46-51.

[5] See supra 64-65 n. 5. The three-line fragment from Anakreon (*PMG* 28) quoted by Hephaistion as illustration of the priapean meter (10.4, Consbr. 34), cannot be associated with any particular cult or primitive ritual. Most of the glyconic and pherecratean fragments of Anakreon (*PMG* 3-28) are related to his own feelings. However, the use of hymn forms to express personal emotions is one of the steps in the evolution of classical poetry, occurring for the first time probably in Sappho where her artistry in language is heightened by being worked out within traditional frames.

[6] *Casina* 815; "Hymen hymenaee o hymen," *Casina* 800 & 808. As the

All these factors would lead to a hypothesis that the priapean meter must have been associated with rural, phallic, fertility rituals, but as evidence is insufficient, the point will not be labored further.

This résumé of subjects particularly associated with the glyconic and pherecratean cola is not absolutely essential to the understanding of Catullus' metrics, but it indicates that he chose his meters purposely to reinforce the subject by emphasizing the tradition. When it comes to an actual analysis of his handling of the meter, the comparative method is somewhat complicated by the two different ways of using the cola. Since Latin predecessors and contemporaries are virtually non-existent, a percentage comparison with them is of little value. Therefore, the emphasis will be entirely upon Catullus with references to the fragments of Anakreon, Aristophanes *Eq.* 973-996, Euripides *Ion* 184-190, 194-200, and the usage of Latin authors who seem relevant, particularly Seneca and Boethius.[1] The two cola will be treated separately whether

---

complexity of Plautine metrics, inextricably bound up with the *brevis brevians* law (see Raven, *LM* 26), is beyond the scope of this paper, this is the only example of Plautus' use of the glyconic and pherecratean cola which I shall discuss. An evaluation can be found in F. Leo, "Die Plautinischen Cantica und die hellenistische Lyrik," *AbhGött Phil Hist Klasse*, n. f. 1, 1897, 7. See also F. Eckstein, "Neue Untersuchungen zu Plautus und Terenz," *Philologus* 80, 1925, 421 ff. The discussion by Lindsay, *ELV* 302-305 is anything but clear, for he quotes a great many lines without marking what he thinks are the quantities of the syllables. The comment of Raven (*LM* 147) re Aeolic in comedy is apt: "Occasionally more complex patterns are found, but the overall rarity of Aeolic in comedy often makes analysis uncertain (as at Pl. *Cas.* 217 ff.). Because of this rarity and uncertainty, the whole subject is best ignored by all except specialists."

[1] The lines from Seneca and Boethius have been chosen because they are examples of stichic glyconics, whereas Horace's glyconics are always part of a stanza containing other Aeolic rhythms: Seneca *Med.* 75-92; *HF* 875-894; Boethius *Consol.* 1.6. The same reasoning applies to the choice of lines from Aristophanes and Euripides, although the percentages obtained from so few lines can only be suggestive or relative. The fragments of Anakreon are *PMG* 3, 4, 12, 13, 15-19, 21-25, 27.1, 29.3, a total of thirty-five glyconics and twelve pherecrateans. A limited comparison of most frequent breaks in the glyconics of Alkaios, Sappho, Anakreon, Sophokles, Euripides, Catullus, and Horace was made by L. J. Richardson, "Greek and Latin Glyconics," *CPCP* 2, 1915, 257-265. He attempted to prove that if there were two different concepts of the meter, a Greek trochaio-iambic approach and a Latin dactylic approach, the works of Catullus and Horace did not substantiate it. However, he did not mention which lines of which poets he used for his percentages, so they have little value. Furthermore, his judgments were hampered by the determination to differentiate between diaereses and caesuras, "always an important clue to verse structure." (258) In general, it is an outmoded

they occur stichically or consecutively in one line, followed by a very brief treatment of vocabulary, since general subject matter has already been discussed.

When it comes to the distribution of words according to the number of syllables, certain differences are noticeable in Catullus' treatment of the eight-syllable colon from that of the seven-syllable.[1] When one studies the location of trisyllables, one discovers that initial trisyllables are more frequent in the glyconic than in the pherecratean colon, although the reverse is true of Anakreon and Euripides.[2] The lines from Aristophanes reveal no initial trisyllables in the pherecratean. The difference between their employment in the two cola, however, is not very great. With final trisyllables, on the other hand, there is a greater disparity, with the exception of the long poem 61. The others show much greater use of trisyllabic ending in the seven-syllable colon than in the eight. There is also a difference between Catullus' handling of the end of the fifteen-syllable line and that of the priapean poem of uncertain authorship.[3] Here, again, Anakreon shows the opposite tendency from the Latin, together with Aristophanes.[4] In this case, the word shape is different, being either cretic or dactylic in the case of glyconics, and bacchaic or ∪ _ ∪ in the case of pherecrateans. In no

article lacking in thoroughness, but at least shows awareness of the correct approach to the subject of word position in the metrical frame, with relation to the number of syllables in each word.

[1] Tables supporting general statements concerning Catullus are to be found at the end of the chapter.

[2] This statement covers all initial trisyllables, whether cretic, molossic, or bacchaic in shape since it seems evident that in Aeolic meters the number of syllables in a word is more important than their quantity. Initial trisyllables in Anakreon, glyconics 26%, pherecrateans 58%; Euripides, glyconics 10%, pherecrateans 50%; Boethius, glyconics 15%; Aristophanes, glyconics 11%, Seneca, glyconics 18%.

[3] 71% of the lines in *Priapea* 85 end in a trisyllable, while only 38% of Catullus 17 do so. This is every bit as important in metrical stylistics in determining authorship as are the more standard comparisons such as trochaic or spondaic beginnings or elisions as treated by Zarker *op. cit.* (supra 42 n. 3). The one glyconic line of Ticidas and in a trisyllable as well as the portion of a glyconic from Calvus (supra 67 n. 3). The percentage of trisyllabic ends in the phalaecean hendecasyllable is double that of the glyconic colon, although both have the same word pattern, 42% against 22%. The total percentage for the pherecratean is a little higher than for the glyconic, 26%.

[4] Anakreon, glyconics 23%, pherecrateans 8%; Euripides, glyconics 10%, pherecrateans 25%; Aristophanes, glyconics 33%, pherecrateans 17%. 40% of Seneca's glyconics end in a trisyllable, while 38% of Boethius' have this ending.

case does conflict of ictus and accent occur. The only other trisyllable of comparative interest in the two cola is the dactylic
3-5. One would assume that a central word of that shape would
be about equal in both cola, since neither conflict of word and
verse accent nor monosyllabic ending is involved. The statistics
show, however, a much greater use of this word shape in the eight-
syllable cola than in the seven, except for Catullus 34, while in
the Greek authors it is rare in both cola.[1] A trisyllable in the 3-5
position in a seven-syllable line, unless preceded or followed by
monosyllables (and even then the tendency is there), tends to divide
the line into three symmetrical units. This symmetry seems to have
been avoided in Greek, and in Catullus' long wedding poem particularly. On the other hand, central choriambic words in the 3-6 position in the glyconic have a higher percentage in Greek than in
Catullus,[2] although the highest incidence for these is found in
Seneca.[3] Anapaestic trisyllables are slightly higher in Latin than
in Greek, and the proportion increases in the later Latin authors.[4]

When it comes to the distribution of disyllables in Catullus'
glyconics and pherecrateans, the highest percentage occurs in the
final position in both cola, although in all but poem 34 the glyconics have a slight edge over the pherecratean. Catullus 34 and
Priapea 85 are also interesting because in both the spondaic initial
word in the glyconic has a greater frequency than the trochaic.
This is similar to the Greek usage,[5] but in Latin the difference is

---

[1] The percentage is virtually zero except for 6% in Aristophanes' glyconics,
and 8% in Anakreon's pherecrateans. The percentage of dactylic words in
Seneca is 29%, while in Boethius it is 23%. The fragment of Ticidas, a glyconic line, contains a dactylic word.

[2] Anakreon 14%, Euripides 20%, Aristophanes 11%. The highest percentage in Catullus occurs in poem 34, 11%. Choriambic words are not found
in the seven-syllable line.

[3] Seneca 24%, Boethius 14%.

[4] Anakreon 14%, Euripides 10%, Aristophanes 17%, Seneca 19%,
Boethius 24%. The highest percentage in Catullus occurs in poem 61, 23%.
On the other hand, the fifteen-syllable *Priapea* 85 has an incidence of 27%
in contrast to Catullus' fifteen-syllable poem 17 with only 12%. Both lines of
Varro's glyconics contain anapaestic words.

[5] The percentage of initial and final disyllables in Anakreon's glyconics
is virtually the same, 37% vs. 35%. There are more disyllabic ends in his
pherecrateans, 33% to 17% initial. The percentages are equal in Euripides
for both cola: 20% initial and final in the glyconic, 25% initial and final in
the pherecratean. There is a marked disparity in Aristophanes: in the glyconic, initial disyllables are 44%, while final are 28%. Of the pherecrateans,
66% commence with a disyllable, but there are no final disyllables.

not significant because in either case the word accent corresponds to verse accent and falls on the first syllable.[1] Perhaps the most interesting difference between the handling of the glyconic and that of the pherecratean occurs in the incidence of pyrrhic words. Here, again, one would assume no reason for a difference in frequency, yet in Catullus' handling of the two cola, nearly twice as many pyrrhic words occur in the glyconic as in the pherecratean.[2] Such a pronounced disparity exists only in Aristophanes in Greek, while in later Latin the pyrrhic becomes much less common.[3] Is is also interesting to note that though the incidence of initial monosyllables is fairly high,[4] iambic words in the 2-3 position are frequent only in poem 61 where the constant repetition of the word *hymen* in both the seven- and eight-syllable colon raises the percentage.

Before monosyllables are discussed, a few words can be said about Catullus' use of four- and five-syllable words. One might expect to find more polysyllabic words in the fifteen-syllable line poem, whereas the reverse of this is true. As the tables show, the actual incidence of polysyllabic words is not high in any poem, with the exception of 34, which contains the highest percentage of four-syllable words.[5] Here, again, a comparison can be made between

---

[1] The patterning of initial and final disyllables shows no increase in later Latin: Seneca initial 50%, final 58%; Boethius initial 55%, final 45%. Both lines of the Varro fragment end in a disyllable, as does the pherecratean line of Calvus. The high incidence of disyllabic ends in both cola is interesting in contrast to the small percentage in the phalaecean hendecasyllable. The total percentage in the three poems of Catullus using the seven and eight-syllable cola of disyllabic ends is 54% for the glyconic (the highest percentage, 65%, is found in the long line poem) and 42% for the pherecratean (again, poem 17 shows a much higher percentage, 62%). The percentage of final disyllables in the phalaecean hendecasyllable is only 17%. (See Cutt 14.)

[2] The total is 27% against 15%. The percentage of pyrrhics in the hendecasyllable is a little higher than that in the glyconic colon, 29% according to Cutt 15. In poem 17, however, the percentage in the two cola is equal, 15%.

[3] Anakreon   pyrrhics in glyconics 14%, in pherecrateans 17%
Euripides   pyrrhics in glyconics 30%, in pherecrateans 35%
Aristophanes pyrrhics in glyconics 28%, in pherecrateans o
Seneca   pyrrhics in glyconics 16%, in pherecrateans o
Boethius   pyrrhics in glyconics 5%, in pherecrateans o
The only pyrrhics in the Latin fragments are in the pherecratean line of Calvus. Interestingly enough, the two lines of Calvus, one a section of a glyconic, and the other a pherecratean, both contain pyrrhics.

[4] See infra 77.

[5] The percentage is in no case large, but see tables infra 85-86. An interesting

34 and *Priapea* 85 which has an extraordinarily high percentage of four-syllable beginnings in the pherecratean.[1] However, quadrisyllabic ends in the pherecratean, which show a high incidence in Greek, are extremely rare in Catullus, except for poem 61 where *Hymenaee* fills the position fifteen out of the total eighteen times.[2] Four-syllable words other than choriambic words [3] are extremely rare in the later Latin authors, and five syllables non-existent.

The interest in monosyllables lies not only in their position, but also in the fact that their incidence decreases in later Latin.[4] As is to be expected, there are more long monosyllables than short, and the highest percentage occurs at 1.[5] More significantly, however, in the practice of Catullus, although the short second syllable is far more common than the long, there are no short monosyllables at 2.[6] The next most frequent monosyllable is at 6, also the site of

---

point relevant to Anakreon as the model for Catullus is the fact that 23% of Anakreon's lines end in a five-syllable word, while a five-syllable ending occurs only four times in all of Catullus' glyconics or pherecrateans, less than 1%, in contrast to a 9% incidence in hendecasyllables, for instance. Five-syllable words do not occur in either Seneca or Boethius. The number of four- and five-syllable words in the hendecasyllable, on the other hand, is considerably higher. See tabels in Cutt 10 and 11.

[1] 34-50%; *Priapea* 85, 48%.
[2] Infra 79 n. 4, 81 n. 5, 86 n. 4.
[3] Supra 74 n. 2 & 3.
[4] Hellegouarc'h's statements *op.cit.* (supra 9 n. 1) 298 about the trend toward fewer monosyllables in the hexameter are also true in other meters. His words about the reason for their location is valid insofar as it goes, but the "rhythmical elements of the line" are, to some extent, a subjective acoustical point of view of the individual poet: ". . . leur répartition est commandée par la recherche d'une correspondance entre les éléments syntaxiques de la phrase et les éléments rhythmiques du vers. Lorsque cette harmonie est réalisée au mieux les monosyllabes deviennent moins voyants et s'insèrent plus discrètement dans le schéma métrique."
[5] For this reason the relatively small number of monosyllables in Catullus at 2 is interesting, particularly as they appear only in the long priapean line, while in Seneca they occur a the rate of 16%, and in Boethius 14%. These percentages of monosyllables at 2 are even higher than two of the Greek authors: Anakreon 11%, Aristophanes 12%; Euripides, however, has 20%. A monosyllable at 2 in the pherecratean is only found once, in Aristophanes *Eq.* 96. The non-existent short monosyllable in the glyconic colon at 2 in Catullus also marks another difference between 17 and *Priaepea* 85, where in twenty-one lines it occurs twice. See note 3 in tables, page 84. A short monosyllable at 2 in the glyconic colon of *Priapea* 85 appears twice although one is an example of an elided disyllable. There are no short monosyllables in the pherecratean colon at 2.
[6] Of the fifty-two examples in Catullus of a monosyllable at 6, fourteen are elided. Anakreon 32%, Euripides 60%, Aristophanes 39%. The highest

the most number of elided monosyllables.[1] These statements refer to the eight-syllable colon; monosyllables in the seven-syllable pherecratean are rare except at 1.[2] An interesting use of the much less frequent short monosyllable can be seen in Catullus 17.22 where the verb *sit* is repeated three times at unusual spots, 4 and 7 in the glyconic half, and 2 in the pherecratean half. This line is also noteworthy because it contains six monosyllables, none of which are elided. In fact, the great number of monosyllables in 17 distinguish it considerably from the only other poem in priapean meter of any length, *Priapea* 85.[3] Catullus' use of monosyllables in respect to frequency and elision is one of the most conspicious aspects of his metrics, and is particularly noticeable in the short line-cola in contrast to later Latin.[4]

The preceding section illustrates the various possibilities of word positions in the Catullan treatment of the glyconic and pherecratean cola by relating it to his Greek predecessors and Latin successors. It also shows that, contrary to most commentators' opinion, it is an oversimplification to call Anakreon Catullus' model, for there are more dissimilarities than similarities in word division, not to mention the generally short 2 in Catullus as compared to the generally long 2 in Anakreon. Catullus' treatment is actually closer to that of the dramatists Euripides and Aristophanes, though no commentary ever mentions this.[5] However, an eight-

---

percentage of initial monosyllables in Catullus occurs in 17: 44% in the glyconic half and 50% in the pherecratean.

[1] This contrasts with the Greek where the next highest number is at 3.

	ANAKREON	EURIPIDES	ARISTO-PHANES
mono 3	35%	40%	33%
mono 6	9%	10%	11%

[2] The percentage is higher in poem 61 than in 34 because of the repetition of the hymen cry. For the Greek authors: Anakreon 25%, Euripides 25%, Aristophanes 11%.

[3] This factor was also not mentioned by Zarker in his article proposing Catullan authorship for *Priapea* 85 (supra 42 n. 3). For example, *Priapea* 85 has only a 14% incidence of initial monosyllables in contrast to Catullus 17 with 42%.

[4] Initial monosyllables in Seneca and Boethius, 27%. At 6 there are none in Boethius, and only one in thirty-eight lines of Seneca. The early Latin specimens reveal a monosyllable at 3 in Calvus' pherecratean fragment. The hymen cry in Plautus *Cas.* 800, 808, has an elided monosyllable at 6, but the eight-syllable line is not a true glyconic.

[5] "Il primo libro dell' edizione Alessandrina d'Anacreonte pare fosse in

or seven-syllable line is actually too short to reveal a great deal of significant patterning, for a poet must create as much variety as possible in order to prevent monotony. This becomes quite clear in reading the stichic glyconics of Seneca or Boethius whose patterns are more repetitious than those of Catullus. The following table indicates the most common patterns of words according to their syllabic count.

Word-Syllable Patterns in Latin Glyconics

				VAR. (1)	TIC. (1)	CAL. (1)	PRIA-PEA 85 (21)	CATUL-LUS (226)	SENE-CA (38)	BOE-THIUS (22)	9th cent.[1] (20)
2	3	3			I		2 10%	18 8%	8 21%	6 27%	1 5%
2	4	2					2 10%	13 6%	7 18%	2 9%	3 15%
3	2	3				I	1 5%	8 4%	3 8%		1 5%
2	1	3	2[2]				1 5%	13 6%			
1	2	3	2					20 9%	2 5%	2 9%	4 20%
2	3	1	2[3]					7 3%	1 2%		
3	3	2		2			2 10%	7 3%	4 10%	4 18%	1 5%

The early Latin samples are included to show where some of the patterns are found. It is interesting to note that the last pattern does not occur either in Euripides or Aristophanes, and in Anakreon only once, *PMG* 17.2. One is struck, also, in comparing the

gran parte composto di strofe di questo tipo, e fu certamente il modello metrico di Catullo," says G. B. Pighi, "La Struttura del carme LXI di Catullo," *Humanitas* 2, 1948, 47. Fordyce 238 is hardly thorough when he says of 61: "The poem is written in strophes of four glyconics and a pherecratean, a system used by Anacreon (fr. 2D), and no doubt by others." Lafaye, *op. cit.* (supra 6 n. 1) 78-81, mentions only Anakreon and Sappho as models for the cult hymn, although both Greek tragedy and comedy are full of short ones and there are also the long ones of Pindar with their varieties of Aeolic cola combinations. (See supra 69-70). One Italian scholar, R. Avallone, has done some important work on the relation of Catullus to Aristophanes and Euripides. However, the two articles, "Catullo e Aristofane," *Antiquitas* 2, 1947, 11-49, and "Catullo ed Euripide," *ibid.* 3, 1948, 112-181 (henceforth *C&A*, *C&E*), are full of nebulous terms like "colore aristofanesco" or "temperamento tragico" which tend to obscure some of the real value of his comparisons. He uses words such as "stylistic" and "linguistic" much too loosely, and fails to mention metrical similarities. However, the two articles do contain many valuable comparisons, as well as references to the Greek Anthology.

[1] Here and infra 80 a 9th century experiment with the two cola is inserted for comparison sake. However, as these were quite clearly scholarly exercises in the learned world, they cannot be considered as part of a developing trend. This one is found in *PLAC* 4[3], 1077, III.

[2] This is the pattern of the Greek hymen cry in Euripides *Tr.* 310, 314, 331.

[3] This is the pattern of Plautus' hymen cry *Cas.* 800, 808.

Greek patterns with the Latin, by the frequency of the short 4 monosyllable in the former in contrast to its rarity in Catullus.[1] In the pherecratean colon, none of the patterns are repeated very often in Catullus. The only ones of enough frequency to give a percentage are: 1 2 4,[2] 19%; 3 2 2, 12%; 4 3, 14%; and 2 3 2, 9%.[3] The most significant difference between the Greek and the Latin pherecratean is the high percentage of quadrisyllabic endings in the former and the comparative rarity in the latter.[4]

The final point in connection with word distribution in Catullus' glyconics and pherecrateans concerns the location of most frequent word-ends. Here, a table can be set up showing his relationship to other Latin authors.

Table of Most Frequent Word-Breaks in Glyconics

After	VARRO	TICIDAS	CATULLUS	PRIA-PEA 85	SENECA	BOETHIUS	9th century
3	2/2		58%	62%	39%	41%	40%
5		1	49%[5]	42%	45%	32%	30%
6	2/2		58%	57%	58%[6]	45%	50%

[1] 8/35 or 23% in Anakreon, 1/10 or 10% in Euripides, as against 5/226, or less than 2%, in Catullus. In the lines of Aristophanes under discussion, the monosyllabic 4 does not occur. However, it is found in *Eq.* 563.

[2] This pattern is found only in Catullus 61 where it is filled by the hymen cry. It occurs twice in Aristophanes, *Eq.* 988 and 992, and in the long line fragment of Anakreon, *PMG* 28.2.

[3] The most common Greek pattern is 3 4, 50%, in Anakreon, and 25% in Euripides. It also occurs in the Kallimachos fragment in glyconics, Pf. 401.3. *Priapea* 85 shows the highest instance of the 4 3 pattern, 38%, and considerably higher than that of Catullus 17 with only 8% following this pattern.

[4] The rarity in Latin of quadrisyllabic endings is notable also in hexameters, the "adonic tag" in the sapphic stanza, and in anapaestic systems, all of which have the identical patterns for the last five syllables as the pherecratean ⏤ ⏑ ⏑ ⏤ ⏤. (This is a typical ending in a system of anapaests in Seneca, for instance, but not the only ending.) To fill these five syllables, a trisyllabic ending is the most common in Vergil, Ovid, and Seneca, in hexameters and anapaests, while in the adonics of Horace, for instance, the most common is a disyllable (Zinn II, 29). A 1 4 ending is so rare as to occur only six times in the *Eclogues*, *Georgics*, and *Aeneid*, once in Horace, *CS* 16, and not at all in Ovid's *Metamorphoses* or in Seneca. A final quadrisyllable preceded by two or more syllables occurs forty-eight times in Vergil, and only seven times in Ovid. (These statements are based on E. O'Neill's findings in *WAFS*, 337, 340, 347). Interestingly enough, of the fifty-four quadrisyllabic endings in Vergil, fifteen are filled by some form of *hymenaeus*, while, although this word occurs fourteen times in the total works of Ovid, it never occupies the final position. (See infra 81 n. 5 for complete discussion of the location of this word).

[5] It is interesting to note the difference in Catullus' percentages for the 15-syllable line alone to get a better perspective on comparison with *Priapea*

In the Greek practice, the percentage of breaks after 3 is considerably higher than that of the Latin, as well as much higher than
that after 5.[1] However, the large number of monosyllables in the
Greek line tends to offset the importance of word-ends in general.
Because of the decrease in monosyllables, the line tended to become a three-word line in the practice of Seneca and Boethius.[2]
As far as word-ends in the seven-syllable colon go, the patterns
reveal the most contrast between Catullus 17 and *Priapea* 85.
However, the table below covers the total number of Catullus'
pherecrateans, but includes for comparison sake percentages from
a twenty-two-line poem in stichic pherecrateans from the 9th
century.[3]

Table of Most Frequent Word-Breaks in Pherecrateans

After	CALVUS (1)	CATULLUS (82)	PRIAPEA 85 (21)	9th century (22)
4		27% [4]	67%	9%
5	1	43% [5]	29%	68%

These are not the word-ends, however, which are high in Greek
usage.[6] Thus, the conclusion from all this is that, in general, the
two cola are too short to fall into prominent patterns, but that the
fifteen-syllable line has even less clear-cut arrangements than are

85. In poem 17 alone the word breaks after 3 are 46%, and after 5, 50%.
The percentage after 3 is thus much lower than the *Priapea* 85 shows; but if
the number of monosyllables at 3 is subtracted to show significant word-end,
the percentage is decreased to 19% in Catullus 17, and 29% in *Priapea* 85.

6 This figure is all the more significant when one remembers that a monosyllable at 6 in Seneca occurs only once as against 52 in Catullus, 5% against
23%.

1 After 3: Anakreon 71%, Euripides 80%, Aristophanes 61%; after 5:
Anakreon 34%, Euripides 20%, Aristophanes 39%.

2 61% of Seneca's glyconics are three-word lines, 64% of Boethius.
Catullus' stanza glyconics show only 31% as three-word lines, and in a large
number of these a monosyllable is one of the words. This is also the case with
Horace. (See Zinn II, 107.)

3 *PLAC* 4[1], 414, III.

4 For poem 17 alone the percentage of word-ends at 4 is much higher, 38%,
but still considerably less than *Priapea* 85.

5 Here there is a great disparity between Catullus' handling of the pherecratean in the 15-syllable line and that of *Priapea* 85. In 17 alone the percentage of breaks after 5 is 61%.

6 Euripides shows a 25% incidence for each break, Anakreon 33% for the
break after 5, and only 8% for that after 3. Aristophanes has no break after
5, and only 7% after 4. His most frequent break is after 3, 50%, as is true of
Anakreon, 67%, and Euripides, 75%.

evident in the stanzaic forms of the two cola. Moreover, there are considerable differences between Catullus 17 and *Priapea* 85, particularly the lower incidence of monosyllables and few pyrrhic words in both cola, which certainly should be mentioned in a comparison of the two poems. Above all, it is clear that if one is going to go into the subject of Catullus' Greek models, Euripides and Aristophanes should be given a close scrutiny, as Catullus' patterns more often reflect theirs than they do those of Anakreon.

A discussion of the subject of vocabulary similarities is limited by the lack of Latin predecessors who used the meter. The difficulty of analysing Plautine glyconics and pherecrateans has already been mentioned. However, at *Casina* 815, which Lindsay interprets as an example of priapean meter,[1] the last two words, *nova nupta*, fill the same position as in the four-times repeated pherecratean line in Catullus 61, *prodeas nova nupta*.[2] The similarity of the hymen cry in the same play has already been noted,[3] but although it occurs in an eight-syllable line, it is difficult to be sure of the quantities of the syllables.[4] An interesting fact concerning the relationship of the Greek hymen cry to the Latin is that nowhere in poem 61 does Catullus commence with the divinity's name. The monosyllabic outcry, either *O* or *Io*, always precedes. In Greek, the monosyllabic cry generally comes after the divinity's name so that the line starts 2 1 instead of 1 2, as in Latin.[5] Undoubtedly, this is related to the ambiguity concerning the quantity of the *y* (the transliteration of the Greek υ, also ambiguous in quantity). However, in the hexameter poem 62, Catullus adopts the Theocritan long *y* in order to place the god first.[6] The syncopation [7]

---

[1] *ELV* 305.   [2] 61.95, 100, 110, 120.
[3] Supra 69 n. 4, 71, 77 n. 4, 78 n. 3.
[4] Lindsay was not troubled by the long at 5, or the two shorts occurring at 3 and 4 instead of 4 and 5, in his statement about the glyconic, *ELV* 303: "It is 'par excellence' the metre of song (e.g., the marriage chorus of *Cas.* 800, 808 . . ."
[5] 'Υμήν, ὦ 'Υμέναι', 'Υμήν as in Euripides, *Tr.* 331, a glyconic example, or 'Υμὴν ὦ 'Υμέναι' ὦ as in Aristophanes, *Av.* 1736, a pherecratean. *Io Hymen, Hymenaee io* as in Catullus 61.144 is one glyconic example. *matris o Hymenaee Hymen* as in 61.59 is another glyconic example of the Euripidean pattern, 2 1 3 2. Catullus' pherecratean pattern is always: *O Hymen Hymenaee*, with *Io* instead of *O* in the latter part of the poem. For a complete list of the forms of the hymen cry in both Greek and Latin, see Mangelsdorff, *op. cit.* (supra 69 n. 4) 4-5.
[6] Theokritos 17.58.
[7] See definition of term infra 127 n. 6.

suggested by beginning the glyconic with ⏑ − − was avoided by Catullus everywhere but in the controversial first stanza of 34. In this poem Catullus seems to be working most tightly within the traditional frames of the paean to a cult-divinity, and may be deliberately imitating the more primitive syncopation.[1]

The only other similarities to the vocabulary in Latin authors, contemporary with or preceding Catullus, in the eight- or seven-syllable colon are in the fragments of Calvus and Ticidas, as the two-line fragment of Varro in a semi-philosophical mood bears no resemblance in the matter of vocabulary to Catullus.[2] There are only three examples of the same word in the same place in the line, two instances of similar vocabulary not in the same place, and one grammatical similarity, of interest.

Position	Word	TICIDAS fr. 1	CALVUS fr. 4	CATULLUS 61
1-2	solus	sol(e)		sola 147
2-4(-5)	amor	amoribus		amore 33
1-2	nympha		nympha (pherecratean) nympha quod	nympha (glyconic) nympha quos
	candidus		6-8 candido	1-3 candido 115
	vaga		vaga 4-5 pherecratean	vaga 117 7-8 glyconic
6-8	abl. pl. in - bus	talibus		floribus 6 omnibus 111, 223

In connection with vocabulary, this is probably the place to refer briefly to fragment 1 of Catullus, which was left out of the statistics, in connection with *Priapea* 85. Here, similarities which did not exist between Catullus 17 and *Priapea* 85 appear. The first line of the fragment begins with a 1 2 2 pattern not found in *Priapea* 85, but found in Catullus 17. However, it does contain the 2 2 3 pattern and the 4 3 pattern in the pherecratean, the second of which is found eight times in the twenty-one lines of *Priapea* 85. The trisyllable ending is filled twice in both poems by the god's name:

---

[1] However, as there is linguistic evidence that the *i* of Diana was originally long, this may be an example of using an archaic form rather than an attempt at more primitive rhythm. See L. Havet, "Mélanges latins sur la prononciation des syllabes initiales latines," *MemSocLing* 6, 1889, 11-12. The poem has other Greek and archaic features, such as the use of *Latonia* for Diana, *nothus*, a Greek adjective, *deposivit* and *sospites*, archaic Latin forms.

[2] See supra 67 n. 3.

> *Priapea* 85. 17   Priapost
>   20   Priapus
> Catullus fr. 2.1   Priape
>   2   Priape

The dative of the personal pronoun fills the pyrrhic of the glyconic half:

> *Priapea* 85.10   mihi
> Catullus fr. 2.1   tibi

The verb *colo* occurs in both, though not in the same position or same form:

> *Priapea* 85.5   7-8 glyconic   colunt
> Catullus fr. 2.3   4-5 pherecratean   colit

These similarities are not sufficient to lend weight to a theory of authorship for *Priapea* 85, but they do show a similar treatment on the same subject which does not exist between these two priapean poems in priapean meter and Catullus 17.

In conclusion, it can be said that although Catullus shows preference for words of a particular number of syllables in a particular place in the line, such as the initial disyllables, greater frequency of the pyrrhic word, and final disyllable in the glyconic, or a technique that involved using more short words in the fifteen-syllable line than in the glyconic and pherecratean cola when they form a stanza, the word-patterning is difficult to detect or to divorce from the subject matter in this particular meter. In this respect, one could say that in his glyconics and pherecrateans, Catullus is most Greek, in that the rhythm grows out of the logic of the poem with a unique synchronization of λογος and ἔργον, the concept and the energizing force. This is, of course, somewhat a matter of opinion and difficult to prove by statistics. The other aspect of the very Greek nature of Catullus' handling of the meter is its lack of involvement with word and verse accent. Perhaps this is the way the awareness of "aiolische Freiheit" in the Greek originals made itself evident in Latin. Even the great pattern creator, Horace, never really systematized the eight-syllable colon. For although he wrote 264 glyconic cola, he used forty different patterns in these lines, and the highest percentage for any pattern, in his case the 3 3 2, is only 10%.[1] It is probably this very lack

---

[1] Statistics based on Zinn II, 107. The five top frequency patterns are: 3 3 2, 10%; 2 1 3 2, 9%; 2 3 3, 9%; 2 4 2, 8%; 1 2 3 2, 7%. Of these,

of regularization, and the difficulty of achieving coincidence of ictus and accent without a tedious repetition of only a few patterns, principally 2 3 3, 2 2 4, 1 1 3 3, which caused the meter to have little appeal for the Latin writers of the Middle Ages, when vowel quantities no longer had any acoustical reality.

WORD LOCALIZATION IN THE GLYCONIC COLON [1]

	CATULLUS				PRIAPEA 85 [2]
Poem	17	34	61	fr. 1	
No. of Lines	26	18	182	4	21
I. Monosyllables					
A. —					
at 1	11 42%	6 33%	66 36%	3 75%	3 14%
at 2	4 15%		2 1%	1 25%	1 5%[3]
at 3	5 19%	2 11%	24 13%		6 29%
at 6	8 38%	3 17%	41 23%	1 25%	2 10%
B. ∪					
at 4	1 4%		4 2%		
at 5			6 3%		
II. Disyllables					
A. _ ∪					
1-2	7 27%	2 11%	62 35%		4 19%
3-4	1 4%	1 5%	6 3%		2 10%
B. ∪ _					
2-3	4 15%	1 5%	50 27%	1 25%	
5-6	4 15%	1 5%	5 3%		1 5%
7-8 [4]	17 65%	7 38%	103[5] 56%	1 25%	11 52%
C. ∪ ∪					
4-5	4 15%	7 38%	51 28%	2 50%	6 27%
D. _ _					
1-2	3 12%	3 17%			7 33%
2-3	1 4%	2 11%	1 5%	1 25%	

only the third has "Kongruenz," so that he writes: "Auch im Glyconeus kommt durchgehende Kongruenz nicht häufig vor; die Inkongruenz am Versschluss wird durch die verschiedensten Mittle gedämpft, besonders dann, wenn dieser Vers eine vierzeilige Strophe abschliesst," *ibid.* I 64.

[1] Certain rare types of words, particularly those resulting in a final monosyllable, are omitted.

[2] In view of the importance of Zarker's suggestion as to the possibility of Catullan authorship for this poem (supra 42 n. 3), statistics for *Priapea* 85 and Catullus fr. 1 have been included to facilitate comparison.

[3] The only example of a short monosyllable at 2 is found in *Priapea* 85.17. (Another possible example is line 1 *eg(o)*.)

[4] All final ancipitia are counted as long for the purposes of this table.

[5] Six of these are examples of synapheia. However, only one is an example of a run-over word, 61.46. The others are cases of elision: 61.122, 142, 147,

	CATULLUS				PRIAPEA 85
III. Trisyllables					
A. _ ∪ _					
1-3	1 4%	4 22%	34 19%		2 27%
6-8	4 15%	7 38%	40 21%	3 75%	5 29%
B. _ _ _					
1-3		Diana (2)	4 2%		2 10%
C. _ ∪ ∪					
3-5	4 15%	1 5%	23 12%	1 25%	3 14%
D. ∪ ∪ _					
4-6	3 12%	1 5%	42 23%		6 29%
E. ∪ _ ∪					
2-4	3 12%		10 5%		
F. _ _ ∪					
2-4	2 11%		1		
IV. Quadrisyllables					
A. Initial					
_ ∪ _ ∪		1 5%	8 4%		
_ _ _ ∪	1 4%	1 5%	2 1%		1 5%
B. _ _ ∪ ∪					
2-5	1 4%	1 5%	2 1%		
C. 3-6 choriambic	1 4%	2 11%	13 7%		2 10%
D. ∪ _ ∪ _					
5-8	1 4%	4 22%	13 7%		1 5%
E. ∪ ∪ _ ∪					
4-7			12 6½% [1]		
V. Five Syllables					
A. Initial	2 7%		2 1%	1 25%	
B. 2-6			2 1%		
C. Final	1 4%		2 1%		

WORD LOCALIZATION IN THE PHERECRATEAN COLON

	CATULLUS				PRIAPEA 85
Poem	17	34	61	fr. 1	
No. of Lines	26	6	46	4	21
I. Monosyllables					
A. _					
at 1	13 50%		16 35%		6 29%
at 3	3 11%		1 2%		1 5%

191, 234. Elision after a final disyllable in the long line occurs in Cat. 17.4, 24, 26. For the purposes of this table they are counted as final as well as the one example of elision with the following line after a final trisyllable, 34.22, and the elision between the two joined cola in 17.11, after a final trisyllable.

[1] All but one of these is filled by the hymen cry *hymenaee*. Line 209 ends *numerare volt*.

	CATULLUS				PRIAPEA 85
B. ⏑					
at 2	2 7%		1 2%		
at 5	2 7%				1 5%
II. Disyllables					
A. _ ⏑					
1-2	6 23%	2 33%	8 17%	1 25%	4 19%
3-4	2 7%		2 4%	1 (?)	2 10%
B. ⏑ _					
2-3	4 15%		15 33% [1]		
5-6			2 4%		
C. ⏑⏑ pyrrhics					
4-5	6 23%	1 17%	7 15%	1 25%	1 5%
D. _ _ finals	16 62%	3 50%	14 30%	2 50%	6 29%
III. Trisyllables					
A. _ ⏑ _		1 17%	10 22%	1 25%	1 5%
B. 2-4	4 15%		1 2%		3 14%
C. _ ⏑ ⏑	2 7%	2 33%	4 9%		1 5%
D. ⏑ _ _ finals	8 38%	3 50%	8 17%	2 50%	15 71%
IV. Quadrisyllables					
A. Initial	4 15%	3 50% [2]	6 13% [3]	1 25%	10 48 %
B. 2-5	3 12%				2 10 %
C. Final	1 4%		18 39% [4]		1 5% [5]
V. Five Syllables					
A. Initial	3 12%		3 6½%	1 25%	
B. Final	1 4%		2 4%		

---

[1] In this position only the word *hymen* occurs.
[2] In the pherecratean at the end of the first stanza, the form is ⏑ _ _ ⏑.
[3] Line 235 has the form _ _ _ ⏑.
[4] Only three times is this position not filled by *hymenaee*: 30, *Aganippe*; 90, *venientem*; and 200, *remorare*.
[5] *Priapea* 85 and Cat. 17 show the greatest similarity in the frequency and position of three- and four-syllable words.

IAMBIC TRIMETER

$$\begin{array}{ccc|c||cc|cccccc}
1 & 2 & 3 & 4 & 5 & 6 & 7 & 8 & 9 & 10 & 11 & 12 \\
\times & - & \cup & - & \times & - & \cup & - & \times & - & \cup & \times
\end{array}$$

The word trimeter generally refers to the iambic[1] six cycle line commencing *in arsi* and ending *in thesi*, of which the six arses in the original Greek pattern alternate between being either short or long. As there is a normal expected word-limit after 5, the colometric pattern in terms of arses is *C B C open* followed by *B C B closed*.[2] However, when one looks at the Latin treatment of

---

[1] The origin of the word *iambos* is uncertain. The earliest use of the noun occurs in the works of Archilochos, *L&B* 249, "ἰάμβων." However, the various translations of the word ἴαμβοι in the three most recent editions of Archilochos, "poèmes," in *L&B* 69; "iambics" in G. Davenport, *Carmina Archilochi* (Berkeley 1964) 29 no. 70; and *"iambi"* in J. M. Edmonds, *Elegy and Iambus* II (*LCL* 1931) 109 no. 22; illustrate scholarly uncertainty concerning what the noun was supposed to mean at this time in the history of poetry. The term eventually came to be associated with the idea of the lampoon because of the vituperation in Archilochos. An interesting theory developed by M. Puelma-Piwonka, *Lucilius und Kallimachos* (Frankfurt 1949) 202-203, is that the Latin translation of the Greek "ἴαμβος" is really *sermo*, so that the Archilochean lampoon found its home in Roman satire. This theory is not unique with Puelma Piwonka, but it is well set forth. However, the concept of an iambic "genre" for vituperation did not become firmly entrenched until the time of the late grammarians, such as Marius Victorinus, Keil, *Gr. Lat.* 6.44.25.

[2] The most common variants of this are *C B rising, C B open, C B closed,* or *C B open, C B falling, C B closed*. Of course, in Catullus there are only B arses. The *B C B closed* colon was, early in the history of metrical studies, sensed to be an important unit in iambic meter. It acquired the name "lecythion," probably from the lecythion refrain in Aristophanes' *Frogs*: 1208, 1213, 1217, 1226, 1233, ληκύθιον ἀπώλεσεν, which completes the lines after the break at 5. Hephaistion is the earliest to use the term, *Ench.* 6.2 (Consbr. 18): "δίμετρον μὲν καταληκτικὸν τὸ καλούμενον Εὐριπίδειον ἢ Ληκύθιον," and the interest in the origin of the term led two of the scholiasts on the passage, A (Consbr. 122. 17-25) and Choiroboskos (Consbr. 230. 16-25) to attempt even further analysis of the word. For an interesting discussion of these two passages, see E. Reitzenstein, "Zur Erklärung der Cataleptongedichte," *RhM* 79, 1930, 89-92 (*Catalepton*). However, Quintilian's awareness of the colometric structure of verse is extremely interesting. His testimony, 9.4.71-76, indicates that the initial and closing cola (*pars prior, pars posterior*) of iambic and dactylic verse were so perceptible to an audience, that used in the wrong place in an orator's speech, they indicated bad taste on his part. He quotes a group of four words from Cicero which he says is a trimeter ending, "Quo me vertam, nescio" (9.4.75), and, therefore, should not be used as a clausula in prose.

the meter prior to the time of Catullus, one discovers that though
the line was considered to have six strong pulses, the freedom of
resolution in both theses and arses makes the basic colometric
pattern difficult to distinguish. The mere fact that the name
"senarius" was needed in Latin indicates that the six pulses were
more important than the colometric pattern of the Greek.[1] What
distinguishes Catullus' handling of the meter from the senarii of
early Latin drama is his assimilation of the colometry of the early
Greek iambographers and their heirs in fifth century drama.
On the other hand, Catullus goes to further extremes than even the
sixth century poets in that not only is there no incidence of resolution,[2] but even the arses which are frequently long in Greek
practice, 1, 5 and 9, are always short. The reason for this is very
probably the extreme popularity of the well-established Roman
comedy of Plautus and Terence, not to mention the tragedies of
Ennius and Accius, or the well-known Lucilius. In the free senarii
of these poets, virtually any syllable can be resolved so that the
only guide post is the short at position 11. By his strict handling
of the meter, Catullus disassociated himself completely from the
popular and well-known, and particularly from Roman drama.[3]

---

[1] Every metrician since the time of Quintilian has felt it important to
differentiate between the terms senarius and trimeter on the basis of whether
the line was divisible into six feet or three metrons, neither of which concepts
have a phonetic reality in the language. Quintilian suggests the terms may
be interchangeable *loc. cit.* (supra 87 n. 2). Even Horace, who wrote iambs,
seems to contradict himself, implying in one place three beats to a line, *Sat.*
10.43, and in another six, *A.P.* 253. See also Marius Victorinus and Rufinus,
Keil, *Gr. Lat.* 6. 79. and 555.22 ff. for typical testimony of the Latin grammarians. For a summary of ancient discussion on the subject, see J. Perret, "Un
Equivalent latin de la loi de Porson," *Hommages à Léon Herrmann, Coll.
Latomus* 44, 1960, 594 n. 1. W. R. Hardie, *Res Metrica* (Oxford 1920) 89,
defines trimeter as a line which has the third and seventh anceps short, as in
Catullus, and a senarius one which has 3 and 7 long. He does not take up the
problem of resolution. J. Soubiran has a more Greek-oriented approach,
including both the above groups in Hardie as one, trimeter. Thus he can
discuss the poets, Catullus, Horace, Seneca, Petronius, and Avienus, one
type: "Recherches sur la clausule du sénaire (trimètre) latin: les mots longs
finaux," *REL* 42, 1964, 439. Since his topic is final four-syllable words, he
also is not troubled by the presence of resolution.
[2] Resolution occurs occasionally in Archilochos and Semonides, and is
more frequent in comedy than in tragedy. Hardie *op. cit.* (supra n. 1) does
not think there is any significant difference between Archilochean usage and
that of tragedy. Others distinguish between the iambographers, tragedy and
comedy by the amount and location of resolved syllables. See Koster, *Traité*
100-114 for a summary of this view, and Schein, *op. cit.* (supra 3 n. 1 11-12.
[3] The similarities R. Avallone finds between Catullus and early Latin

The long history of the iambic six-cycle line, and the enormous amount of literary criticism which has been devoted to it, are subjects far beyond the scope of this study.[1] In Latin alone the number of poets who used the meter is considerable. Outside of the drama,[2] the principal examples of the meter occur in the works of Lucilius, Varro, Catullus, Horace, Petronius, Martial, Phaedrus, Ausonius, Boethius, as well as in the Catullus-inspired *Priapea* and *Catalepton*.[3] However, the Catullan pattern, *B B B open* followed by *B B B closed*, is found elsewhere only in the *Priapea*,[4] *Catalepton*,[5] and *Epode* 16 of Horace, where the iambic line alternates with a dactylic hexameter line. Thus, in order to make some

fragments and dramatists of the Republic are those of vocabulary and subject matter, *C&MR*. He does not concern himself with the crucial topic of metrical similarities. This failure is the chief drawback of the book (supra 6 n. 1).

[1] An excellent summary of such literary criticism, particularly on Greek practice, can be found in Schein's dissertation, *op. cit.* (supra 3 n. 1) 11-12. The most careful recent work on Latin iambics has been done by Perret and Soubiran, (supra 88 n. 1). See also the latter's "Monosyllabes élidés au debout du vers dans la poésie latine archaique," *Pallas* 6, 1958, 39-53. M. Burger, "Le Vers accentual en bas-latin," *REL* 37, 1959, 230-246, and D. Norberg, *Introduction à l'étude de la versification latine mediévale* (Stockholm 1958) discuss the trimeter as it evolved in Medieval Latin. See also E. Tamerle, *Der lateinische Vers ein akzentuierender Vers*, II (Innsbruck 1938) 131-344; and B. Axelson, "Die zweite Senkung im jambischen Senar der Phaedrus," *Vetenskaps-Societeten i Lund Årsbok*, 1949, 45-68.

[2] In the field of Latin drama, particularly on the position of Seneca, the most thorough treatment is that of L. Strzelecki, "De Senecae Trimetro Iambico," *RWF* 65 s. 3. 20, 5, 1938, 1-109. It also contains a good bibliography, 107-109. He compares the trimeter of Seneca with that of Petronius in a section of a later article, "De Rei Metricae Annaeanae Origine Quaestiones," *Eos* 53, 1963, 159-162. See also Soubiran, *op. cit.* (supra 88 n. 1) 447-450 on final quadrisyllables in Seneca's trimeter. O'Neill discusses Seneca's trimeters briefly in *WAFS*, 348. In Christian Latin poetry the meter occurs in Hilary, Prudentius, Paulinus of Nola, Eugenius of Toledo, and others. Cf. M. Burger, *Recherches sur la structure et l'origine des vers romans* (Paris 1957) 88-90. (*Recherches*).

[3] For discussion and brief commentary on the individual poems of the *Catalepton*, see *RE* 8A[1], (1955), 1070-1088. As is the case with the *Priapea* (supra 42 n. 3), most of the scholarly endeavor has been to prove or disprove Vergilian authorship. Of the works mentioned in the *RE* article, the most worthwhile are those by Birt *op. cit.* (supra 42 n. 3), Reitzenstein, *Catalepton*, 65-92; and the careful dissertation of P. Sommer, *De P. Vergilii Maronis Catalepton* (Halle 1910). This last includes a brief discussion of some metrical aspects, chiefly location of caesuras and unusual resolutions, 93-99. For information on the *Priapea*, see supra 42 n. 3.

[4] *Priapea* 82, forty-five lines; 84, twenty-one lines. The only fragment in Varro of this type is 385.2.

[5] *Catalepton* 6, six lines; 10, twenty-six lines; 12, nine lines.

sort of comparison between Catullus and his Latin predecessors, it is more profitable to take the normative pattern which incorporates the C arsis as the standard. However, as there are no examples of resolution in Catullus, lines from his predecessors which show resolution are only included if they are part of a longer passage of regular *C B C* pattern. Such criteria eliminate all predecessors, with the possible exception of Lucilius,[1] except Varro. Of his 142 iambic six-cycle lines,[2] about fifty [3] fit the *C B C open, B C B closed* scheme. Thus, these can be compared with the fifty-five iambic trimeters of Catullus in poems 4, 29, and 52.

---

[1] Here and there in Ennius, Pacuvius, Accius, or other writers of early Republican verse, an iambic line of the *C B C* pattern may be found, as well as in Plautus or Terence. However, these lines are the exception, rather than the normative scheme. The rules for Plautine senarii given by Lindsay, *ELV* 269 are applicable to all Latin iambic six-cycle lines before Catullus. The percentage of *C B C open, B C B closed* cola in Lucilius is only about 2%, for instance. (I use "about" because this figure is based on Soubiran's table, *op. cit.* (supra 88 n. 1) 438. However, it is a little disgraceful on his part that a work so recent should rely on out-dated texts, particularly in the case of Lucilius. Nevertheless, as I am not going to discuss any poets prior to Varro, the accuracy concerning Lucilius is perhaps not vital. Observations concerning Lucilius' iambs are complicated by the uncertainty about the correct order of the fragments of books 28 and 29, as well as the many fragmented lines which can be construed as iambs, trochees, or dactyls, depending on the point of view. For example, a line which could be a perfect six-cycle iambic line, lacking the final cretic, is given four different ways by four different editors:

Müller Book 28.20   amicula aspera atque praecox $- \cup \times$
Marx Book 3.130   amicula aspera <praecox> (in hexameter
              section)
Warmington Book 3.99 annicula aspera equa atque/praecoca (in the
              hexameter section)
Lindsay Nonius I, p. 219 amicula aspera atque *praecox.*

For this reason very few scholars have attempted to study the iambs of Lucilius in books 28-29. See, however, J. Stowasser, "Vulgärmetrisches aus Lucilius," *WS* 27, 1905, 211-230; F. Skutsch, "De Lucilii Prosodia," *RM*, n.f. 48, 1893, 303-307; Soubiran, *op. cit.* (supra) 438-440. Thus, statistics obtained from the only two certain lines in Lucilius which are examples of the *C B C open, B C B closed* pattern, W 949 and 884 (M 823, 939), are of little value.

[2] This total is based on the most recent edition, the reprint of Bücheler, 1963. Soubiran, *loc. cit.* (supra n. 1) using the 1865 Riese edition, has only 126, and F. Crusius, *op. cit.* (supra 15 n. 6) 79, credits Varro with only 124 senarii, although he does not give the source of his total.

[3] There are actually only forty-eight whole lines and three incomplete lines: frgs. 37, 77, 95, 96, 111, 171, 218, 247, 269-273 (omitting 272.3), 306, 349-355, 385, 485, 486, 578.

In such a comparison, the first observation is the constanzy of the normative *C B C open, B C B closed* scheme; in Varro the frequency is 82%; in Catullus there is a drop to 73%.[1] However, although 82% of Varro's lines show the *C B C open* initial colon, only 66% have a strong accent at 4 and 1% have a weak accent at 4. This is because he permits monosyllables at 5 quite frequently, but only twice has a monosyllable at 4 also, which would carry the weak accent. In Catullus the percentage is about the same, 64% with a strong 4 accent, and 7% with a weak 4. These facts are significant in pointing up the differences between choliambic meter and the normal iambic trimeter, where in Catullus the percentage of accent at 4 is 86% and in Varro 90%. In the rest of the line there is even greater difference between the practice of Varro and that of Catullus. 58% of Catullus' iambic lines have a coinciding ictus and accent at 8, while only 14% have this coincidence in Varro.[2] For a medial accent Varro has a larger percentage at 6, 62%. At 10, however, Varro and Catullus are again similar, Varro preferring a strong accent in 72% of his lines and Catullus 65%. None of these figures, on the other hand, are as close as the various authors' treatment of choliambs (infra 156-158), revealing that even within the limiting frame of *C B C open, B C B closed* a much greater freedom or variety was permissible. Whether it was the effect of word accent that played a part, there is no way of telling. One factor which Soubiran emphasizes in his article already mentioned (supra 88 n. 1) is the use, or lack of use, of four-syllable words at the end of an iambic six foot line. Clearly, a four-syllable word at this position will not affect the ictus and accent coincidence at 10, but it will remove any strong accent at 8, since 8 then becomes a final syllable. And it is just here that the biggest difference can be seen between Varro and Catullus. Only 20% of Catullus' lines end with a quadrisyllable, while 46% of Varro's have this close, and the number for Varro would, of course,

---

[1] Of the other *C B C open, B C B closed* iambics (supra 89), the *Catalepton* show 77%; the *Priapea*, 88%; Horace *Epod.* 16, 97%; 17, 96%. I do not use for comparison the other epodes of Horace where iambic six-cycle lines occur, since only 16 and 17 are the Catullan *B B B open, B B B closed* type, and only 17 is an example of stichic iambs, the latter being the principle reason. For purposes of reference, Horace's other iambic poems are *Epod.* 1-10, where six-cycle iambs alternate with four-cycle, and *Epod.* 11 where six-cycle iambs alternate with a line composed of dactyls and iambs.

[2] Such a coinciding accent is not found at all in the two fragments mentioned supra 90 n. 1 of Lucilius, for instance.

be greatly increased if all his six-foot iambic lines were under discussion.[1] It is not really possible to know the reasons for Catullus' slight usage of this ending, and guesses are always a matter of opinion. Clearly, his iambics with their indefatigable short syllables are a tour de force, as far from dramatic iambics as possible, and perhaps the avoidance of the four-syllable final word is related to this.[2] It is worthwhile mentioning that nine out of these eleven instances have also other less usual features in Catullus. One of these is the cretic at 6-8 which occurs only five times in his iambic trimeters, four of which are in this group of lines ending with a quadrisyllable. The cretic in this position is found in Varro 46%, as against only 9% in Catullus. What makes this statistic so interesting is that "outer" metrically it is a perfectly logical place for such a word. (For example, it has a 20% frequency in Semonides, and is also common in Aeschylus' trimeters.) [3] However, it does focus the accent at 6. Perhaps this strong accent divides the line too severely, or is too choppy after an already sharp accent at 4. Whatever the reason, Catullus does not favor it, although in the choliambic lines it is perfectly permissible.[4]

If, however, a four-syllable word-end or a cretic at 6-8 does not change coincidence of ictus and accent, the coincidence is affected by the choice of a disyllabic or trisyllabic ending. A strong accent at 10 is felt by both authors to be important, and a three-syllable word-end guarantees this accent.[5] But although the two authors

[1] Soubiran gives a table, *op. cit.* (supra 88 n. 1) 438 of quadrisyllabic endings in other Latin trimeters for the particular purpose of showing that the ending is virtually non-existent in Seneca. There must be considerable discrepancy in the French text he uses from Kroll's text whereby he arrives at a total of sixteen lines ending with a four-syllable word, while my count is eleven, or 20%.

[2] This is a good place to quote Quintilian's famous words about one word filling two metrical "feet:" "Est in eo quoque nonnihil, quod hic singulis verbis bini pedes continentur, quod etiam in carminibus est praemolle . . ." 9.4.65. Of the Greek iambographers, Archilochos and Solon use a quadrisyllable as a normative end of the line, and the count is high in Semonides, also. See Schein, *op. cit.* (supra 3 n. 1) 23-24.

[3] See Schein, *ibid.* 24, and 47-48, and table p. 118.

[4] See tables of word localization at end of this chapter and of choliambic chapter. Cf. Knox, *H &C* (infra 103 n. 2) 250 who claims that Greek writers of lyric iambs avoided a *B C B closed* colon with the word-syllable combination 3 2 2.

[5] This is in effect what happened to trimeter when it became accentual. Lines had to end with a word of three or more syllables. Cf. Burger, *Recherches*, 107, and W. Beare, *Origin*, 3-20.

are close in their percentages of strong accent at 10, 65% for Catullus and 72% for Varro, they vary considerably in their use of
this final cretic: Catullus 36%, Varro 22%.[1] Thus, more than
half of Catullus' lines with a strong accent at 10 end in a cretic
word, while this is true of less than a third of similarly accented
lines in Varro.

One other word-type is of interest from the point of view of
the relationship between ictus and accent, the disyllable. Any
iambic disyllable is in opposition to the metrical ictus since, with
rare exceptions, the normal Latin word-accent does not fall on the
ultima.[2] The percentage of those in 1-2 place in Catullus is 18%,
while in Varro it is 38%. Of these ten occurrences in Catullus
(4.2, 5, 15, 16, 19, 26; 29.3, 12, 24), all but two have a special
reason for being first in the line, to emphasize the word.[3] The
most obvious are *ait* in 4.2 and 15, *senet* 4.26, *Mamurr(am)* 29.3,
socer 29.24. However, two-syllable beginnings occur too often in
Varro for one to assume he uses them on purpose.[4] Moreover,
although most of Varro's fragments have survived because they
contain some lexicographical peculiarity, these words are not
found to have any particular position of importance in the line.
Certainly conflict of ictus and accent at 2 played no role, nor
perhaps did it figure as much at the end of a line as the high percentage shows. For the choppiest of all endings, two disyllabic words at
the end of a line, occurs twelve times in the fifty lines under discussion, but it is found only once in Catullus' iambics, 29.1, a line
whose *s*'s and *t*'s and sharp word-ends are a deliberate attempt
of the poet to make the words fit the contemptuous mood of the
whole poem.[5]

---

[1] Horace shows variety himself: *Epod.* 16, 54% cretic end, *Epod.* 17, 34%.
In the *Priapea* the statistics show 29%, while in *Catalepton* they show 41%. A
final cretic in Greek iambs is very infrequent, related to the avoidance in
general of word-end at 9. See Schein, *op. cit.* (supra 3 n. 1) 30-32, where
he discusses the significance of this in relation to Porson's law, and
47-48.
[2] Concerning words with the final syllable accented, see Fraenkel, *op. cit.*
(supra 7-8 n. 4) 273-299, and Palmer, *LL* 212. See also supra 56 n. 3.
[3] Perhaps not so true of *opus* 4.5, or *simul* 4.21.
[4] It is true that his lines are fragmentary, but they are sufficiently numerous to permit comparison with Catullus.
[5] This line examplifies the less frequent but chief variation of the common
initial colon, the *C B rising, C B open, C B closed* or tripartite line.

Quis hoc potest videre, quis potest pati

The position of strong accent is related to the last point, Catullus'
placing of words for aesthetic function. This has already been
alluded to briefly in connection with the disyllable in the 1-2
position and the rare cretic at 6-8, but it is also true of the relationship between lines with a view to artistic expressiveness.[1]
What gives poem 4 its sense of fluidity and deceptive ease is not the
regularity of alternating short and long syllables, but the way
Catullus handles polysyllables, especially three-syllable words,
and his echoing of phrase units.[2] Trisyllables are important both
in respect to their sound and to their position, and particularly
the latter, since no matter where placed, they provide coincidence
of ictus and accent in iambic trimeters.[3] Yet many lines of Varro
also have coincidence of ictus and accent, but do not show awareness
of rhythmical word localization. So other factors must be involved.
Clearly, the nature of the syllables themselves is one. Lines full
of harsh consonants will be harsh. This aspect of literary criticism
is too obvious to need discussion here. But the distribution of
words with relation to the number of syllables in each word, as well
as the sound of the syllables, is also involved. It is here that Catullus'
genius, especially in contrast to Varro, is most marked. For the
former seems to be aware of certain combinations of words which
produce rhythmical flow, and he uses them or rejects them with
relation to the sense of the poem and the effect he wants to convey.[4]

[1] Wilkinson has not been very observant when he says in reference to
the *nugae* of Catullus: "There is hardly any artistic word patterning,"
GLA 219. The criticism of Quinn is much more perceptive. See particularly
his comments about poem 4, *Docte Catulle* 45-46.
[2] Quinn has noted this type of echoing in poem 4 (*loc. cit.*) to which
could be added the significant point that lines 2 and 15, though syntactically dissimilar, are phonemically similar, as well as similar in the distribution of the number of syllables in the words. Moreover, the trisyllable
phasellus, which is the subject of the poem, the initial trisyllable in line
1, occupies the key position, 5-7 in line 10 (see infra 98, 111, 115 n. 3, supra
44-45), and has a further parallel in the initial trisyllable of the final line,
gemelle. In addition, note poem 29: the parallelism within line 1 echoed in
line 22, or *Gallia* and *Britannia* in 3 and 4 echoed in 21. 13 and 14 both end in
a 4-3 pattern. Other lines exhibit syllabic parallelism within the line, such as
15 *ducentiens, trecentiens,* or 7 *superbus, superfluens.*
[3] However, a trisyllable ending at 4 occurs only three times in both Catullus and Varro, possibly because it throws the strong accent on 2. Trisyllables
at 6-8 are also rare. See supra 92.
[4] See Quinn, *Docte Catulle*, 46: "The poem develops a kind of somni-
ferous, repetitious rhythm suggesting the way the yacht goes on and on

There is a certain smoothness about a three- or five-syllable word in contrast with the two or four in an evenly alternating rhythm such as iambic trimeter.[1] However, an iambic line cannot be composed of only trisyllables without destroying the important colometric break at 5, or at 4 and 7. Thus, no iambic six foot line can contain more than three trisyllables. Catullus' skill in using two or three trisyllabic words is noteworthy. The line which produces the greatest smoothness will be one which has an initial and closing three-syllable, plus coincidence of ictus and accent at 4, 8, and 10.[2] Here are two possible lines:

$$\begin{array}{cccccccccccc} 1 & 2 & 3 & & 4 & 5 & & 6 & 7 & & 8 & 9 & & 10 & 11 & 12 \end{array}$$

a) ∪ _ ∪ | _ ∪ | _ | ∪ _ ∪ | _ ∪ ×

b) ∪ _ ∪ | _ ∪ | _ ∪ | _ ∪ | _ ∪ ×

Line (a) is found four times in poem 4, line (b) not in Catullus at all.[3] In both, the initial trisyllable urges the flow toward the strong 4 accent, but to Catullus' sensitivity three disyllables in a row, as in line (b), are too many, perhaps too choppy. Also with line (b) there is no clear differentiation of accent at 4, 6 or 8. In line (a) the monosyllable at 6 minimizes an accent in that place and serves to facilitate the phrasing of the line. Thus, the ideal smooth line may be defined as one composed of five words [4] whose syllables are 3 2 1 3 3. Two alternative patterns are 3 2 4 3 [5] and 1 1 2 3 1 4, but the latter is the antithesis of the "ideal."[6]

---

about its achievements. The contribution of the rhymes in lines 15 and 17 is striking (a pair of rhymes—*origine, cacumine*—followed by a third near-rhyme, *aequore*, each in a word stressed on the ante-penult; ...." Notice the illustration concerns trisyllables.

[1] This would also be true of trochees. Although this is admittedly a subjective-aesthetic appraisal, it is based on the observation that in a two-unit meter, such as iambs or trochees, trisyllabic ends are placed so as to divide the unit. Disyllables are either the same as the unit or reciprocals, while quadrisyllables are even multiples of the unit.

[2] The frequency of initial trisyllables in Catullus is 33%, in Varro 12%; of final trisyllables, Catullus 36%, Varro 22%. See diagram, graph infra 150, 152.

[3] This pattern is found once in Varro, fr. 95.

[4] Note again the importance of the odd number.

[5] Interestingly enough, these are not the most frequent word breaks in the patterns of the Greek cola, particularly because of the Greek avoidance of word-end at 9. See Schein, *op. cit.* (supra 3 n. 1) 23.

[6] The word "ideal" is purposely chosen as the variety of word patterning is too great to determine a "norm." In this connection it is interesting to

Can Catullus be said to use these patterns intentionally? Here, of course, the metrician cannot avoid the element of subjectivity. But the "ideal" pattern seems to have a function in poem 4. It is the pattern of the first line, the last line, the central line 13, as well as line 20.[1] Line 13 is particularly significant because of the unusual proper names and compound words. Yet in spite of the innate harshness of the words if taken individually, Catullus turns them into poetry by incorporating them into the smoothest iambic pattern, the 3 2 1 3 3.

Amastri Pontica et Cytore buxifer

This is a good example of Catullus' success with a technique of which Varro does not seem to have been aware. Varro could have welded many lines, in spite of their strange vocabulary, into poetry by a sensitivity to the importance of word localization. However, this most fluid of line-patterns is seen only once in Varro's iambics under discussion, one of the rare lines which creates a poetic image, fr. 273.[2]

Propontis unda quam liquenti caerula

Taken alone by itself with the author unknown, it could easily be assigned to Catullus' poem 4.[3]

Now, if the 3 2 1 3 3 line is the ideal smooth line, it should not appear in the two vituperative poems, 29 and 52. This is exactly the case. What does figure in these poems, by contrast, is the use and position of four-syllable words. These occur twice as often in poem 29 as in 4.[4] From the standpoint of meaning, they seem to have most significance in the 6-9 position. Four of the five times

---

note the two fragments of Lucilius which observe the *C B C open, B C B closed* scheme. W 949 has a word-syllable pattern of 5 1 1 1 4; W 884 has 3 2 2 1 2 2. Neither of these are found as whole lines in either Varro or Catullus. However, Catullus twice uses an initial colon of one five-syllable word. The *C B C open* colon of 3 2 is frequent in both other authors, while the lecythion 2 1 2 2 never occurs in Catullus and is found once in Varro (fr. 349.1).

[1] This is a fitting pattern for the favoring breezes.
[2] This fragment will be discussed under the vocabulary section because of the word *Propontis*, (141).
[3] Horace has this 3 2 1 3 3 line twice in *Epod.* 16 with the pure alternating iambs, but not in 17.
[4] The percentages of four-syllable words in the three poems are: 4-30%, 29-62%, 52-50%.

where they occur in this position, the lecythion of which they are a part has the same word pattern, 4 3.[1] The four-syllable words in these lines are witheringly clever: *imperator, occidentis, diffututa, perdidistis*. Moreover, the four lecythia, the first three in succession in the center of the poem, the fourth the last line, taken together contain all the elements of the perfect lampoon: sarcastic address, ironic criticism, dirty words, and total condemnation, in that order of build-up of intensity.

imperator unice
occidentis insula
diffututa mentula
perdidistis omnia

There is nothing in Varro that even approaches this genius for rhythmical and aesthetic word-localization. It can be argued that his fragments are too short to produce a possibility for artistic intensification. However, a glance at the fifty lines under scrutiny here shows that repetitious patterning does occur in the *Marcipor* fragments about the storm and shipwreck. But the result is not build-up of tension, only unalleviated monotony. The repeated word pattern 2 3 3 4 [2] is at variance with two of Catullus' principles, sparing use of initial disyllable, and avoidance of the cretic at 6-8. This last is used here in the extreme of nine out of twelve lines, resulting in the deadly sing-song of strongly accented 4 and 6. The worst line of all is fr. 272.2:

quarum bipennis fulminis plumas vapor

Here, the most cumbersome syllables are set down one after the other, while the end of the line is chopped in pieces by the two final disyllabic words. It is possible that Varro is trying to create a word-image of a thunderstorm, and such an interpretation could be justified if the line were taken alone. But taken in context with the other lines in the passage, it fails to give a poetic impression of a storm. Rather, the lines give the feeling of a scholar interested in odd words and using them in a grandiloquent manner to poke fun at epic writers on the same subject.

---

[1] The five lines are 11-13, 17, 24. Omitting 17 the four have the pattern: 3 2 4 3, 2 3 4 3, 1 2 2 4 3, 2 3 4 3.

[2] Fr. 269.3, 270.2-3. Closely related are the two lines which have the same beginning but which chop up the end of the line, 2 3 3 2 2: 270.1, 272.2.

Catullus, on the other hand, uses repetition consciously, often in pairs or groups of three. For example, the 5-7 word usually is found in two successive lines, as if Catullus felt that the change from the normative *C B C open* colon ought to come twice in a row so that the audience sense perception could make the adjustment.[1] The same is true of four-syllable words, either at the 6-9 or 9-12 position.[2] These examples could be multiplied almost *ad infinitum*, but they are sufficient to make the point clear. There is most certainly artistic word-patterning in the iambics of Catullus, while it is the lack of such patterning which causes Varro to fail as a poet, though he succeeds as a satirist and metrician.[3] In the words of two eminent scholars, Catullus possesses that particular sensitivity to the "phonetic subtleties of metrical phenomena,"[4] an aesthetic sensitivity by which "he fits his material into the given pattern," yet "continually varies his method of realizing the form."[5]

When it comes to a discussion of vocabulary similarities, there is only a very small amount of comparable material. Interestingly enough, it is in the one passage in Varro which bears a metrical resemblance to Catullus where a topical resemblance also exists. This is the group of *Marcipor* fragments on the storm at sea where Varro seems "most poetic" to the modern reader.[6] Actually, a more careful examination of the fragments, 269-273, show that Varro by using epic vocabulary in iambic meter, is poking fun, if not at Ennius, at least at those who tried to write epic on grandiloquent themes but empty content.

Repente noctis circiter meridie   *Marcipor* 269
cum pictus aer fervidis late ignibus
caeli chorean astricen ostenderet

Nubes aquali frigido velo leve   270
caeli cavernas aureas obduxerant
aquam vomentes inferam mortalibus

---

[1] 4.5 & 6, 9 & 10; 29.14 & 15, 20 & 21.

[2] 4.7 & 8, 15 & 16; 29.2-8, 11-13.

[3] In other words, they succeed in structural metric, but fail in rhythmical. See Porter, *op. cit.* (supra I n. I) 20 n. 42.

[4] E. O'Neill, Jr., "The Importance of Final Syllables in Greek Verse," *TAPA* 70, 1939, 267.

[5] Porter, *op. cit.* (supra I n. I) 25.

[6] These are the lines which J. W. Duff translates in his *Literary History of Rome: Golden Age* (London 1910) 337, to "illustrate the poetical side of the *saturae*," claiming that they "form the best example of Varro's style in iambics." See supra 96.

Ventique frigido se ab axe eruperant 271
phrenetici septentrionum filii,
secum ferentes tegulas ramos σύρους

at nos caduci naufragi ut ciconiae, 272
quarum bipinnis fulminis plumas vapor
perussit, alte maesti in terram cecidimus [1]

Propontis unda quam liquenti caerula 273
× _ ‿ _ natantem perfundit, cape

Most of the basic sea vocabulary above can be found in Catullus' short epic poem 64: *nubes, velum, caelum, ventum, maestus, caerula*; while the word *naufragus* occurs in 68. All of these words are standard in epic vocabulary concerning the sea. The novelty lies in their being used in iambics. A few of them are found in poem 4.[2]

Word	Author	Position in line
Propontis	Varro 273.1	1-3
Propontida	Catullus 4.8	1-4
natantem	Varro 273.2	5-7
natantis	Catullus 4.3	5-7[3]

Neque at 1, followed by elision at 2, is found in Catullus 4.3 and 22 and occurs in Varro 352. Here an exception to the *C B C open* colon has to be made for Varro, as 3 is long. But the line is part of the sequence of eight fragments so cannot be discarded. More striking, perhaps, is the occurrence of the noun *palmula* in both Varro and Catullus. The word may well have been a Varronian invention since in his context it means "little hand", but elsewhere in Latin, Catullus 4.17 and Vergil A.5.163, it means "the blade of an oar." In both Varro 355 and Catullus 4.17 the word fills the 6-8 position. Lastly, one further word deserves mention, showing probably the relation of both authors to comedy when obscene vocabulary is required. This is the noun *cinaedus* and its related adjective *cinaedicus*. Catullus uses the noun eight times in his verse, twice in iambic trimeters, 29.5, 9, and once in iambic septen-

---

[1] The second colon of this line does not conform to the *B C B closed* pattern, since 7 is long and 10 is resolved. It is included because it is part of the fragment.

[2] The subject of this poem is a Greek diminutive, *phasellus*, which is also found in a fragment of Varro, 85, a sotadean line: *phaselon*.

[3] For the sake of comparison, Lucilius fr. W 884 contains two words found in Catullus' 4.18 in the same word position, 11-12, *fretus*, Catullus' form is *freta*.

arius, 25.1. In these three locations it fills the 1-3 position. The adjective is used by Varro in 353 in the 5-8 position, an unusual place for a four-syllable word. He uses the Greek spelling of the noun in the same satire, "Ονος λύρας, 357, in a septenarius.[1]

No one would dispute that the similarities outlined above are of negligible importance. If one were making a study of only vocabulary usage regardless of meter, a great many more parallels could be found, but as far as subject matter goes, it is clear that there is not much similarity between Catullus' iambic trimeter and that of Varro under discussion. What stands out in Catullus' iambics, however, perhaps more than in any other of his meters, is his awareness of significant places in the line which highlight a word. This is more important in a regularly alternating meter such as iambic trimeter, than in a meter with varied arses not in regular alternation, such as the phalaecean hendecasyllable or the glyconic. In these the meter itself provides a certain amount of variety, whereas in iambics the variety must be achieved in the patterning of the semantic units. For this reason the aesthetic word-localization has been emphasized in this meter more than in the others where it undoubtedly occurs, but is considerably less noticeable.

WORD LOCALIZATION IN IAMBIC TRIMETER

1 2 3 4 5 | 6 7 | 8 9 10 11 12
× ‿ ‿ ‿ × | ‿ ‿ | ‿ × ‿ ‿ ×

		VARRO		CATULLUS	
I. Monosyllables						
A. ‿						
1			2	4%	21	37%
3			1	2%		
5					6	10%
7			1	2%	11	1%
9			1	2%[2]	4	7%
B. —						
2			4	8%	8	15%
4			2	4%	6	11%
6			8	15%	14	26%
8			4	8%	8	15%
10			1	2%	5	9%
12			1	2%	1	2%

---

[1] Here it is the last word in the line, while in Catullus 25.1 it is the first. The noun and adjective occur several times in the last act of Plautus' *Stichus*.

[2] There is one example of a long monosyllable at this position in Varro, fr. 351.1.

	VARRO	CATULLUS
II. Disyllables of the type ◡ — [1]		
A. 1-2	19 38%	10 18%
B. 3-4	6 12%	8 15%
C. 11-12	15 30%	18 33%
III. Trisyllables		
A. ◡ — ◡, × — ◡, ◡ — ×		
1-3	6 12%	18 33%
3-5	16 32%	9 16%
5-7	2 4%	13 24%
7-9	4 8%	12 22%
9-11		
B. — ◡ —, — × —		
2-4	3 6%	3 5%
4-6	1 2%	
6-8	21 42%	5 9%
8-10	1 2%	8 15%
10-12	11 22%	20 36%
IV. Quadrisyllables		
A. — ◡ — ◡, — × — ×		
2-5	6 12%	3 5%
4-7		2 4%
6-9	5 10%	9 16%
B. ◡ — ◡ —, ◡ — × —, × — ◡ —		
1-4	3 5%	1 1%
5-8	2 4%	
7-10		
9-12	23 46%	11 20%
V. Five Syllables		
A. 1 word first colon		1 2%
B. — ◡ — ◡ —, — ◡ — × —, — × — ◡ —		
6-10	1 2%	2 4%
8-12	1 2%	4 7%
C. × — ◡ — ×		
5-9	1 2%	

---

[1] Disyllables of the type — ◡ are not significant in terms of accent conflicts. Catullus has a disyllable at 7-8 twice, but both times the monosyllable *et* is on either side of the disyllable. 29.2 and 10, not in the smoother *phasellus* poem. It occurs six times in Varro.

CHOLIAMBICS

1 2 3 4	5 ‖ 6 7	8 9 10 11 12
✕ – ◡ –	✕ ‖ – ◡	– ◡ – – ✕

This meter is generally discussed as a variation of iambic trimeter. However, as it has aspects, such as the preference for an initial anceps and the characteristic ending of three long syllables which made it particularly adaptable to the Latin language with its preponderance of long syllables,[1] and since Catullus wrote more than twice as many choliambic lines as he did trimeter,[2] it will be treated separately here. It consists in its normative state of two cola, the *C B C open*, followed by the *B B A C falling*.[3] It is the unusual juxtaposition of theses 10 and 11, as well as the fact that the line begins in arsis and ends in arsis which distinguishes it sharply from trimeter, and gives the meter its so-called "limping" effect. Two of its commonly used names, scazon and choliambic, are derived from Greek words meaning "lame", σκάζων and χωλός. It is also called hipponactean after the poet who first used the meter widely, Hipponax of Ephesos [4] (c. 540 B.C.), who seems to have used it chiefly as a vehicle for invective.[5] Interest in the meter was revived by the Cynic philosophers of the fourth century B.C., and it en-

---

[1] This so-called spondaic beginning and end of a line coupled with the frequent series of three longs in a row in the 3 4 5 position led one scholar to the conclusion that the essential element of the choliambic is a spondee. Cf. W. Weinberger, "Der Lateinische Choliamb", *Serta Harteliana* (Vienna 1896) 118.

[2] Catullus wrote 126 lines in the choliambic meter and fifty-five in iambic.

[3] The picture of syllable sequences given above is the "norm." Syllable 9 is occasionally found long, resulting in a line ending with five long syllables, or "ischiorrogic" sequence, causing metrical theorists much headache. For a clear discussion of the conflicting opinions, see O. Masson, *Les Fragments du poète Hipponax* (Paris 1962) 23-24.

[4] All the grammarians writing on meter testify to the Hipponactean origin. Cf. Hephaistion *Ench.* 5.18 (Consbr. 17), and the index to Keil, *Gr. Lat.* 6.

[5] The most recent works on Hipponax are Masson *op. cit.* (supra n. 3), and A. Farina, *Ipponatte* (Naples 1964) which contains an excellent bibliography.

joyed tremendous vogue among the Alexandrians.[1] Chief among
these were Kallimachos, Phoinix of Kolophon, and the mime-
writer, Herondas,[2] all of whom were contemporaries aware of the
works of the others.[3] In Latin literature the earliest specimens of
choliambics also fall within a very narrow period of time, the close
of the second century and the beginning of the first century B.C.,
the so-called Age of Sulla. The pre-Catullan authors are Laevius,
Matius, and Varro; Catullus' contemporaries are Cinna and Calvus.[4]

---

[1] For a discussion of the choliambic meter in Greek and Latin, see A.
Meineke, "Ceterorum Poetarum Choliambi" in Lachmann's edition of
Aesop (Berlin 1845); J. Pelckmann, *Versus Choliambi apud Graecos et
Romanos Historia*, Diss. Greifswald (Keil 1908), (Pelckmann, *Chol.*); A.
Gerhard, *Phoinix von Kolophon*, Teubner (Leipzig 1909) 202-227. No one
article gives a complete discussion, and of course all were written before the
publication of the Kallimachean papyrus fragments, for which see R. Pfeiffer,
Callimachi Fragmenta (Oxford 1949) and C. M. Dawson, "The Iambi of
Callimachus," *YCS* 11, 1950. Gerhard concerns himself with listing all the
names of those who wrote choliambics and summarizing their works and lives
where possible. He fails to mention Ausonius, however. Pelckmann is concerned with developing a theory for the origin of the meter and the deviations
from "the norm." He omits Cinna.

[2] Important works bearing on the choliambics of these writers are:
Gerhard, *op. cit.* (supra n. 1).
W. A. Knox, *Herodes, Cercidas, and the Greek Choliambic Poets* (LCL 1929).
W. A. Knox-W. Headlam, *Herodas* (Cambridge 1922).
W. A. Knox, "Herodes and Callimachus," *Philologus* 81, 1926, 241-255 (*H &C*).
W. A. Knox, "The Early Iambus," *Philologus* 87, 1932, 18-39.
G. Puccioni, *Mimiambi* (Florence 1950). This is the most recent, though
   not most accurate, text of Herondas, but it contains a valuable index to
   Herondas' metrical peculiarities.
J. Irigoin, "Lois et règles dans le trimètre iambique et le tétramètre trochaï-
   que," *REG* 72, 1959, 67-80.
A. Ardizzoni, "Callimaco 'Ipponatteo'," *AFLC* 28, 1960, 3-16.
G. Perotta, "Il poeta degli epodi Strasburgo," *StItal* n.s. 15, 1938, 17-19.
G. Morelli, "Studi sul trimetro giambico," *Maia* 13, 1961, 143-161; 14, 1962,
   149-161, gives the most modern points on Knox's laws expounded in
   Philologus (supra), and also discusses Perotta's observations.

[3] The "floruit" for these authors is generally given as the first third of the
third century B.C., or the reign of Ptolemy II Philadelphos 285-247. Dawson
op. cit. (supra n. 1) 136-138, and Knox, *H &C* 248, 253, think that
Herondas and Kallimachos are making veiled references to each other in
their respective poems, Mime 8 and Iambus 13, possibly claiming superiority
in metrical technique. For peculiarities in the spelling of Herondas' name,
see A. Lesky, *A History of Greek Literature* (New York 1966) 747 n. 3.

[4] Choliambics are found at the end of the first century B.C. or last third of
the century in the *Catalepton* 2 & 5, a total of nineteen lines, and in the
Priapea, containing eighty-one choliambic lines: 31, 36, 47, 51, 58, 63, 78,
79. For information on the *Catalepton* and *Priapea*, see supra 42 n. 3, 87
n. 2.

Since the fragments of these five authors are not located in the
same volume, they are given in full below for the reader's convenience.

Laevius

\<Se\> seque in alta maria praecipem misit	12
inops \<et\> aegra sanitatis herois	
scabra in legendo reduviosave offendens	25

Matius

Iamiam albicascit Phoebus et recentatur	9
commune lumen hominibus voluptatis.	
Quapropter edulcare convenit vitam	10
curasque acerbas sensibus gubernare.	
Nuper die quarto, ut recordor, et certe	11
aquarium urceum unicum domi fregit.	
Sinuque amicam refice frigidam caldo	12
columbulatim labra conserens labris.	
Iam tonsiles tapetes ebrii fuco,	13
quos concha purpura imbuens venenavit.	
In milibus tot non videbitis grossum.	14
Sumas ab alio¹ lacte diffluos grossos.	15
pressusque labris unus acinus arebat.	17
Meos hortulos plus stercoro, \<ut scias\> quam holero.²	16

Varro

ne me pedatus |— ◡ | versuum tardor	57 *Bimarcus*
refrenet arte compari rhythmon certum	
donec foras nos intus evallaverunt ³	109 *Epitaphiones*
tum denique omnis cum lucerna combusta est	219 *Inglorius*
in lucubrando olivitasque consumpta est.	
aut ille, cervum qui volabili currens	293 *Meleagri*
sparo secutus tragulave traiecit.	
equi colore dispares item nati	358 ΄Ονος λύρας
hic badius, iste gilvus, ille murinus	

¹ This is O. Crusius' emendation for the crux *a basilio* in the manuscript.
Cf. *Herondae Mimiambi* (Leipzig 1914⁴) 96. (*HM*).
² This line, quoted by Priscian for the use of the word *holero* (Cf. Morel,
FPL 50) is full of complications. F. Leo, *op. cit.* (supra 40 n. 1) 277 n. 2,
makes it a choliambic by saying *meos* is an example of synizesis, and place
11 is resolved. *ut scias* is also a conjecture.
³ Bücheler and della Corte list this fragment as a senarius which seems
more difficult to construe since a senarius must have a short syllable at
place 11, than to consider it as an example of an "ischiorrogic" ending of
a choliambic line. (See supra 102 n. 3). Cf. Weinberger, *op. cit.* (supra 102
n. 1) 119, who explains differences of various scholars' conjectures and
gives *evallaverunt* with *e* short.

omni opstat in mysterio invidum tabes	373	*Papia Papae*
neque in polubro mystico coquam carnes, quibus satullem corpora ac famem ventris	401	Περὶ αἱρέσεων
nec multunummus piscis ex salo captus helops neque ostrea illa magna Baiana quivit palatum suscitare _ _ _	549	Τὸ ἐπὶ τῇ φακῇ μύρον

Calvus

Sardi Tigelli putidum caput venit.   3

Cinna

somniculosam ut Poenus aspidem Psyllus   10

On the problem of trying to associate the choliambic meter with a certain type of subject matter, that is, classifying it as a specific genre, the thirty-three and a-half lines of fragments just quoted do not shed much light. Nor can so few lines from such diverse areas reveal much in the way of content that can be compared either to the various Greek poets who used the meter, or to the eight complete poems of Catullus.[1] Only Matius offers a possible exception. Gellius, writing in the second century A.D., may imply a connection between Matius and Herondas when he gives the title of Matius' work *Mimiambi*, the same as that of Herondas.[2] A grammarian of the sixth century A.D. discoursing on meter, Terentianus Maurus, wrote twenty-one lines of choliambics to illustrate the rules for the meter. Here he mentions Matius and his mimiambi,[3] saying that he was a "bard flavored with Attic thyme."[4] Some scholars have even seen selections of Hipponax in Matius' fragments.[5] However, since among the Greeks from the time of Hipponax to the Alexandrians of the third century B.C. the meter seems to have been used to cover as wide a range of subject matter as invective, proverbs, epic-myth, informal literary criticism, diatribe,

---

[1] Poems 8, 22, 31, 37, 39, 44, 59, 60.

[2] *NA* 10.24. 10.

[3] Keil, *Gr. Lat.* 6. 297. 2416-2418.

> hoc mimiambus Mattius dedit metro:
> nam vatem eundem est Attico thymo tinctum
> pari lepore consecutus et metro.

[4] For fuller discussion on their possible relationship and Attic qualities in Herondas, see Knox-Headlam, *op. cit.* (supra 103 n. 1) 419, xxix, and Leo, *op. cit.* (supra 40 n. 1) (276-277.

[5] See Leo, *ibid.* 277 n. 2. The fragment of Hipponax he discusses is No. 13 in Mazon's edition and No. 19 in Farina (the most recent editions). See note on Matius 11 in Morel 50. The subject matter of both is the breaking of a cup.

moral, didactic, philosophic, and scientific principles, fables, and
dramatic amusement, very little can have been excluded from the
"genre."[1] Nevertheless, invective and diatribe were most commonly
associated with the meter. Therefore, of great interest is the very
observable absence of invective in the Latin fragments, in contrast
to the virulence of Hipponax or the salacious abusiveness of
Catullus. Of the latter's eight poems, four are usually omitted
from school texts: 37, 39, 59, 60, and a fifth, 22, is full of snide
insinuations and scurrilous remarks.[2] But in the fragments, while
there may be a few disagreeable words or ones with negative
poetic content, such as

stercoro	manure	Matius 16
scaber [3]	scabrous	Laevius 25
reduviosus	full of hang-nails	Laevius 25
putidum [4]	stinking	Calvus 3

there is no evidence of anything which could be classed as invective.
On the other hand, when it comes to the subject of love, Catullus
was not the first Latin poet to use scazons. To some extent fragments 10 and 12 of Matius (both quoted by Gellius to show Matius
as a clever coiner of words) [5] have a little of the flavor of the
eighth poem of Catullus with its famous exhortation to remain firm
when the beloved is lost. Compare:

Miser Catulle, desinas ineptire,   8:1-2, 10-11
et quod vides perisse perditum ducas.
. . . .
                          nec miser vive,
sed obstinata mente perfer, obdura.

Quapropter edulcare convenit vitam   Mat. 10
curasque acerbas sensibus gubernare.

But, whereas Catullus' words are violently, personally directed
toward himself, Matius is only being generally didactic, as the use
of the word *convenit* makes abundantly clear. Kissing also exists
in Matius, but, as the contrived reference to doves, and affected
juxtaposition of heat and cold show, the poet is obviously playing

---

[1] Cf. Gerhard, *op. cit.* (supra 103 n. 1) 216-223.
[2] Even Fordyce, in his annotated edition in 1961, felt he must omit 37
and 59.
[3] Word used by Catullus in elegiacs: 68.151.
[4] Used by Catullus six times, but not in scazons: 17.10; 14.11, 12, 19, 120;
98.1.
[5] *NA* 15.25.2; 20.9.2.

with words and sound-effects. There is no indication of being emotionally upset.

> Ibi illa multa tum iocosa fiebant, 8.6-7; 17-18
> quae tu volebas nec puella nolebat.
>
> . . . .
>
> Quem nunc amabis ? cuius esse diceris ?
> Quem basiabis ? cui labella mordebis ?
>
> Sinuque amicam refice frigidam caldo Mat. 12
> columbulatim labra conserens labris.

Compare also the slight, but significant, difference in vocabulary for the same things.

CATULLUS	MATIUS
puella	amica [1]
labella	labra [2]
basiabis	labra conserens labris

The subject of nature appears in Matius, but it is impossible to tell from the fragmentary nature of the lines whether the gardener is Matius himself, or just any gardener, or what was the context of the lines about figs, manure, and berries (fr. 14-17). In 16 occurs the only instance of a diminutive in Matius, perhaps implying a genuine interest in the gardens: *hortulos*. Certainly the frequent diminutives in Catullus increase the personal element in his poems. In the two relating to his love of nature, 31 on Sirmio and 44 on his Tiburtine farm, the use of the word *ocelle* at the beginning of line 2 in 31 betrays Catullus' affection for the spot. No such warmth is felt about his villa on the edge of town in 44. It is a place to escape to, not to long for.

After Matius, the only other possible similarity of subject matter in the fragments and in Catullus is found in Varro. Two lines from the satire on philosophers, Περὶ αἱρέσεων, mention feeding the belly (fr. 401) with somewhat the same derogatory tone that Catullus mentions the bad effects on the belly of sumptuous dinners (44.8-9).[3]

---

[1] In the poems of Catullus the *amica* at best is the kept woman or paid girl-friend, and the cheap whore at worst. Cf. 41.4 and 43.5 in hendecasyllables; 72.3 and 110.1 in elegiacs.

[2] The noun occurs in Catullus only once, when he is jeering at someone for what he considers rather disgusting homosexual practices. (80.8) *Labella*, the polite word is used at the beginning; *labra*, the coarse word is used at the end.

[3] Fordyce 197, interprets the poem as "a vehicle for the pun on *frigus*", an interpretation which would increase the similarity to the satire in Varro.

neque in polubro mystico coquam carnes   Varro 401
quibus satullem corpora ac famem ventris
Non inmerenti quam mihi meus venter   44.8-9
dum sumptuosas adpeto, dedit, cenas.

Much more evident than similarity of subject matter in these four lines, however, is the use of the same noun in the same position in the line. The word *venter* is common enough in Latin, but always a little strong in poetry, and in both cases here probably meant to arouse some disgust in the reader. Other similarities in vocabulary are:

frigidus:	Cat. 44.13	Matius 12
	gravedo frigida	frigidam amicam
mare:	Cat. 31.3	Laevius 12
	mari vasto	alta maria
reficio:	Cat. 44.16	Matius 12
	refectus	refice
sinus:	Cat. 37.11, 44.14	Matius 12
	meo sinu, sinum	sinu caldo
	(of the farm)	
versus:	Cat. 22.3	Varro 57
	plurimos versus	versuum

However, none of these words can be compared in terms of similar word-position in the line. Only *certe* Matius 11, and *certum* Varro 57 have position in common. On the other hand, there is one final similarity of usage to be noted in the position of the verb form *est* in position 12.[1] The two lines of fr. 219 of Varro end *combusta (e)st*, and *consumpta (e)st*. There are six examples in Catullus of this "enclitic" *est*,[2] and two of *est* as a separate final monosyllable where it has a more special emphasis.[3]

tergo (e)st 22.21
indignum (e)st 37.15   dens est 39.20

---

[1] It would be interesting to trace the similarity between choliambic and iambic word- and line-ends and hexameter usage, where the preferred break is after 5, next common after 7, and *est* the most frequent final monosyllable. For the analogy between hexameter and trimeter, see Schein, *op. cit.* (supra 3 n. 1) 26-27, 146 n. 68.

[2] Later examples of the enclitic *est*, as Pelckmann (*Chol.* 23) calls it, as the last word of the line are Martial 3.7.6; 4.65.2; 7.26.3; 8.44.1, 2, 9; 9.1.10; 11.61.9, 80.6, 98.22; 12.51.2; Ausonius 19.87.7, 8.

[3] Other examples of final *est* without elision are: *Priapea* 36.11; Martial 1.10.3, 6.26.2, 9.6.3. For unusual monosyllabic endings, see Pelckmann, *ibid.*, *Catalepton* 2.3.

ventum (e)st 39.2   non est 44.2
ubicumque (e)st 39.6
nulla (e)st 39.16
cordi (e)st 44.3

Now it may seem disappointing that these comparisons of vocabulary and subject matter give no definitive result. This is probably inevitable because of the scanty fragmentary evidence. What is more remarkable is that any similarities exist at all. Therefore, all the more striking is the uniformity in metrical practice and word-localization discernible in these authors which places them in a position of setting the norm for later choliambists.[1] The first observation is that there is a definite normative opening colon in the choliambics of these five authors: the *C B C open.* Moreover, the preference for this opening colon is much stronger in choliambics than in trimeter; for the alternative opening, the *C B rising;* that is, a break after the fourth syllable and not after the fifth, occurs in only 5% of Catullus' choliambics in contrast to 24% of his trimeters.[2] Examination of the fragmentary lines, surprisingly enough, reveals a similar percentage: 6% of the total thirty-three and two-thirds lines, or 7% in Matius and Varro, and not at all in the others. The converse of this is significant: 95% of the choliambics of Catullus and 97% of the fragmentary choliambics (93% for Matius and Varro, 100% for Laevius, Cinna and Calvus) have the *C B C* opening colon.[3] For a practice so much

---

[1] Pelckmann (*Chol.* 36-44) gives instances of certain deviations from the norm in Greek choliambists, and for Latin, 46-50, 52-54. However, he is not talking in terms of words, but of the various types of feet, spondees, dactyls, anapaests, tribrachs, etc. His statistics are interesting, but not of much help in analyzing the basic word units of a line or their functional properties.

[2] These statistics are valid only if one considers word-ends even where there is elision. Pelckmann (*Chol.* 46) takes the other point of view, but this produces strange lines with long cola, such as Cat. 31.10 with only a break at 10, "desideratoqu(e) acquiescimus lecto," or 22.8 with a line ending in a seven-syllable word: "directa plumb(o) et pumic(e) omni(a) aequata," which the ear and sense comprehension of the listener or reader could not have tolerated. Similarly, E. O'Neill, "The Localization of Metrical Word-Types in the Greek Hexameter," *YCS* 8, 1942, 108-110, (*Localization*) using the principle of metrical violations and unexampled practices for his arguments, defends his point that enclitics and particles, etc., should be treated as separate words. This heretical approach throws Knox's theories (as well as countless others) to the wind. Cf. Knox's articles in *Philologus* (supra 103 n. 2). Perhaps the riddle, "When is a word not a word?" is unanswerable.

[3] Percentages for later choliambics: *Catalepton* 89% (twice in eighteen lines the *C B rising* colon occurs), *Priapea* 100%, Petronius 87½% (seven out of eight lines), Persius 100%, Martial 98%, Ausonius 93%, Boethius 100%.

more regular in Latin than in Greek, one is tempted to see if there could be some reason. And this is the danger point involving "the spirit of the times" and "personal idiosyncrasy."[1] Nevertheless, some point of view must be taken if only to enable another to refute it more concisely. It is possible that the Latin choliambists did not make much use of the *C B rising* opening colon because they were trying to follow the strictest Greek usage. But since this colon occurred often enough in Greek not to be considered a rarity [2] (and was employed more freely by Catullus in his trimeters, as has been stated), it is more likely that its avoidance was connected with the psychological or subjective dislike of clash of ictus and accent at place 4 (the inevitable result if a word break occurs at 4), since the line also contained the sudden change of beat at the end: the juxtaposition of two theses at 10 and 11 with no intervening arsis, which does not occur in regular trimeters. Moreover, because of the overwhelming percentage of lines which feature the *C B C open* colon, one is inclined to think that the dominant accent was on 4, and that 2 was much less important, contrary to what many handbooks on meter imply.[3] If one is absolutely strict and substracts the percentage of monosyllables at place 5 which are not preceded by a monosyllable at 4 or contain elision, both of which would place a weak accent on 4, the number of lines showing a 4 accent is still high.

	CATULLUS	FRAGMENTS
C B C open	95%	97%
Mono. at 5	18%	18%
Strong 4	77%	79%
Mono. at 4	6%	—
Elision at 5	3%	3%
Total Accented	86%	82%

---

[1] With apologies to Porter, *op. cit.* (supra 1 n. 1) 29.

[2] Statistics for the Greek choliambists on this point do not exist, but only on where a break after 4 occurs. These are not entirely uncontroversial because of different interpolations and emendations, and differences of opinion between Pelckmann, Gerhard, and Knox. Nevertheless, for some idea on the subject, see the authors (supra 103 n. 1 & 2).

[3] "Since Bentley's time it has been the fashion to hold that the ictus on the first, third, and fifth feet (that is on 2, 6, 10) was heavier than that on all remaining feet. In all modern editions the ictus, if marked at all in iambic trimeter and similar verse, is marked on that principle." E. Post, *Selected Epigrams of Martial* (Ginn & Co. 1908) xliii n. 2. B. L. Gildersleeve and G. Lodge, *Latin Grammar* (New York 1963) 466.

This apparent preference for a strong accent at 4 is also illuminating in the light of the development of later accentual verse. Theories about this are, of course, conflicting. Of considerable interest, however, is Burger's statement that iambic trimeter had become, by the time of the fifth century, a line of twelve syllables, having, without exception, a caesura after 5 and an accent at 4, and at the end of the line an accent on 10 if the line ended in a trisyllable, or 11 if it ended in a disyllable.[1] This would tend to strengthen the conclusion that there was a definite pattern of expectancy associated with the iambic rhythm which became more dominant, so that eventually any deviation from this was semantically as well as structurally unacceptable.

Closely related to the fact of the predominant *C B C open* colon, or rather to its converse, the rare *C B rising*, is the function of the word which fills the 5-7 syllabic space when the *C B rising* does occur. It is practically always the crucial word of the line.[2] This is more difficult to state categorically in respect to the fragments. *Tapetes*, Matius 13, fills the 5-7 position and should be the significant noun in the passage. But the poet was also conscious of his cleverness in using the adjective *ebrii*. To Varro in 373, where *mysterio* fills the 5-7 place, the unusual use of *invidum* may be as important, or the final disyllable *tabes*. The practice of Catullus, however, is clear. To fill the 5-7 space he uses only verb forms, twice the present indicative, and four times the infinitive:

reponit	31.8	perisse	8.2
renidet	39.7	sectare	8.10
		putare	37.5 [3]
		bibisse	39.21

Of these, *renidet* best examplifies the importance of the 5-7 position, for the whole poem pivots around the verb *renidoe*. *Perisse* and *sectare* are equally illustrative of the functional importance of the

---

[1] Burger, *Recherches* 107. As an example he quotes a line which has the accentuation of a choliambic, 108: "A quo refĕcti laudes dicamus Dĕo."

[2] This is in general true of 4-7 words in later choliambics. *Catalepton: amator* 2.1; *tyrannus* 2.3; Petronius 5.6 *addictus*; Martial 1.77.1-5 *Charinus*; 3.93.20 *sarire*; 4.37.4 *fundisque*; 4.61.14 *crudelis*; 5.14.8 *deiectus*; 5. 37. 13 *sciurus*; 5. 37.24 *accepit*; 8.44.3 *Titulle*; 9.13.2 *donare*; 12.32.11 *grabatus*. *Fundisque* and *sciurus* are less obviously important, perhaps.

[3] The first part of 37 pivots around the verb *putare* where it occurs four times in nine lines. Cf. N. Herescu, "Autour de la 'Salax Taberna'" in *Hommages à Leon Herrmann* (supra 88 n. 1) 431-435.

5-7 position. The mad love of Catullus' life, with its agony and
intense joy, is over; he is not to pursue it any longer. That is what
poem 8 is all about. *Reponit* conveys the whole mood of 31, the
relief of real relaxation at Sirmio, away from pretense. Thus, it
would seem that a change from the normal *C B C open* colon was
made to focus the attention on the central word as the emphatic
one, as well as just for variety.[1]

Another point, not to be passed over in connection with the
nature of the *C B C open* colon, is the preference for a long syllable
at 5, or the tendency toward the anceps at 5. The percentage for
the total lines of the fragments is 7% (or broken down by
authors: Laevius 33%, Matius 64%, Varro 71%, Cinna and
Calvus 100%) and for Catullus 64%.[2] Here, the percentages are not
so high, but all except for Laevius are over 60%. This strengthens
the conclusion that the *C B C open* colon was a unit of metrical
structure as was the "lecythion" (*B C B closed*) or the "adonic
tag" (*D C falling*). For just as in hexameter, the final unaccented
syllable had the value of a long even when short,[3] thus marking
the end of a line or phrase pattern, so the unaccented fifth syllable
in iambic meter tended to become always long, as later history
of the meter shows, because it also marked the end of a colon or
phrase pattern.[4] Furthermore, though ancient metrical analysts
were not aware of it, this colon was the fundamental unit of iambic
meter, and not a metron composed of two iambic feet.[5]

A fourth metrical observation concerns the use of resolution. Here,
again, a normative pattern among the five authors can be traced,

---

[1] Varro himself made one of the earliest attempts in literary criticism to
analyze the need for the break after 5 or 7 in hexameters. He explained its
existence as necessary to preserve a geometrical ratio. This theory could be
applied to trimeter also. The fragment is quoted by Gellius in a brief passage
discussing metrical peculiarities of iambics and hexameters, *NA* 18.15.2.

[2] The percentages are even higher in later Latin choliambics with the exception of the *Catalepton* 56%, and Ausonius 64%. *Priapea* 70%, Petronius
75%, Persius 79%, Martial 79%, Boethius 72%.

[3] O'Neill, *Localization* 112. In general it can be said that colometric ends
are often marked by ancipitia.

[4] In Seneca's trimeters, for instance, 87% have a colometric end at 5
which is long. See O'Neill, *WAFS* 348.

[5] The *loci classici* for earliest mention in Latin of the two-foot metron are
Horace, *Ars Poetica*, 251 ff., and Quintilian 9.4.75. The *C B C open* colon is
also clearly a unit of the Alcaic stanza, and in Horace the fifth syllable is
always long.

and this time one which distinguished them from the later Latin choliambist. In contrast to the considerable freedom of the Greek poets in handling of resolution,[1] the Latin writers who first adopted the meter restricted themselves to resolution only of the theses at place 2, 4, 6 or 8, never allowing a resolved arsis.[2] In "Silver Latin" and later, on the other hand, a resolved initial anceps becomes almost the norm, and place 3 can also be resolved.[3] Concerning the general practice of resolution, it is interesting to note the curve from a fairly high percentage in the earliest fragments to a low point with Catullus, his contemporaries, the *Catalepton* and *Priapea*, back to very high by the time of Martial and later.[4] The percentage of resolution in the fragmentary authors is 24% (Matius 36%, Laevius 66%, Varro 7%, Cinna and Calvus 0%), while in Catullus it is only 2%. This might be connected with Catullus' wish to be completely distinct from the various iambic rhythms of drama, or because he felt a strict meter made the pattern clearer. Another fact concerning resolution can be observed from the tables of word localization; namely, that in no case is an anapaestic word substituted for an iambic word.[5] This practice also differs from Martial's. Resolutions are never divided between two words, nor is there any example of a disyllabic word of two shorts (the pyrrhic). In the five authors, words of three short syllables can occupy the 2-3, 6-7, or 8-9 position.

---

[1] Pelckmann's statistics, a bit spread around (*Chol.* 26-27, 30-32, 36-39, 41-43, 59), are not totally accurate because of variant readings and new fragments, but they are sufficient to show that the percentage of resolution in Greek choliambics is considerably higher than in Latin.

[2] This is one argument against Baehrens' rendering of Laevius 25, *FPR* (Leipzig 1886) 290:

animi impos aegra sanitatis herois

which results in an initial resolved anceps. The initial resolution occurs first in Petronius, 5.8.

[3] Information about resolution in Latin writers in Pelckmann, *Chol.* 50, 52-54, 56, 59, again depends to some upon extent readings. Cf. Lachmann-Meineke, *op. cit.* (supra 103 n. 1) xii-xiii.

[4] There are only fourteen pure choliambic lines in Martial and resolution in proper nouns is the rule rather than the exception. Cf. H. J. Isaac, *Martial* I, (Paris 1933) xxx.

[5] This would result in a conflict of ictus and accent. But in Martial such practice is permitted: Intro. 3, occupying the 3-4 position is *theatrum*, which would be normally accented *théa-trum*, but its position in an iambic foot requires the odd *theatrúm*.

2-3	6-7	8-9
Varro 258 badius	Matius 12.1 refice	Matius 17 acinus
	Laevius 12.1 maria	
	Catullus 59.3 rapere	

Even as the disyllable at 6-7 is more frequent than at 2-3 or 8-9,[1] possibly to strengthen the accent at 6, so a tribrach word is found in the 6-7 place the most. Anapaestic words occur in the 4-5 place once in Catullus and once in Matius, while a strange combination of anapaest and elision is also found in Matius at the important 11-12 position.[2]

4-5	11-12
Matius 15 alio [3]	Matius 16 qu(am h)olero
Catullus 22.19 aliqua	

Lastly, there are three examples of resolution in words of more than three syllables.[4]

5-8	1-3
Matius 9.2 hominibus	Catullus 37.5 confutuer(e)

5-9
Laevius 25 reduviosav(e)

The five poets are not only set apart in their restricting resolution only to a thesis, but even Catullus is separate from the others in using it so little.

Finally, a few other observations can be made. The first of these concerns elisions. Although examples can be found in every place except 12 (disregarding the enclitic *est* as do the following statistics), the most common elisions occur at 2, 6, and 8.

	2	6	8
Fragments	12%	12%	9%
Catullus	10%	8%	11%

---

[1] 36% Matius, 33% Laevius, 40% Varro, 100% Cinna, 27% Catullus.

[2] See (supra 104 n. 2) and Müller, *CTP* 92. Because of emendations and variant readings, it is not possible to make absolute statements about the localization and types of resolution.

[3] This is one of the fragments of Matius with uncertain reading. Cf. Morel, *FPL* 50, Müller, *ibid.* and Crusius, *HM* 96.

[4] Pelckmann includes in his statistics a dubious fragment of Matius (*Chol.* 48) which Morel 184 fr. 84 does not consider to be by Matius, but rather places in the section of uncertain fragments after the Augustan Era, Keil, *Gr. Lat.* 6. 563. 5-6.

The elision at 2 is related to another observation, the prevalence of a monosyllable at 1, a particularly distinctive feature of Catullan use of words.[1] Over 43% of his choliambs commence with a monosyllable, and these added to the 10% showing elision at 2 show that more than half of his lines in his meter alone have an initial monosyllable, as against 39% of the fragments.[2] An interesting illustration of this can be seen in poem 39, nine of whose last eleven lines begin with a monosyllable, and line 19 has the elision at 2 *dent(em) atque*, a word deliberately placed to emphasize Catullus' contempt for the polished teeth of Egnatius' grin.[3] If the elision at 2 is prominent to emphasize the initial monosyllable, perhaps the elision at 6 has a much clearer purpose, to preserve the important break after the fifth syllable; that is, to preserve the *C B C open* colon. The elision at 8 is more difficult to analyze, however. It may have some connection with word accent as its presence generally places a two-syllable word in the 6-7 position, making a strong accent at 6. Indeed, 70% of Catullus' choliambs have a break at either 7 or 8, causing 6 to have a dominant accent according to penultimate law, 6 7 | 8 |, whereas the percentage of strong 6 in the fragments is 65%.

It is doubtful whether any conclusions can be drawn from examining the localization of words of more than three syllables as to accent or position for the sake of emphasis. Their distribution is regulated by the demands of the iambic meter and the *C B C open* initial colon. In spite of this regulation, however, they could be employed more than Catullus or the other authors use them. Of four-syllable words, the favored positions are the 9-12: thirteen times in Catullus, four times in Matius; and the 6-9: nine times in Catullus, three times in the fragments.[4] As for five-syllable words, one occurs three times filling the

---

[1] For instance, of Catullus' 537 hendecasyllabic lines, 279 commence with a monosyllable, according to Cutt (supra 34 n. 2) 7. Twenty-two out of fifty-five trimeter lines have initial monosyllable, etc.

[2] Monosyllabic beginnings are less than 50% in Martial.

[3] The word for tooth occurs in different cases four times in the twenty-one lines, as well as the form *dentatus*. The verb *renideo* occurs five times, and once in the important 5-7 position (supra 44-45, 94, 98, 111).

[4] 9-12 Cat.: 8.1; 22.5, 13; 31.8, 14; 37.4, 14, 17; 39.8; 44.11; 59.2; 60.1. 6-9: 8.19; 22.10; 37.8, 20; 39.17, 19; 59.5; 60.3. See also localization tables p. 117.

C B C open colon in Catullus, once in Matius 12, a coined word:

Matius   columbulatim
Catullus   desideratoqu(e) 31.10
            cuniculosae   37.18
            Bononiensis   59.1

A five-syllable ending occurs twice in Catullus and once in Varro:

Varro 109   evallaverunt
Catullus   contubernales 37.1
            insularumque 31.1

In Catullus, five-syllable words are found more often in the 6-10 position, a total of six times, but they never occur in the fragments in this position. Varro, however, has one very odd place for a five-syllable word, 5-9, resulting in an unpoetic, although metrically correct, line: *olivitasque* 509. However, as the total of four- and five-syllable words in any position in Catullus is less than 50%, and only 21% in the fragments, they were probably felt to be too cumbersome in iambic rhythm. In contrast, the preference for disyllables is so high that just at 11-12 alone the percentage in both Catullus and the fragments is 56%. This is one of the interesting differences between trimeter, which prefers a trisyllabic end [1] and choliambics. It serves to emphasize the juxtaposition of the two theses at 10 and 11 and the dominant 11 accent.

In conclusion, it is helpful to sketch an "ideal" choliambic line to illustrate the normative pattern against which the poet plays.

1	2 3	4 5	6 7	8 9 10	11 12
×	– ⌣	⊥ ×	⊥ ⌣	– ⌣ –	⊥ ×

The words are the masonry, the iambs the formal structure, and the pattern is achieved by the location of two- and three-syllable words, so that the strong accents, 4 and 11, are the most constant. In the normative line sketched above, however, ictus and accent also coincide at 2 and 8, which if it were true of every line, would result in extreme monotony. The norm can easily be

---

[1] The percentages of later choliambics which have a disyllabic end increases from 56% in the *Catalepton*, to 70% in the *Priapea*, 75% in Petronius, 72% in Martial, 80% in Ausonius, 72% in Boethius. Only Persius seems out of line with just 50%, (See supra 92).

varied by shifting every break, except the fifth, one place to the left:

$$ \times - | \cup \perp \times \| - | \cup \perp \cup | - \perp \times $$

This keeps the accent at 4 and 11, but 6 becomes subordinated to 8. There is, of course, no argument here that Catullus or any other poet sat down and drew a similar picture and then thought up words to fill the spaces. Rather, these word divisions were an unconscious semantic aspect of Latin. Catullus differs from his predecessors, contemporaries, and followers in seemingly instinctive awareness of handling these varieties of phrase pattern, in contrast to their studied and experimental awareness, in a way which only jars the expectation of the listener or reader for a particular purpose. Coupled with this, his skillful placement of words and phrase patterns in a line with relation to the normal Latin word accent to achieve the highest efficiency of sense, sound, and rhythm, sets him apart from any of his predecessors. The purpose of this chapter has been to point up a few of his metrical-semantic subtleties in the handling of the choliambic meter.

WORD LOCALIZATION IN CHOLIAMBICS

```
 1  2  3  4  5 | 6  7  8  9  10  11  12
 ×  -  ∪  -  × | -  ∪  -  ∪   -   -   ×
```

	MATIUS	LAEVIUS	VARRO	C & C	CATULLUS
	(14)	(3)	(14-2/3)	(2)	(126)
I. Monosyllables					
A. ∪					
1. 1	1 7%	1			6 5%
2. 5					2 2% [1]
B. —					
1. 1	3 21%		6 41%		57 45%
2. 5	3 21%		1 7%	1	17 13%
3. at 6	2 14%		2 14%		50 40%
II. Disyllables					
A. ∪ —					
1. 1-2	1 7%	1	3 20%		8 6%
2. 3-4	1 7%		1 7%		10 7%
3. 9-10			5 34%	1	29 23%

---

[1] The two instances of a short monosyllable at 5, 39.8 and 44.11, are elided with the preceding word.

	MATIUS	LAEVIUS	VARRn	c & c	CATULLUS
	(14)	(3)	(14-2/3)	(2)	(126)
B. _ ◡					
4-5	3 22%	2	3 20%		13 10%
C. _ ×					
1. 4-5	1 7%		1 7%		23 18%
2. 11-12	8 57%	1	8 55%	2	70 56%
III. Trisylllables					
A. _ ◡ _					
1. 2-4	3 21%		1 7%		5 4%
2. 6-8	3 21%		3 20%	1	19 15%
3. 8-10	5 36%	1	2 14%	1	13 10%
B. ◡ _ ◡					
1. 1-3	1 7%		1 7%		16 13%
2. 3-5			2 14%		17 14%
3. 5-7	1 7%				5 4%
C. ◡ _ ×					
3-5	2 14%	1	4 27%	1	21 17%
D. × _ ◡					
5-7			1 7%		2 2%
E. _ _ ×					
10-12	1 7%	2	5 34%		31 25%
IV. Quadrisyllables					
A. _ ◡ _ ◡					
1. 2-5					4 3%
2. 6-9			2 14%		9 7%
B. _ ◡ _ ×					
2-5	1 7%		4 27%	1	21 17%
C. ◡ _ _ ×					
9-12	4 29%				13 10%
V. Five Syllables					
A. × _ ◡ _ ×					
1-5	1 7%				3 3%
B. _ ◡ _ ◡ _					
6-10					6 5%
C. _ × _ _ ×					
8-12			1 7%		2 2%

Notice in all cases that 5 when final, or a monosyllable, is predominantly long, in particular Catullus: mono short 2%, long 13%; disyllable short 13%, long 23%; trisyllable short 14%, long 21%; quadrisyllables short 3%, long 17%; five syllables 100%.

GALLIAMBICS

$$\text{I}\ \text{I}\tfrac{1}{2}\ \mid\ 2\ 3\ \mid\ 4(4\tfrac{1}{2})\ 5\ \mid\ 6\ 7\ \parallel\ \text{I}\ \text{I}\tfrac{1}{2}\ 2(2\tfrac{1}{2})\ \mid\ 3\ 4\ \mid\ 4\tfrac{1}{2}\ 5\ 6^{\,1}$$

$$\smile\ \smile\ \mid\ \_\ \smile\ \mid\ \_\ \ \smile\ \mid\ \_\ \_\ \parallel\ \smile\ \smile\ \ \_\ \mid\ \smile\ \smile\ \mid\ \smile\ \smile\ \times$$

In many ways the galliambic meter is one of the most interesting of all the meters employed by Catullus. The first reason for this is that more than any other meter it is tied to its subject, the cult of Cybele, the Phrygian Mother Goddess,[2] and her priests, the Galli, from whom most of the ancient grammarians assumed the name of the meter was derived.[3] The second reason is that Catullus 63 is the

---

[1] This is only the most basic scheme. The most frequent variation of the first half is $\_\ \_\ \smile\ \_\ \smile\ \_$, and for the second $\smile\ \smile\ \_\ \smile\ \_\ \smile\ \times$. A third variety for each is $\smile\ \smile\ \_\ \smile\ \smile\ \smile\ \smile\ \_\ \_$, $\_\ \_\ \smile\ \smile\ \smile\ \smile\ \times$.

[2] There is no need to give the history of the legend here, particularly as the number of articles, books, and chapters of books on the subject are endless. General information can be found in *RE* 11[2], 2250-2298, and Ellis, *op. cit.* (supra 57-58 n. 2) 251-261. The most thorough treatment of the legend and cult is contained in the two old stand-bys, H. Graillot, *Le Culte de Cybèle* (Paris 1912), and H. Hepding, *Attis, seine Mythen und sein Kult, Religionsgeschichtliche Versuche und Vorarbeiten* (Giessen 1903) Bnd. I. This last not only discusses the origin and spread of the cult and its relationship to other mystery cults, but quotes in the first chapter every important Greek or Latin text, as well as many inscriptions, which pertains to Attis and Cybele. For the connection between Catullus and the cult, see V. Bongi, "Il Carme 63 di Catullo e il culto di Cibele e di Attis," *La Civiltà Moderna* 7 (Florence 1943). For a religious-psychological study of the cult and Catullus, Varro, and Lucretius, see O. Weinreich, "Catulls Attisgedicht," *Mélanges F. Cumont, AnnPhilHist* 4, 1936, 463-500, the first page of which contains an excellent bibliography. For some of the more recent discussions about the cult, see P. Lambrechts, "Attis: Van Herdersknaap tot God," *Verhand. Vlaamse Acad. voor Wet. van België Kl. der Lett.* 46, 1962; "Les Fêtes 'phrygiennes' de Cybèle et d'Attis," *BIBR* 27, 1952, 141-170; "Attis à Rome," *Mélanges George Smets* (Brussels 1952) 461-473; all of which works have the thesis that Cybele was in Rome in the Republic, but that Attis was left behind in Phrygia until the first century A.D. This was the main argument sixty years earlier of G. Showerman, "Was Attis in Rome Under the Republic?" *TAPA* 31, 1900, 46-59. C. B. Pascal, *The Cults of Cisalpine Gaul,* Coll. Latomus 75, 1964, 57-58 stresses how firmly entrenched the cult was. M. J. Vermaseren, *The Legend of Attis in Greek and Roman Art* (Leiden 1966) contains an excellent bibliography, p. 2 n. 1, as well as a thorough catalogue of sculptures, coins, frescoes, plaques and plates. An interesting art-oriented treatise based on recent excavations is M. Floriani Squarciapino, *I Culti orientali ad Ostia* (Leiden 1962) 1-18.

[3] Marius Victorinus in Keil, *Gr. Lat.* 6. 154. 24-26; Terentianus Maurus *ibid.* 410, 2889-2891; Choiroboskos, *Commentarius* (Consbr. 245). Ovid, who has a

only extant poem in either Greek or Latin in the meter. Thus the
knotty problem of his models and predecessors has occupied the
wits of more scholars and the pages of more journals than practically any other Catullan question.[1] Of course, one must not
overlook the meager two lines in Greek quoted by Hephaistion.[2]

passion for giving the reasons for things akin to that of Kallimachos, derives
the name of the priests from the river in Phrygia, the Gallus, which the
priests in celebrating the rites, drank, and then went mad: *Fasti* 4.361-366.
It is interesting to note in passing that the concept of religious fervor so
intense that the celebrants castrate themselves is associated with insanity.
The same concept is found in the attitude toward Dionysiac rites. What
shocks the modern mind is the castration or the sexual indulgence. What
shocked the Greek and Roman was the abandonment of the well-ordered
world to elemental and primeval wildness.
   [1] Wilamowitz was one of the chief figures in the discussion, insisting on
Kallimachean authorship for the fragment in Hephaistion (*PMG* adesp. 112)
and Catullan translation. See "Die Galliamben der Kallimachus und Catulls,"
Hermes 14, 1879, 194-201; *HD* 291-295; and the footnote on Wilamowitz in
J. P. Elder, "Catullus' Attis," *AJP* 68, 1947, 394 n. 2. Lafaye *op. cit.* (supra
6 n. 1) 82-90 is clearly under the spell of Wilamowitz, convinced of Catullan
dependence on Alexandrianism and Kallimachos. Critics since 1929 seem to
be free from the insistence on Kallimachos, but they are still searching for a
model: "Il s'agit maintenant de savoir si Catulle trouva ce thème remanié
ou non par un prédécesseur, et ici se présente le problème de la préexistence
d'un modèle alexandrin, question il y a une trentaine d'années à l'ordre du
jour. C'était alors la mode d'affirmer a priori qu'un Latin étant, par définition,
incapable de rien inventer, partout où on apercevait du nouveau, il fallait
supposer un modèle alexandrin." This is how A. Guillemin sums up the
situation in "Le Poème 63 de Catulle," *REL* 27, 1949, 152. A. Klotz takes an
intermediate stand, insisting that although Catullus 63 cannot possibly be
"eine Urschöpfung," his model was probably somebody who imitated Kallimachos, but not Kallimachos himself: "Zu Catull," *RhM* 80, 1931, 354.
Weinreich *op. cit.* (supra 119 n. 2) 469 punctures the Wilamowitz bubble by
pointing out the differences between the fragment and Catullus. I feel,
however, that if one must play the model-seeker, the most profitable comparisons are those made by Avallone, *C & E* 154-175 where he discusses
similarities between passages of the *Helen* and the *Bacchae* and Catullus 63.
   [2] *Ench.* 12.3 (Consbr. 39):

        Γαλλαὶ μητρὸς ὀρείης φιλόθυρσοι δρομάδες,
        αἷς ἔντεα παταγεῖται καὶ χάλκεα κρόταλα.

In a corrupted epigram by Diogenes Laertius, 8.91, composed of eight lines
in ionic a minore, line 4 illustrates the anacreontic cola, A and γ (infra 122 n. 1,
125). Had 3 and 4 appeared alone in an anthology, they might well have gone
down in history as illustrating the galliambic meter in, Greek.

        ταύρου. κοὐδὲν ἔλεξεν· βοῖ γὰρ πόθεν λόγος;
        φύσις οὐκ ἔδωκε μόσχῳ λάλον ᾿Απιδι στόμα.

However, as lines 1, 2, 6-8, are regular ionic a minore cola, the discussion over
the epigram has centered on its transmission in elegiac form in the Palatine

or the seven and one-half textually corrupt lines in Varro's *Menip-pean Satires*,[1] or the three lines by Maecenas.[2] Nevertheless, critical appraisal of the meter can only rely on Catullus' ninety-three lines for valid statistics. A third reason for the fascination of the Attis poem is the confusion of scholars concerning the nature of the meter itself. Most critics still insist on trying to analyze the meter on the basis of the statements of the ancient grammarians who could understand no meter unless it was derived from another.[3] Thus, because of the great number of short syllables in the galliambic meter, particularly at the end of the line, the different places in the line where these shorts can be resolved into longs, and the fact that in terms of time value a pure ionic a minore dimeter seems equal to the first half of the line, the general consensus has been, and still is, that the rhythm is a form of ionic a minore tetrameter.[4] The association, however, is completely erroneous

Anthology. See note in H. Stadtmüller, *Anthologia Graeca* 2 (Leipzig 1899[1]) 518-520, and F. Dübner, *Anthologiae Palatinae* (Paris 1871) *In Caput VII Annotatio* 513.

[1] Fr. 79, 131, 132, 275, and 540, are given by Bücheler as examples of Varro's galliambics. Of these, however, only the first two are certain in their original manuscript state. The rest have required emendation to make them sensible as well as metrical. They are quoted infra 123-124 where the problem is discussed in full.

[2] Morel, *FPL* fr. 5 and 6. There are also three fragments, Incerti 19, 20, 74, by unknown writers of the empire period which add another two and one-half lines to the total. Of interest in illustrating the learning of the Renaissance are the poems quoted and discussed by D. Campbell, "Galliambic Poems of the 15th and 16th Centuries," *HumR* 22, 1960, 490-510. These poems are, of course, only imitations of Catullus 63 and reveal nothing concerning a genuine historical development of the meter.

[3] Caesius Bassus, Keil, *Gr. Lat.* 6. 261-262, is a good example of the deriva-tion technique in the galliambic meter. Cf. Terentianus Maurus, *ibid.*, 410. 2885-2900.

[4] Hephaistion *loc. cit.* (supra 120 n. 2) equates the meter with ionic a minore catalectic requiring anaclasis, or inversion of the syllables. Marius Victorinus, Keil, *Gr. Lat.* 6. 93, follows Hephaistion, as does Atilius Fortuna-tianus, *ibid.*, 290.4. Bassus, *ibid.*, 262. 26-28 suggests a possible iambic origin, but the general consensus of the grammarians in Keil 6 agrees with Hephaist-ion, even though they all notice that the first half of the line is an anacreontic colon, which in its original location in the poems of Anakreon should never have been called ionic, but rather a variation of the Aeolic *D B alternating* colon. The harm done by Hephaistion has been perpetuated by metricians since. For an interesting scholarly battle during the last decade of the 19th century, see G. Allen, *The Attis of Gaius V. Catullus, Bibliothèque de Carabas* (London 1892) for ionic theory; R. Tyrrell, "Grant Allen on the Attis of Catullus," *CR* 7, 1893, 44-45, against ionic, saying ancients were misled, and promoting iambic first half and trochaic second; E. S. Thompson, "The

because the *A* arsis, which gives true ionics and bacchiacs their
syncopated punch, is missing. The first colon of the line is easily
explained as a *D B B C open* colon.[1] The second half of the line,
because of the succession of short syllables at its close is more
difficult to analyze. Still, if the pattern is determined from the
practice of Catullus, the second half can be described as the catalectic twin of the first half, a *D B B rising* colon in which the
thesis between the two *B* arses is normally resolved. The problem
is complicated by the responsion in the Hephaistion fragment
with an ionic final colon of the form *D A D A open* which also
occurs twice in the fragments of Varro, 132.1, 2. Since the pure
ionic a minore initial *D A D A rising*[2] colon is found only once
in Catullus, 1.54, concerning which Fordyce writes in his apparatus criticus "multis suspectum,"[3] and the *D A D A open* never
occurs, it does not seem likely that Catullus was attempting to
write ionics, although undoubtedly he was aware of their possibility
for metrical responsion. The following study of word localization
and vocabulary in comparison with Varro and Maecenas, however,
is not aimed at proving ionic affiliation or no, but rather to show
the handling of disyllables and trisyllables, the role of word accent,
and the type of vocabulary that accompanies the meter.

Galliambic Metre," *CR* 7, 1893, 145-146 (Thompson 1) against ionic, holding
both halves iambic; G. Dunn, "The Galliambic Metre," *CR* 7, 1893, 146-148,
imaginatively calling it logaoedic tripodies and tetrapodies composed of
irrational dactyls, irrational trochees, and irrational spondees, and dividing
the line in the middle of a word; and a final parting thrust in the same volume
of *CR* by Thompson, "The Galliambic Metre," 354-355 (Thompson 2)
likening it to a mixture of 3/4 and 6/8 rhythm in music. W. R. Hardie,
"The Galliambic Metre," *CR* 7, 1893, 280-282, sweepingly condemns Messrs
Tyrrell, Thompson, and Dunn, and brings the argument to an end with a
plug for ionic a minore. Thus the 20th century has returned to Hephaistion,
following the confident lead of the German tradition headed by W. Christ,
Metrik der Griechen und Römer (Leipzig 1874) 523-525. In addition to all the
well-known books on Greek and Latin meter cited in Koster, *Traité* 9-11,
there are also individual articles such as those of Klotz (supra 121 n. 2),
Campbell (supra 120 n. 1), Elder (supra 119 n. 2), T. Goodell, "Word
Accent in Catullus' Galliambics," *TAPA* 34, 1903, 27-32, G. B. Pighi,
"Il Canto di Attis," *Rivista Musicale Italiano* 39, 1932, 34-40 and R. C.
Ross, "Catullus 63 and the Galliambic Meter," *CJ*, 64, 1969, 145-152.

[1] This colon is often known as the anacreontic, after Anakreon where it
first occurs (*PMG* 50), and more commonly in the imitations of Anakreon
found in the *Anacreontea* (*PLG* 3. 297-309).

[2] It is also possible to interpret this pattern as a *D A D C open* colon,
which makes it closer to the anacreontic *D B B C open*: Thus the possibilities
of responsion between the two are easier to understand.

[3] Fordyce 44. For further mention of this *F* colon, see infra 126, 127 n. 1.

In order to make accessible the material of the other Latin examples, the lines are quoted below. The value of percentages derived from such texts, however, limited as they are by their fragmentary nature and, in the case of Varro, by their uncertain readings, is only relative. For a critic it is difficult to resist the temptation to use an emendation which suits what he is trying to prove.[1]

VARRO [2]

Cycnus

    tua templa ad alta fani properans citus itere   79

---

[1] Although the text of Nonius Marcellus' *Compendiosa Doctrina* made by Lindsay in 1903 is generally accepted, there are many readings of the fragments of Varro's *Menippean Satires* which are open to conjecture. The innocent reader of Bücheler's 1963 edition of the *Menippean Satires* is little aware that there may be several Varros until he starts to compare Bücheler with the version of the fragments as found in Lindsay. The lines from fragment 132 (infra n. 2) have been worked over more than any others with such appallingly different results that one really wishes for the original manuscripts of Nonius in order to make up one's own mind. If meaning is all that one is after, the differences in emendations are not very crucial. But when word localization, metrical patterns, and vocabulary comparisons are the subject of the study, arbitrary changes in word order, or a substitution of a final disyllable for a trisyllable, can wreak havoc with statistics. The protagonists in the battle for a better text of Varro's *Satires* are principally the Germans of the last century: G. Röper, "M. Terenti Varronis Saturarum Menippearum quarundam reliquiae emendatae," *Philologus* 9, 1854, 223-278 (*MQR*), "Epimetrum Varronianorum," *ibid.* 567-573, "Varronische Vindicien I," *Philologus* 15, 1860, 267-302, II 17, 1861, 64-102, III 18, 1862, 418-446 (*VV* I, II, III); J. Vahlen, *In Varronis Saturarum Menippearum reliquias coniectanea* (Leipzig 1858) (*MRC*); F. Bücheler, "Bemerkungen über die Varronischen Satiren," *Kleine Schriften* I (Leipzig 1915) 169-198 (*Bemerkungen*), "Über Varros Satiren," *ibid.* 534-580 (*UV*); O. Ribbeck, "Über Varronische Satiren," *RhM* 14, 1859, 102-130 (*VS*); A. Riese, *M. Terenti Varronis Saturarum Menippearum Reliquiae* (Leipzig 1865) (*VSM*), "Kritisches und Exegetisches zu Varros Satiren," *RhM* 21, 1866, 109-122 (*KVS*); K. Lachmann, *Kleinere Schriften* (Berlin 1876) 56-57. J. H. Onions' labors over the manuscripts of Nonius are also important: "Noniana Quaedam," *JP* 16, 1888, 161-182, "Verisimilia Noniana," *CR* 3, 1889, 247-249, "Adversaria Noniana," *JP* 18, 1890, 89-119 (*AN*). E. Norden, although mainly concerned with understanding the satires, also alludes to textual problems: "In Varronis Saturas Menippeas Observationes Selectae," *Kleine Schriften* (Berlin 1966) 1-87. The twentieth century has remained content with Bücheler's text with the exception of an occasional lone voice here and there, mainly in Italy, where F. della Corte is preparing a new edition. Two relevant articles of his are "Per il testo delle 'Menippee'," *RIF*, n.s. 20, 1942, 201-213 (particularly 208 ff.) and "Rileggendo le Menippee" (supra 41 n. 2) 69-76. See also supra 40 n. 1 and 35-36, n. 4.

[2] The only uncontested line of these Varronian fragments is 79. The most

Eumenides

Phrygius per ossa cornus liquida canit anima   131
tibi typana non inani sonitu matri' deum   132
tonimus *chorus* tibi nos, tibi nunc semiveri
teretem comam volantem iactant tibi famuli

Marcipor

spatula eviravit omnes Veneri vaga pueros   275

Testamentum

sic ille puellus Veneris repente Adon   540
cecidit cruentus olim

MAECENAS

Ades, inquit o Cybebe, fera montium dea,   5
ades et sonante typano quate flexibile caput.

Latus horreat flagello, comitum chorus ululet   6

INCERTI

O qui chelyn canoram plectro regis Italo   19

Rutilos recide crines habitumque cape viri   20

Cybele rotabo crines ∪ ∪ — ∪ ∪ ∪ ∪ ×   74

---

worked-over fragment is 132. The most imaginative version of that fragment is by Vahlen *MRC* (supra 123 n. 1) 22, quoted with exaggerated condescension by L. Müller, *De Re Metrica Poetarum Latinorum* (Leipzig 1861[1]), (*MPL*[1]) 35.

tibi typana non inanis sonitus tibi tonimus
tibi nos cymbala crepimu'. tibi nunc semeviri
teretem comam volantem iactant. tibi Cybele
Phrygius per ossa cornus liquida canit anima

Onions would like to substitute *tubam* for the uncertain *chorus* in line 2 suggesting that *"Tubam"* would easily drop out before as similar a word as *tibi*," *AN* 94. For other versions, see Ribbeck, *VS* 111, Riese, *VSM* 132, Röper, *MQR* 234, Müller, *op. cit.* 37, and Lachmann, *loc. cit.* The French editor, L. Quicherat, *Nonii Marcelli de Compendiosa Doctrina* (Paris 1872) avoided such problems by citing all the doubtful fragments of Varro as prose, and putting a felicitous statement in the apparatus, such as "in duo versus plerique docti dividunt," 273. Since it is not the purpose of this paper to establish a text of Varro, I have followed that of Bücheler, although it seems to me, from my study of Varro as a poet, that he was such an experimenter, and possessed so little sensitivity in the metrical field, that he might well have written *Galli* (132.3) as it stands in the manuscripts where Bücheler has emended the line to end with the requisite three-syllable word *famuli*. For Bücheler's reasoning for his versions, see *UV* 561. Lachmann, *loc. cit.* suggests *galluli*, which might well be a satirical invention on the part of Varro, but the word is not attested anywhere else in Latin. On the other hand, *Galli* turns the line into two pure ionic cola; the final *A D A closed* colon is equal in terms of responsion to the *D A D rising* colon found in the Alexandrian fragment (supra 120 n. 2). Considerable disagreement also exists concerning fr. 540; cf. Röper, *V V* III 455-457, Müller, *MPL*[2], 1894, 109-110, the apparatus in Bücheler 321, della Corte, *MVF* 312.

Before the location of individual words is examined, it is worthwhile to look at the colometric patterns of each line segment. To simplify comparison the first half of the line will be called 1, the second half 2; colon 1 will be assigned Latin letters for the different patterns in alphabetical order of frequency, colon 2 Greek. The following table results:

1	2
A. ⏑⏑ — ⏑ —⏑ — —	α. ⏑⏑ — ⏑⏑⏑⏑ ×
B. — — ⏑ —⏑ — —	β. — — ⏑⏑⏑⏑ ×
C. ⏑⏑ — ⏑⏑⏑ ⏑ — —	γ. ⏑⏑ — ⏑ — ⏑ ×
D. ⏑⏑⏑ ⏑⏑⏑ —⏑ — —	δ. ⏑⏑⏑ ⏑⏑⏑ — ⏑ ×
E. — — ⏑⏑⏑ ⏑ — —	ε. — — ⏑ — ⏑ ×
F. ⏑⏑ — — ⏑⏑ — —	ζ. ⏑⏑ — —⏑⏑ ×
G. ⏑⏑ ⏑⏑⏑⏑⏑⏑ — —	
H. — — — ⏑⏑ — —	

These patterns are the total varieties found in both Latin and the two-line Alexandrian fragment in Hephaistion. H and ζ do not occur in Catullus, and are patterns which have caused problems for scholars in emending the text of Varro.[1] F and α are the pure ionic a minore *D A D A rising, D A D A open* cola so common in the choral lyrics of Euripides' *Bacchae*.[2] A and α are by far the most common patterns, 75% and 91% respectively in Catullus, 75% and 43% respectively in Varro,[3] and 67% and 60% in the remaining Latin samples.[4] The following are the possible combinations and their percentages:

---

[1] See supra 123-124. They are two of the patterns found in the Alexandrian fragment (infra n. 4, 126 n. 1).

[2] See particularly the opening chorus, 64-71, 78-87, 94-104, and the one commencing at 370. With the first of these Avallone, *C &-E* (supra 77-78 n. 5), 162-163 makes valid comparisons concerning verbal parallels and "struttura sintattica" (161) found in Cat. 63. However, he fails to mention the metrical similarity such as the anacreontic A colon *Ba* 530-535, 550-554, or Φρυγίων in the initial word position, *Ba* 86, and *Phrygium* and *Phrygiam* in Cat. 63.2, 20. Colon α occurs in *Ba* 372. When one looks at O. Schröder's version of Euripides' choruses, however, one can be easily frustrated in any attempt to make metrical comparisons. The strange abbreviations and the unnatural line divisions prevent some of the most obvious colometric patterns from being noticed (*Euripides Cantica* Leipzig 1928). A new appraisal along the lines set forth by Porter (supra 3 n. 1) is needed.

[3] It must be remembered that the Varronian percentages are based on Bücheler's text, which in turn is based on many reasonable emendations but very little certainty.

[4] In connection with the ionic a minore theory, as well as that of Catullus' imitation of the Alexandrian fragment so important to Wilamowitz (supra 120 n. 1), it is significant that the fragment contains neither of these

	VARRO	CATULLUS	MAECENAS & INCERTI
A α	3 43%	65 75%	2 40%
A β	1 14%	3 3%	
A γ		2 2%	1 20%
A ζ	1 14%		
B α		7 8%	
B β		1 1%	1 20%
B ε		1 1%	
C α		6 6%	
C γ		1 1%	
C δ		1 1%	
D α		3 3%	
D ζ	1 14%		
E α		1 1%	
E β		1 1%	
F α		1 1%	
F or H β [1]	1 14%		
G α		1 1%	

There are no examples of the H or ζ colon in Catullus, and F is questioned (see infra 127 n. 1). Varro lacks B, C, E, G, δ, and ε. Maecenas and Incerti contain only A, B, α, β, and γ.[2]

For the purpose of analyzing word positions, it is necessary to devise some system of numbering the syllables. As will be seen on the first page of the chapter illustrating the principal colometric patterns, those with ½ after the number indicate the second of two shorts which are occasionally resolved into one long, in which case the whole number stands for the one syllable. Upon close

two major cola, and only one combination that is found in Catullus. The pattern of its first line is H-ζ and that of its second E-β found in Cat. 63.22. Neither ionic a minore cola, F or ζ occur in the later galliambics.

[1] The problem with fr. 540 is that it is either missing two initial short syllables or one initial long. The latter results in the very unusual H pattern found only in the Alexandrian fragment, and rare even in regular ionic a minore sequences such as those of Euripides. *Ba* 81 is an example of the H colon. However, as an illustration of the difficulty metricians face, what Schröder calls an ionic, Sophokles *El.* 830, Pohlsander calls a pherecratean. See *Sophoclis Cantica* (Leipzig 1907) 86, and *op. cit.* (supra 64-65 n. 5) 56, respectively. Whatever its name should be, it is an example of the H colon. Analysis becomes much more simple when one abandons the attempt to give the frame a traditional name and includes it under heading 10 c. of propositions: those systems which use two or more kinds of arses not in regular alternation. (See supra 4). However, by changing *Adon* to *Adonis* the line can be construed as an ionic a majore, without adding anything at the beginning. See della Corte, *MVF* (supra 40 n. 1) 112 fr. 544, and apparatus in Bücheler 321.

[2] Maecenas 5.2 is the only example of a resolved 6, *typano*.

scrutiny of the patterns it becomes clear that, in spite of the many variations and the different places permitting resolutions, there are a few constants, at least in Catullus. These are: in colon 1, the short 3,[1] and the ∪ _ _ at 5, 6, and 7; in colon 2, the short 3, and the ∪ × at 5 and 6. These factors are instrumental in understanding colon 2 as a catalectic version of colon 1. In addition to these quantities which remain constant, there are also word-types which are interesting. All critics discussing this poem have noted the effect of rapidity which the four or five short syllables at the end of the line give, and the connection between this rapidity and the frenzied nature of the subject of the poem.[2] The number of syllables in words in this position, however, has not been assessed.[3] Attention has also been drawn to the effect of the so-called anaclasis and the frenzied movement,[4] or to conflict of ictus and accent as the cause of the agitation.[5] But if one looks at the types of words in the lines, their syllabic length, and where located, the true reason for the phrenetic nature of the meter becomes apparent. The extreme variety of word-length in the second colon, and the syncopation of word-accent as a result,[6] coupled with the phonetic qualities of the syllables,[7] are the devices by which Catullus achieves a μίμησις

---

[1] The one exception to the constant short 3 occurs in the questioned line 54 already mentioned (supra 122) which, as it stands, is the F, or straight ionic a minore *D A D A rising* colon. For a brief discussion of emendations for this line, see L. Müller, "Zu Catulls Attis," *RhM* 25, 1870, 167, where he calls *omnia* a "Flickwort."

[2] For an excellent recent appraisal of this technique, see T. Oksala, "Catulls Attis-Ballade," *Arctos*, n.s. 3, 1962, 208-210. See also Elder, *op. cit.* (supra 120 n. 1) 397; F. R. Dale, "The Attis of Catullus," *G&R* 11, 1964, 43-44; Tyrrell, *op. cit.* (supra 121 n. 4) 45, and Thompson 1, *op. cit.* (supra 121 n. 4) 146; Weinreich, *op. cit.* (supra 119 n. 2) 473.

[3] Goodell, *op. cit.* (supra 621 n. 4) 30-32, discusses trochaic and iambic word-types in hopes of strengthening his argument that a coincidence of word and metrical accent assists the reader to "read the poem in a true galliambic rhythm" (32). See infra 130 n. 6.

[4] Goodell, *op. cit.* (supra 121 n. 4) 31; Fordyce 263.

[5] Thompson 2, *op. cit.* (supra 121 n. 4) 355. See Ross, *op. cit.* (supra 121-122 n. 4) 148-150 for comparison with hexameters.

[6] Syncopation is a term not necessarily applicable only to music, for it implies a shifting of any normal or expected accent by stressing the unaccented or unexpected beat, a situation which can be found in poetry and dance, as well as music. In this case I am using the word to indicate the effect produced by accenting the unexpected: ×́× ×́××, ×́×× ×́×. (See infra 130-131.) A metrical-ictus syncopation in contrast to word-accent syncopation is achieved by the use of the A arsis, which results in the juxtaposition of two theses. See supra 102.

[7] Most critics mention assonance as one of the features of the poem, without

of phrenetic fanaticism with words. An evaluation of the table of word localization is helpful in this respect, coupled with an examination of the most frequent word patterns.

To begin with, one of the first unusual features of the galliambic is the comparatively small percentage of monosyllables in general, and particularly initial monosyllables, so prominent in the rest of Catullus' meters.[1] There are only ten initial monosyllables in colon 1, and half that in colon 2. The highest percentage, the long at 2 in both cola, is only 23% and 12% respectively. In addition, what is interesting in connection with monosyllables in the galliambic meter is the number of times they are used at the end of colon 1, although in most meters they are infrequent as colometric ends. Yet although they occur in position 1:7 fourteen times, only twice are they preceded by a cretic word, the preference being for an iambic word. A second feature is that disyllables are unusually numerous, considering the potential of the long lines. The word-type with the highest frequency in both cola is the initial pyrrhic, although the first colon is 10% higher than the second. Another interesting metrical point is that although position 2 colon 1 is resolved into 2-2½ four times, and position 4 is resolved into 4-4½ ten times, a word division between 2 and 2½ never occurs, and one between 4 and 4½ only twice. In colon 2 on the other hand, position 2 is resolved only once and undivided, but 4-4½ forms a long 4 only four times and is frequently divided. Thus, although the second colon is undoubtedly a catalectic version of the first, the same word-types are not used to fill the corresponding positions. A further illustration of this is that although the long 4 in colon 1 is resolved ten times, no 3-4-4½ tribrach occurs; but this tribrach

---

being very specific. Elder, *op. cit.* (supra 120 n. 1) couples assonance and alliteration (397) without illustrating and makes a brief reference to similarity of sounds, 402 n. 29. Further on in the article he mentions the "iterative device" of the same word in the same metrical position (400). No one would quarrel with his citing of these words, but he fails to note how often morphemic similarities such as the ablative plural or the present participle also fill the same metrical position. T. Means, in a very brief article, "Catullus LXIII," *CP* 22, 1927, 101, calls attention to the number of times the name of the hero of the poem occurs in the 6-7 position in colon 1, with the helpful comment, "Catullus must have meant something."

[1] See tables of word localization at the ends of other chapters as well as 25 n. 2, 47, 75-77, 115 n. 1, Cutt, *op. cit.* (supra 34 n. 2) 7, and Hellegouarc'h, *op. cit.* (supra 9 n. 1) 26-29 for number and types of initial monosyllables in Catullus' hexameters.

occurs in the corresponding position in colon 2 twelve times. A third statistic showing the difference in treatment between the two cola is the frequency of trisyllables of any shape. In colon 1 there are 76; in colon 2, 105; and the word shape which both have in common, the initial anapaest, is found nineteen times in 1, but twenty-nine times in 2.

Perhaps what is most interesting in terms of word-type and metrical requirements, however, is the use and distribution of words of more than three syllables. The total number of quadrisyllables is just about evenly distributed in both cola, eighteen in 1, twenty-one in 2. They are slightly more frequent in the initial position than in the final position. In contrast to this uniformity, on the other hand, is the location and frequency of pentasyllabic words. In a meter with as much metrical variety in pattern such that, using all the resolutions possible, colon 1 can have as many as ten syllables, the rarity of five-syllable words is remarkable.[1] None occur in colon 1, for instance, although the word shape ∪ _ ∪ _ ×, metrically suited to the 3-7 position, comprises 71% of the pentasyllables in the phalaecean hendecasyllable.[2] In galliambics the pentasyllable occurs only in colon 2 initially, 1-4, or finally 3-6. Of the six occurrences of the former, five are ablative plurals, lines 24, 28, 39, 48, and 59. Three of these illustrate the use of similar sounds in the same metrical position in the line, having the ending -antibus, a fourth is -atibus, and the fifth -oribus.[3] The sixth initial five-syllable word is actually a quadrisyllable with an enclitic -que (line 16). These five pentasyllables are illustrative of a distinctive feature of the galliambic meter, the extensive use of the ablative case, particularly ablative plurals, and its

---

[1] There is no dearth of five-syllable words in Latin. Any trisyllable of the third declension, for instance, becomes a pentasyllable in the dative and ablative plural. There are innumerable pentasyllabic comparative adjectives and adverbs as well as the many coined poetic compound pentasyllables. See della Corte, "Varrone e Levio" (supra 34 n. 1) 376-377 for a list of polysyllables coined by Laevius, many of which are pentasyllabic.

[2] See Cutt, op. cit. (supra 34 n. 2) 33.

[3] The present participle occurs in the 1-1½-2 position in the second colon five times so that the -ans or -ant morpheme falls on 2: 28, 30, 39, 47, 77. This is an illustration of what Schein, op. cit. (supra 3 n. 1) 49 has pointed out: "Words which are found in certain shapes *do* tend to a certain extent to be the same part of speech, so that when a wordshape is localized at a particular position, a part of speech tends to be localized at the same position."

corollary the low percentage of monosyllables. Furthermore, of the twenty-nine ablative plurals in the poem, eighteen occur in colon 2.

The second type of five-syllable word, the 3-6, occurs only four times in the ninety-three lines. This illustrates an important point regarding the "flurry of short syllables" [1] at the end of the line. The "inner metrical" [2] requirement is that these syllables be divided. For although it is true that pentasyllables composed of only short syllables do not exist in great numbers in Latin, it cannot be doubted that Catullus with his great facility for coining compound words and fondness for diminutives, could have found more than four, had it been rhythmically, in the sense of audio-accentually, desirable. Even the final four-syllable in colon 2 is not frequent, occurring only eight times in the whole poem. The most common divisions of the final five (or four when the last syllable is long) syllables are 2 3, 3 2, () 2 3, () 1 2 2, and () 1 4.[3] If Latin is a language where word accent is noticeable (as has been assumed throughout this paper),[4] a reason can be seen for the word division in the final five syllables. It varies the positions of word accents, thus preventing a pattern of expectancy [5] from being built up in the mind of the audience. This lack of patterned expectancy is the real source of the phrenetic quality of the poem.[6] The ending of five short syllables is simply an outer metrical requirement of

---

[1] Dale, *op. cit.* (supra 127 n. 2) 43.

[2] This is O'Neill's phrase, see supra 5 n. 2.

[3] The respective percentages for these five patterns are 27%, 13%, 20% (where the sign () indicates a word of more than one syllable preceding and incorporated with syllable 3, 4 or 4½), 13% and 10%.

[4] See supra 7-8.

[5] This is Porter's expression, *op. cit.* (supra 1 n. 1) 8.

[6] The relationship of word accent to the frenzy of the poem is what I think Goodell was trying to show in his article, *op. cit.* (supra 121-122 n. 4). He was hampered, unfortunately, by being unable to discard the traditional concepts of ionic feet and trochaic dipodies, and failing to realize that the normative cola were the ones he labeled *anaklomenos.* He did note that the greatest number of iambic word-shapes occurs in the threnody 50-73 "where the tone of excitement is most marked" (31), although he did not enlarge upon this by showing, for instance, that the 3-4 iambic word in colon 1 occurs three times consecutively, 50-52, and then six times consecutively, 57-62. (Line 53, if one takes into account the type of elision, can also be considered an illustration of the 3-4 iamb, *niv(em) et.*) "These marked preferences as regards location of the exceptional iambic words appears to have some significance, but I am not quite sure what." (30-31).

the meter, as the fragments from Varro show, and not a device peculiar to Catullus.[1]

This point has been labored at some length because virtually every article mentioned in the footnotes of this chapter so far, whether specifically on the meter or on the poem in general, contains some kind of reference to the "piling up of short syllables" [2] at the end of the line. But no one has noticed the importance of the word-type used to fill these syllabic spaces. The pattern is basic; it is how the poet uses the pattern, his awareness of the accentual-acoustical qualities of words of varying length, which gives the "Spannung und Entspannung," the "ausdrucksvolle Sprache" and "alpdruckhafte Tempo" [3] so extraordinary in this particular poem. The basic pattern for word division is established in the very first line:

$$1 \; 1\tfrac{1}{2} \; | \; 2 \; \; 3 \; | \; 4 \; \; 5 \; | \; 6 \; \; 7 \; \| \; 1 \; 1\tfrac{1}{2} \; 2 \; | \; 3 \; \; 4 \; | \; 4\tfrac{1}{2} \; 5 \; 6 \,^4$$
$$\smile\smile \; | \; {-}\smile \; | \; {-}\smile \; | \; {-}{-} \; \| \; \smile\smile{-} \; | \; \smile\smile{-} \; | \; \smile\smile\smile$$

This pattern for colon 1 occurs seven times, that for colon 2 fifteen times. Thus, these are the nearest to what one could call normative cola.[5] Against these patterns of expectancy Catullus plays, not only with metrical changes, such as resolution of long syllables, or a long substituted for two normative shorts, but also with change of word-type to fill the metrical shape. An example of this can be seen in the first three lines whose word-syllable patterns are:

$$\begin{array}{lllllll} 1. & 2 & 2 & 2 & 2, & 3 \; 2 \; 3 \\ 2. & 2 & 1 & 2 & 3, & 3 \; 2 \; 3 \\ 3. & 3 & 3 & 2 & , & 4 \; 2 \; 2 \end{array}$$

If one accents the words with exaggerated emphasis according to the normal rules of accent, the switch from the four closely alternating coincidences of ictus and accent of line 1 colon 1 (that is an accented 1, 2, 4 and 6), to the separated accents 1, 4 and 6 of line 3 (where accentually the colon has three light syllables in a

---

[1] Three of the seven lines from Varro, regardless of emendation problems, end in the four or five short syllables: fr. 79, 131 and 275. 132.2, according to Bücheler, is also an example. Maecenas and Incerti probably were copying Catullus, so they offer no proof that this was the standard ending. However, it is worth noting that two of Maecenas' three lines have the standard ending, and both lines of Incerti.

[2] Tyrrell, *op. cit.* (supra 121 n. 4) 45.

[3] Oksala, *op. cit.* (supra 127 n. 2) 213.

[4] Varro fr. 275 is an example of this line pattern 2 4 2, 3 2 3.

[5] See Porter, *op. cit.* (supra 1 n. 1) 11.

row: $1\frac{1}{2}$, 2 and 3, before a return to the expected alternating accent of the norm at 4 and 6), emphasizes the syncopation.[1] As for the second colon, the expectancy is lulled by two repeated accentual patterns, and then shocked by a completely different one. This is not to say that the poem was read, or is meant to be read, in such an exaggerated manner. There is no way of knowing how it was read. But the position of words is as much a matter of form as is the metrical pattern, and the exaggerated reading illustrates this.

If one leaves behind the controversy concerning the question of ictus and accent to study observable phenomena, a few points concerning vocabulary are in order. The iteration of the same word in the same metrical position has already been mentioned by Elder.[2] His findings are included:

For Colon 1			For Colon 2		
Attis	6	6-7 [3]	redimita	2	1-3
Cybebe	5	5-7 [4]	nemora	6	3-4$\frac{1}{2}$
citatus	3	5-7	citus abiit	2	3-6
()cutus	3	6-7	animum	5	4$\frac{1}{2}$-6
itaqu(e) ut	2	1-3	()antibus oculis	2	2-6
quiete molli	2	3-7			

He overlooked:

tympanun	2	2-4	tympana	1	2-4
Phrygi(um)	2	1-2	Phrygi(a)	2	1-2
rapidus	2	1-2	rapid(us)	2	1-2
ego	7	1-1$\frac{1}{2}$ [5]	eg(o)	4	1-1$\frac{1}{2}$
mihi	2	1-1$\frac{1}{2}$	mihi	2	1-1$\frac{1}{2}$
patri(a)	3	1-1$\frac{1}{2}$	Cybele(s)	3	1-2
simul	2	1-1$\frac{1}{2}$	vagus	2	3-4
ubi	5	1-1$\frac{1}{2}$	deae	2	5-6
ibi	4	1-1$\frac{1}{2}$	fero	2	5-6
Ida	3	6-7	forem	2	5-6 [6]

---

[1] This is clearly a term open to controversy (see definition supra 127 n. 6), else how could Thompson 2, *op. cit.* (supra 121-122 n. 4) 355 state that there is no syncopation in Catullus 63? It is interesting also that he can maintain that Catullus "got his effect of tumult by the device of collision between accent and ictus in the last half of the line," when colon 2 in its normative shape has only one apparent metrical ictus, that in position 2, and 2 receives coincidence of ictus and accent forty-one times!

[2] *Op. cit.* (supra 120 n. 1) 401-403. The words are found in other cases than the nominative.

[3] The subject of the poem occurs only in this position in the line. See supra 127-128 n. 7.

[4] Elder adopted the more conventional spelling, *Cybele.*

[5] *Egon(e)* occurs at line 58. The alternation between the initial nominative and the dative of the personal pronoun first person is found only in the threnody, 50-73.

[6] A final disyllable commencing with *f* occurs eight times: 40, 46, 53, 68, 78, 79, 89, 90.

The number of these words, repeated in Catullus and found also in Varro and the later fragments, is significant, although not all are found in the same metrical position. Those in the same metrical position include:

VARRO

Colon 1			Colon 2		
132	Phrygius	1-2	79	citus	3-4
			131	anima	4½-6
			132.1	deum	5-6
			275	vaga	3-4

MAECENAS ET INCERTI

M 5.1	Cybebe	5-7	M 5.1	dea	5-6
I 74	Cybele	1-2			

The list of similar vocabulary, not necessarily in the same position, is even longer:

VARRO			CATULLUS		MAECENAS ET INCERTI		
132.1	typana	1:2-3	9 typanum	1:1-2	M 5.2	typano [1]	
			8 typanum	2:4½-6			
79	properans	2:1-2	30 properante	2:1-3 [2]			
275	Veneri	2:1-2	17 Veneris	2:1-2			
540	Veneris						
			24 ululatibus	2:1-4	M 6	ululet	2:4½-6
			28 ululat	2:4½-6			
132.1	sonitu'	2:1-2	74 sonitus	2:1-2			
79	alta	1:4-5	1 alta	1:2-3			
132.2	chorus [3]	1:3-4	30 chorus	2:5-6	M 6	chorus	2:3-4
132.3	famuli [4]	2:4½-6	52 famuli	1:1-2			
			10 quatiensque	1:2-3	M 5	quate	2:1-1½
132.1	matri	2:4-4½	9 mater	2:2-3			
			15 comites	2:4½-6	M 6	comitum	2:1-2
			11 comitibus	2:4-6			

---

[1] This is an unusual metrical variation, for its location requires a resolution of position 6.

[2] Notice that this word occurs in the same metrical position in both Varro and Catullus, as do quite a few of the rest of the words in the list. For the similarities between Maecenas and Incerti, and Catullus, it is easy to assume imitation. But the relationship between Varro and Catullus is not certain. It is this which makes the large number of coincidences between vocabulary and position of words so interesting.

[3] This word is only an interpolation in Varro.

[4] This is Bücheler's emendation, see supra 123-124 n. 2.

VARRO		CATULLUS		MAECENAS ET INCERTI		
		27 comitibus	1:3-5			
		32 comitata	1:1-3			
275 eviravit [1]	1:2-5	17 evirastis	1:4-7			
132.2 ( )viri	2:5-6	6 viro	2:5-6	I 20	viri	2:5-6
		69 vir	2:2			
540.1 repent(e)	2:3-4	28 repente	1:3-5			
		83 rutilam	1:1-2	I 20	rutilos	1:1-2
		40 ferum	2:5-6	M 5.1	fera	2:1-1½
		53 ferarum	1:5-7			
		85 ferus	1:1-1½			
		89 fera	2:5-6			
131 liquida	2:1-2	46 liquidaque	1:1-3			
131 canit	2:3-4	22 canit	1:5-6			

Two examples of verbs in the common and frequentative form are also found:

132.3 volantem	1:5-7	25 volitare	2:1-3
132.3 iactant	2:1-2	23 iaciunt	2:1-2

It is clear from the preceding list that the similarity of vocabulary and word-type in Varro, Catullus, and the later Latin lines is too extensive to be sheer coincidence. Whether it was Catullus, or someone prior to him who welded the set vocabulary, the Phrygian forest, the lions, the tympana, the hollow flute, the shrieking voices, the echoing cymbals, the flowing hair, the female-male, and the verbs of haste, to the galliambic meter, is an unsolvable mystery. The subject obviously held a fascination for the Alexandrian epigramatists,[2] yet there is no evidence of the galliambic meter in the Anthology. A most intriguing question from the Latin point of view is, what part did Varro play—that of an innovator or imitator—in this meter? [3] Moreover, a third Roman

---

[1] This verb is found in no other classical authors. The fourth principal part, used as a comparative adjective, occurs in Martial 5.41.1, a choliambic poem where the poet, in heaping scorn upon an unpleasant homosexual, compares him to a priest of Cybele. The verb form *ululat* also occurs, 41.3.

[2] See particularly *AP* 6.51, 217-220. For the vocabulary similarities, see the lengthy note in Avallone, *C & E* 168. For a brief discussion of these Hellenistic epigrams, their relationship to each other, and to the development of the cult of Cybele, see Reitzenstein, *op. cit.* (supra 39 n. 7) note pp. 165-166, and J. Geffcken, "Leonidas von Tarent," *NJbb*, supplbnd. 23, 1897, 96-98.

[3] As to Varro's role as a metrician, see della Corte, "Varrone Metricista" (supra 35-36 n. 4) 160-161. However, when he wrote the satires which contain galliambic lines cannot be ascertained. Even the evidence that he had been to Phrygia, Cichorius, *op. cit.* (supra 40 n. 1) 195, 204, does not date the satires. See also Weinreich, *op. cit.* (supra 119 n. 2) 466 n. 3.

poet, contemporary with Varro and Catullus, Lucretius, also became occupied with the implications of the cult.[1] His metrical medium was the hexameter, however. The theory of one scholar that the liturgical development of the cult was purely Roman [2] could go hand in hand with the idea of Roman development of the galliambic meter as a part of the liturgy, if there were any evidence. As it is, the ninety-three lines of Catullus 63, seven uncertain fragments from Varro, three lines from Maecenas, and two and one-half lines of a post-Hadrianic period, are the only material from which to make conclusions. By themselves, they are not sufficient to justify any theories about the nature of the cult. From the studies of the meter, on the other hand, it is clear that it was a highly structured, systematized union of two cola, whose base pattern, A-α, was cleverly changed, not only by metrical variations in the positions of long and short syllables, but by the word-types used to fill the requirements of the meter. What this section has tried to illustrate is that the undeniable brilliance of Catullus 63 lies not just in the "Pathos" and "Ethos" [3] evoked by the tragic nature of the story, nor in the poet's own emotions possibly released in the creation of the poem,[4] but in the extent

---

[1] For an interesting discussion of Lucretius and the cult of Cybele, see J. Perret, "Le Mythe de Cybèle, Lucrèce, II, 600-660," *REL* 13, 1935, 332-357. In many ways Lucretius and Varro are more similar than Catullus and Varro, in the sense that both approach the legend from a philosophical point of view, pointing out the irrationalism behind superstition and the possibilities of concomitant insanity. On Varro the philosopher, see Norden, *op. cit.* (supra 123 n. 1) 70; della Corte, *VMF* 176-180; L. Riccomagno, *Studio sulle satire Menipee* (Alba Sacerdote 1931) 119-141.

[2] Perret, *ibid.* 352-353.

[3] See Oksala, *op. cit.* (supra 127 n. 2) 209-212 for a discussion of the relationship between the severely split line, the poet's split personality, and the division between epic theme and lyric intent which results in a syncretism of Hellenistic and Roman elements. "Das Pathos des Dichters wird mit fortgerissen in das wilde Tempo der Dichtung, während in den letzten Versen sich das Ethos zu heftigem Widerstand erhebt." (212).

[4] The concept that the poem is a reflection of Catullus' mad love, and possible release from this insanity, in his relationship to Lesbia, is most reasonable, as expressed by P. W. Harkins, "Autoallegory in Catullus 63 and 64," *TAPA* 90, 1959, 106-111. For a similar approach to the emotional background of the poem, see G. Highet, *Poets in a Landscape* (New York 1965³) 26-27. Critics are more or less in accord that the poem is not a retelling of the Attis legend: Weinreich, *op. cit.* (supra 119 n. 2) 465; Elder, *op. cit.* (supra 120 n. 1) 394-397; and "The Art of Catullus' Attis," *TAPA* 71, 1940, xxxiv: "Catullus is not interested in tracing the history of the rite—the awesome effect on mankind of sweeping passion affects him;" also Oksala, *op. cit.* (supra 127 n. 2) 211-212. Harkins calls attention to the extensive

to which Catullus exploited the syntactic potentialities of the Latin language within the chosen metrical frame. Assonance and alliteration are only one aspect of this. The alternation of disyllables and trisyllables, particularly at colometric ends, the morphemic similarities in ablative plurals and present participles occurring in the same position in the line, and the iteration of vocabulary are all part of the explanation of the phrenetic quality of the galliambic meter as Catullus handled it.

TABLE OF WORD LOCALIZATION IN
CATULLUS' GALLIAMBICS

I I½ 2(2½) ¹ 3 4(4½) 5 6 7   I I½ 2(2½)   3 4 4½ 5 6

∪∪ _   ∪ _   ∪ _ _   ∪∪ _   ∪∪∪ ∪ ×
  _ ∪∪   ∪∪   _ ∪∪   _

		Colon 1		Colon 2
I. Monosyllables				
A. ∪				
I		6	6%	4	4%
I½		2	2%	I	1%
3		5	5% ²	2	2%
4		1	1%		
5		3	3%		
B. _				
I-I½		4	4%	I	1%
2		21	23%	12	13% ³
4	4-4½	6	6%	5	5%
6		I	1%	2	2%
7		14	15%		
II. Disyllables				
A. _ ∪				
2-3		20	22%	11	12%
4-5		20	22% ⁴		

use of the word *furor* in 63, and its love-connotations in other poems. Modern criticism may go too far in stressing the psychological approach to the understanding of poetry, but the realization that poems are a reflection of a poet's individual paranoia has considerable validity where Catullus is concerned.

¹ A long syllable from 2-2½ will be referred to as 2 since it is the most common form. The same applies to the long syllable from 4-4½.

² Frequencies will not be given in percentages for Varro, or Maecenas and Incerti. The number of times a word type occurs in Varro depends upon the emendation preferred. Frequencies given in these notes are based on Bücheler and included for interest, not for practical comparisons. In colon 1 a monosyllable occurs at 3 twice.

³ A long monosyllable at 2 in colon 1 occurs in Varro twice, in Maecenas and Incerti twice. A long monosyllable at 2 in colon 2 occurs in Varro once. A monosyllable at 7 occurs once in Varro.

⁴ Trochaic disyllables in Varro occur twice in the normal 4-5 position of colon 1, but they also occur in the F colon as 3-4 4½, fr. 540, and ζ colon in

	Colon 1	Colon 2
B. ∪ —		
1½-2	4 4%	2 2%
3-4	30 32% [1]	
5-6	10 11%	11 12%
C. ∪∪		
1-1½	47 50%	37 40% [2]
3-4	1 1%	24 26%
4-4½	7 8%	13 14%
4½-5	1 1%	
5-6 (final)		14 15%
D. — —		
1-2	3 3%	2 2%
6-7	36 39%	

III. Trisyllables

	Colon 1	Colon 2
A. ∪∪∪ [3]		
2 2½ 3	3 3%	1 1%
3-4½		12 13%
4 4½ 5	1 1%	2 2%
4½-6		
4½-6		21 23%
B. ∪∪ — [4]		
1 1½ 2	19 20%	29 31%
4½-6		21 23%
C. — ∪∪		
2-4		11 12%
D. — ∪ — [5]		
2-4	6 6%	1 1%
4-6	2 2%	2 2%

---

corresponding numbers with the F, that is 3-4 4½ also, fr. 132.1. The 2-3 disyllable in colon 1 occurs in Maecenas 5.1.

[1] Iambic words:

3-4	Varro 2	
	M & I 1	
5-6	Varro 1	Varro 1
		M & I 1

[2] Initial pyrrhics:

	Colon 1	Colon 2
	Varro 3	Varro 1
	M & I 2	M & I 2
3-4 pyrrhics		Varro 4
		M & I 2

[3] Tribrachs: Varro: 1: 2 2½ 3   2: 4½-6 (twice)
                 Maecenas: 2: 4½-6 (once)

[4] Anapaestic words: Varro: 1: 1-2 (4)   2: 1-2 (5)   4½-6 (2)
                      M & I   1: 1-2   2: 1-2 (once)   4½-6 (1)

[5] Cretics: M & I   1: 2-4 (once)   2: 2-4 (once)

		Colon 1	Colon 2
E. ∪ — ∪ [1]			
	1½-3		3 3%
	3-5	11 12%	
F. — — ∪			
	1-3	4 4%	2 2%
G. ∪ — — [2]			
	5-7	30 32%	
IV. Quadrisyllables [3]			
A. ∪ ∪ ∪ ∪			
	3-5	1 1%	
	4-6 (final)		6 6%
B. ∪ ∪ — ∪			
	1-3	9 10%	8 9%
C. — ∪ — —			
	4-7 (final)	7 8%	
D. ∪ ∪ ∪ —			
	4-6 (final)		3 3%
E. — ∪ ∪ ∪			
	2-4½		3 3%
F. — ∪ — ∪			
	2-5	1 1%	
G. ∪ — ∪ ∪			
	3-6		1 1%
V. Five Syllables			
A. ∪ ∪ ∪ ∪ ∪			
	4-6		2 2%
B. ∪ ∪ ∪ ∪ —			
	4-6		2 2%
C. ∪ ∪ — ∪ ∪			
	1-4		6 6%

[1] Varro: I: 3-5 (once)
   Incerti: I: 3-5 (twice)
[2] Bacchaic words: Varro: (3) M & I: (3)
[3] Quadrisyllables are rare in both Varro and the five other Latin lines. At colon 1: 2-5 occurs once in Varro, fr. 275. A final choriamb occurs in a ζ colon, 132.2. In M & I there are two quadrisyllables also, both in colon 2: 2-4½, 1-3.

CONCLUSION

This study has illustrated some of the metrical aspects of word localization in Catullus' treatment of the principal types of Greek lyric and iambic cola in his *polymetra*. Furthermore, it has shown how a descriptive classification of quantitative classical verse, in terms of the types of arses occurring between fixed theses, not only simplifies the problems of metrical analysis, but more important, facilitates the recognition of words as the fundamental unit of said verse. In this way, the semantic function of words can be analyzed in relation to their structural organization within the metrical frame, both being formal manifestations of equal importance. These two aspects of form in poetry, the semantic function of words and their structural organization in the metrical frame, play different roles in Greek and Latin quantitative verse because of the syntactic potential inherent in the two languages: the semantic concentration of Greek is on the phrasal unit, while that of Latin is on the individual word.[1] Hence, to comprehend form in terms of semantic colometry is indubitably essential in understanding the metrics of Pindar and Greek choral lyric, and relatively less so in the description of Latin verse techniques. Nevertheless, even here it has an existential importance, for it frees the critic from having to locate and discourse upon the chief "caesuras"—be they masculine or feminine or not present—so that he can concentrate upon the "sense-functions of words . . . (as) part of the expression of metrical form."[2]

It is clear that, from the Augustan period on, the normative Greek colometric patterns became a requisite feature of the formal

---

[1] I doubt that there can be any quarrel with the validity of these statements. They are drawn partly from my own observations and partly from the perceptive analysis of a number of scholars. Chief among these are Howard Porter, and Steele Commager in the second chapter of his book, *The Odes of Horace* (New Haven 1962) 50-98. Other books and articles which I have drawn on include Marouzeau, *op. cit.* (supra II n. 3) 178-189; Quinn, *Docte Catulle* 34-47, and *Latin Explorations* 1-28, 60-75; N. E. Collinge, *The Structure of Horace's Odes* (London 1961); V. Pöschl, *The Art of Vergil*, transl. by G. Seligson (Ann Arbor 1962) 139-173; G. E. Duckworth, *Structural Patterns and Proportions in Virgil's Aeneid* (Ann Arbor 1962).

[2] Porter, *op. cit.* (supra I n. 1) 7.

structure of Latin verse.[1] The device of playing against the patterns of expectancy to achieve variety, emphasis, or create a particular mood,[2] could no longer be employed when the "expected" became the rule, part of the "outer-metrical" requirement, as it were. Thus, the brilliant Augustan poets were compelled to develop the technique (often referred to in connection with the commendatory substantive, "polish") of organizing words on symmetrical principles, through the structural devices of antithesis or parallelism, partly by the syntactic nature of Latin itself, and partly by desire to create variety, emphasis, and mood.

Insofar as the dichotomy between Latin word and "Greek" colometry is real, I have tried to show that Catullus, conscious of both, handles both deftly. His awareness of the functional importance of the individual word is evident, in his *polymetra* at least, not so much in symmetrical location within a line of substantive and modifier, or verb and subject, but in the repetition of the same word, within one poem or in several poems, in the same position. This place is often the final; but locating the emphatic word in the central 5-7 or 4-7 position which bridges a normal colometric end is an even more distinctive feature of Catullus' technique. Consistently in phalaeceans, iambics, and choliambics, the important word, whether it be a verb, an odd proper noun, or a term of abuse, occurs in this position.[3] In galliambics, also, the center of the line is used for significant points: words related to concepts of speed, madness, or the chief proper nouns in the poem, regularly are located as the last word of colon 1, or the first of colon 2. Thus, a pattern can be detected in Catullus' poetry, not a prearranged formal structure such as evident in Horace or Vergil,

---

[1] The contradiction in the case of the hexameter is only an apparent one. Although the preferred word-end in Greek occurs at $5\frac{1}{2}$, while that in Latin, at 5, several subtle factors are involved. The first of these is the high number of monosyllabic particles in Greek filling the $5\frac{1}{2}$ position, which may have enclitic or proclitic force, but which certainly indicate an awareness that word-end at 5 is also normative. (See Porter's tables, *op. cit.* supra 1 n. 1, 59.) The other factors relate to the Latin sensibility for verbal symmetry and the effect of word accent. The coincidence of word accent with the third thesis at 5, which would invariably occur if the break at $5\frac{1}{2}$ were employed, may be related to the less frequent usage of this word-end. The word normative still holds, but must not be confused with regularized.

[2] Schein and Porter have clearly illustrated this technique of playing against the expected colometry for particular effect. See supra 6 n. 5.

[3] See discussion supra 30 n. 2, 64-65, 134, 139, 159, 164 n. 3, 181 n. 3, 188-189.

but one which emerges as the poem proceeds, and throws light on other poems where the same words are emphasized. This emergence of a pattern is akin to that of Greek lyric, and is evidence of Catullus' conscious adaptation of Greek colometry. Moreover, Catullus' "Greek sensitivity" appears clearly in such meters as the Sapphic hendecasyllable, where the varieties of colometric patterns are more evident than a balancing of initial word with final word in the line, or withholding the principal verb till the adonic colon, or other such perfect symmetrical device as found in Horace.[1]

Catullus' interest in the individual word shows itself in another way, concern for the sequence of words related to the number of syllables in the word, especially at the beginning of the line. In sapphics, phalaeceans, iambics, and choliambics, the initial word-syllable patterns occurring most frequently are the 3 2, or the 1 2 2. In glyconic, pherecratean, and galliambic cola, on the other hand, the 2 3 initial pattern is more frequent. In this last mentioned meter it is possible that the focus of interest on the number of syllables in a word and their order in the line is related to word accent. Having established in the first line of the poem the two basic colometric patterns of word-syllable organization, 2 2 2 , 3 2 3, Catullus continually varies these throughout the poem, yet returns to them often enough so that the audience -perception is aware of the basic pattern against which the poet plays.

Thus, one of the chief patterns which emerges in Catullus' poetry is related to his apprehension of the importance of individual words, both with relation to their sequence, depending upon their length, and to their position, depending upon the normative Greek colometry. More needs to be done in analyzing the types of words used to fill various positions in the line, and particularly monosyllables, which are such a distinctive element in Catullus' verse. I hope that this study, in which I have also tried to assemble and correlate a great deal of scattered information on Latin and Greek metrical technique, will stimulate further interest on the word as the crucial element of poetry.

---

[1] Poem 11 is also Greek in its syntactic structure, i.e., the addition of semantic unit to semantic unit. According to a comment of Professor Porter in one of his lectures, "Greek proceeds by adding things, epexegetically, while the Latin view of the world is a closed world turned in upon itself in a shift toward unity from a many-faceted, pluralistic universe." See also his article, *op. cit.* (supra 1 n. 1) 21.

APPENDIX

Septenarii

1	3	5	7	9	11	13	15
×	–	∪	–	×	–	∪	–	×	–	∪	–	×	–	×

In view of the fact that Catullus uses the iambic line of seven and one-half feet in only one poem of thirteen lines, 25, in a form much more restricted than any of the authors who used it before him either in comedy or satire or farce,[1] it seems advisable only to discuss it briefly. Among the grammarians the meter is commonly known as iambic tetrameter catalectic, especially with reference to Greek usage. The application of the term "septenarius" does not seem to have been accepted until about the end of the fourth century A.D.[2] The only example in Greek that is a possible example of the Catullan usage of the meter is a fragment of Hipponax quoted by Hephaistion [3] (a line in which there is no resolution, for instance). Commonly the meter is found in Greek comedy where all sorts of substitutions are permitted.[4] Clearly, from this source the meter gained its foothold in Latin comedy, particularly in Plautus where the rules are virtually non-existent.[5] The septenarius is also found

---

[1] Marius Victorinus mentions Plautus, Caecilius and Turpilius: Keil, *Gr. Lat.* 6. 135. There are also ten or so lines of Varro's *Menippean Satires* in this meter. See metrical index in Bücheler's text.

[2] The first time the term can be said to definitely apply to the seven- and one-half foot iambic line is in a grammarian of the late fourth century, Diomedes, Keil, *Gr. Lat.* 1. 515. "Septenarium versum Varro fieri dicit hoc modo, cum ad iambicum trisyllabus pes additur . . ." The reference in Cicero's *Tusculan Disputations* 1.44.107, is generally thought to be a mistake by the copyist in transcribing the Roman numeral VIII as VII. For after quoting a fragment of Pacuvius (fr. 4.4-5, O. Ribbeck, *TRF*, 1897, 114-115) which is a line of eight iambic feet, the comment Cicero makes is, "Non intellego quid metuat cum tam bonos septenarios fundat ad tibiam."

[3] Consbr. 16: "εἴ | μοι | γένοιτο | παρθένος ‖ καλή | τε | καὶ | τέρεινα
× | – | ∪ – ∪ | – ∪ – ‖ ∪ – | ∪ | – | ∪ – ×
There is no line pattern similarity with Catullus. However, there are a few word pattern parallels: the cretic 6-8 is found in 1, 4, 7, 9, 12, and a final trisyllable in 1, 3, 4, 8. Catullus has three examples of iambic word-feet in the second part of the line, all in the 9-10 position: 3, 6, 12. In no place does he permit two iambic word-feet in sequence.

[4] See Koster, *Traité*, 119-120.

[5] Lindsay, *ELV*, 274-276, gives some detail on comparisons with Aristophanes. The *Dyskolos* of Menander had not been discovered in 1922, but as

in a few fragments of Varro, not all of which are undisputed.[1] In his free handling of the meter he clearly follows the comic tradition, another proof of his close affinity with comedy equally as important as his vocabulary similarities and mock-comic titles.[2] Indeed, the Roman dramatists are even freer in their use of resolution, substitution, and *ancipitia* than the Greek.[3] Catullus, on the other hand, is outside the dramatic tradition, for there is only one line where resolution occurs, and that in a line which has tortured scholars for centuries.[4] The one place where similarity between Catullus and the

Harsh points out in his review (p. 585) of the Martin recension of the new play (*Gnomon* 31, 1959, 577-586) Lindsay's statement, "The self-restrained Menander apparently eschewed this meter of unrestrained rollicking," has to be discarded. Lines 880-958 are in iambic tetrameter catalectic. See M. Treu, *Dyskolos* (Munich, 1960) 142; also W. Kraus, *Menander's Dyskolos* (Vienna 1960) 14 and 117, for unusual usage in line 895.

[1] 133-35, 214, 308-309, 357, 449, 576 are listed in Bücheler's text. Della Corte in his commentary however, though agreeing with 133-35, 308-309, 214 and 756, doesn't commit himself on 357 or 449, while he adds 216 to the list with the words in parenthesis (*ut vid*) See *VMF* p. 47.

[2] F. della Corte connects Varro and Laevius with the comic tradition by deriving the former from the type of poetry in *diverbia* and the latter that of the *cantica*. Cf. *Varrone e Levio* (supra 40 n. 1) 379-382. In his more recent recension of Varro's satires, *VMF*, della Corte continually points out the traces of Plautus in Varro's lines, such as his comment on fragments 133-35 (137-9 in his numbering) 177: "Un gruppo di frr. in settenari giambici ci riportano al perduto finale dell'*Aulularia* plautina, nella quale figura il nome del servo Strobilus, che compare anche negli Hibeh Papyri 1.5." Fragment 139 "risentono di una situazione plautina, in cui il servo Strobilus apparirebbe triste e bastonato." If he were to comment on the meter, he could point up additional similarities to Plautus possibly more significant than subject matter or vocabulary.

[3] This separates the Roman writers of comedy from Aristophanes who practically never has 13 long (Lindsay, *ELV* 275). A long syllable in this position is found in line 11 of Catullus' poem in the uncommon word *conscribillunt*, but not in the few lines of Varro.

[4] The manuscript tradition for line 5 does not make sense. However, many of the various suggestions do not make much sense in the context, either. I lean toward J. Colin's interpretation in "L'Heure des cadeaux pour Thallus le Cinède," *REL* 32, 1954, 106-110, where he gives the reading "cum diva mulierarios intendit oscitantes" since it stays closest to the manuscript tradition while preserving the sense of the passage. I think his point that Thallus is not a petty thief, but an artist in the entourage of Catullus and his friends, is particularly valuable. The crux of his argument is in the interpretation of the words "palam soles habere." According to Colin, this means that Catullus has bestowed gifts often on his homosexual dancing friend, but in a typical change of heart, wants these tokens back. This interpretation gibes with Catullus' character at least, while Putman's suggestion, following Monroe, about Dea Murcia, has missed the logical sense (J. Putman, "Catullus 25.5," *CP* 59, 1964, 268-270). He does, however,

comic tradition would be expected is the break after 8. Here, however, comedy breaks the rule often enough (the Latin authors probably on the basis of Greek example)[1] to put Catullus and Varro in a category by themselves with respect to this mid-line break. However, since there are only thirteen lines from Catullus, and not even ten certain lines from Varro, no definitive conclusions should be assumed.

Since nothing is to be gained by futile comparison, a few interesting factors can be pointed out by looking at Catullus alone. Certainly, no thesis about ictus and accent can be illustrated from this poem. There is universal coincidence at 2 and 14, with the exception of line 9 where 1 and 2 are monosyllables, and the strong accent is thrown to 4. 61% of the lines have strong accent at either 4 or 6, and 10, while only 23% have a strong accent at 12. Two lines show a complete pattern: 2, 4, 6, 10, 14 (lines 1 and 4), but thirteen lines are too few to justify any stand on the subject of ictus and accent. More interesting is Catullus' handling of cretic words, as has been noticed in the section on the iambic six-cycle line. No cretic occurs in the catalectic last part of the line, although it is found in Varro, while in the first half these three-syllable word-types occur in every line but 5, 8 and 13 with a varied pattern which could well be more than just problematical. 6-8 is the most frequent; this is logical as a fitting end for an iambic run. The sequence is: 6-8, 2-4, 4-6, 6-8, (line 5), 4-6, 6-8, (line 8), 6-8, 2-4, 4-6, 6-8. Consciously or unconsciously, the cretic words thus employed produce a rhythmical pattern in a line which, because of its length, would otherwise be too much like normal speech. As a metrical exercise, however, the septenarius seems not to have held much appeal for Catullus other than to prove he could handle the meter with movement,[2] as well as make it a suitable vehicle for his deliberately caustic remarks. Indeed, the poem is an excellent example of the type "tossed off by talented, idle young men, stimulated by intimacy with literature and the exhilaration of outdoing one another in technical competence."[3]

include in his footnotes a valuable listing of other attempts at solving the problem of this line.

[1] Cf. Lindsay, *ELV* 275; J. White, *The Verse of Greek Comedy* (London 1912) 65; and Harsh, *op. cit.* (supra 142-143 n. 5) 586, all giving examples of no break after 8 in comedy.

[2] Cf. Victorinus in Keil, *Gr. Lat.* 6.135.28: "est enim iocosis motibus emollitum gestibusque agentium satis accommodatum."

[3] Quinn, *Docte Catulle* 35.

ASCLEPIADEAN MAJOR

1	2	3	4	5	6	7	8	9	10	11	12	13	14	15	16
×	×	–	⏑	⏑	–	–	⏑	⏑	–	–	⏑	⏑	–	⏑	×

It is difficult to discover who first applied the eponym Asklepiades, the Alexandrian composer of epigrams, to the sixteen-syllable line diagrammed above. Hephaistion, usually the source for naming metrical patterns after Alexandrian poets, as well as famous poets of earlier periods, calls the line a Σαπφικὸν ἑκκαιδεκασύλλαβον,[1] reserving the name "Asclepiadean" only for the twelve-syllable line known in most grammar books as the Asclepiadean minor.[2] The Latin metricians generally discuss both meters under the heading of types of choriambic rhythm.[3] It is clear that the name eventually became attached to the sixteen-syllable line because of the *adiectio* theory of adding two choriambic "feet" in the middle of the twelve-syllable line. If one looks at the Greek patterns and usage of the meter, however, the choriambic nature association is much less evident than in the use of Horace, for instance. This is because Horace, without fail in the thirty-two lines in the meter,[4] isolates the central choriamb by always having a word-end at 6 and 10. The only Greek poet who approaches this high frequency is Theokritos who has a break after 6 and 10 in twenty-six out of fifty-seven lines.[5] It is more suitable in relation to the original Greek handling of the meter to classify it as another of the group "c" meters (supra 5) because of its irregular colometric patterns, because of its early appearance in the poetry of Sappho

---

[1] *Ench.* 10.6 (Consbr. 34). See also Atilius Fortunatianus, Keil, *Gr. Lat.* 6.295.17-296.15.

[2] *Ibid.* 3 (Consbr. 33). See Kolář, *De re Metrica* (supra 35 n. 4) 239-244, who gives an analysis on the tradition of the Latin grammarians, and Koster, *Traité* 243-245. The term "first asclepiad" is also used for the lesser asclepiadean; see Raven, *LM* 142. He calls the great asclepiad the second asclepiad, while Bennett and Rolfe, in their analysis of meters in their edition of Horace, Appendix 35, call the greater asclepiad the "fifth asclepiadean."

[3] See particularly Marius Victorinus, Keil, *Gr. Lat.* 6.167.24-32, 172.1-8; Atilius Fortunatianus, *ibid.* 295.19-296.25; and Sacerdos, *ibid.* 536.23-26.

[4] *Carm* 1.11, 18; 4.10.

[5] 28 and 30. Heinze, *op. cit.* (supra 17 n. 1) 33 gives a count of twenty-seven. See also his footnote on the same page about the fragments of Kallimachos, Pf. 400, and the textually corrupt 527.

and Alkaios,[1] and because of its use in Greek dramatic lyrics along with other *B D C alternating* rhythms.[2]

The pattern for the whole line is simple to grasp, but because of the varied positions of word-ends, different colometric divisions can be made. The whole line, in terms of the arsis patterns, can be described as *C D A D A D B closed*. A break after 6 and 10 results in a *C D A falling, D A falling*, and a *D B closed* sequence of cola. However, a significant break after 7 changes the whole character of the line for it emphasizes the pherecratean similarities, so that the initial pattern seems to be a *C D C falling* colon.[3] As the word-end at 10 is the most universal of all except at 16, a line with a break after 7 and the requisite 10 has the pattern *C D C falling, D A open, D B closed*. It is interesting to note, in connection with this initial colometric ambiguity, the high incidence of mono-syllables at 7 in all examples of the meter excepting those from Sappho and Sophokles.[4]

The following tables illustrate the distribution of words from one to four syllables in Catullus' twelve-line poem.

I. Monosyllables

A. —

at	1	5
	2	4
	3	3
	6	4
	7	6
	10	2
	11	1
	14	2

[1] *PLF* 53-56 for the eight lines by Sappho, and *PLF* Z 16-25 containing nineteen whole lines by Alkaios and several fragmentary lines. According to Hephaistion *loc. cit.* (supra 145 n. 1) all of Sappho's third book was written in this meter.

[2] See particularly Sophokles' treatment in the *Philoctetes*: 175-176, 186-187; 680-681, 696-697; 713-715, 726-727. Relevant discussion can be found in Pohlsander, *op. cit.* (supra 64-65 n. 5) 114-115 and 117-119.

[3] Cola from the group "c" meters which end in two long syllables, or a long and an anceps, have a certain ambiguity concerning the best description, particularly if the colon begins *in thesi*. Thus the pherecratean colon can also be described as a *C D A closed* colon.

[4] In addition to those examples mentioned supra 145 n. 1-4, there survive in Greek two lines possibly by Stesichoros, *PMG* 101, and ten lines from the *skolia*, *PMG* 14, 19-22. The percentage of lines with a monosyllable at 7 is 42% for Alkaios, 13% for Sappho, 17% for Sophokles, 50% for the *skolia*, 50% for Kallimachos (there being only two lines), 23% for Theokritos, 50% for Catullus, and 41% for Horace.

B. ᵕ
   at 4   1
      5   1

II. Disyllables

A. ᵕ —
   9-10   1
   15-16   5

B. — ᵕ
   3-4   1
   7-8   1
   11-12   3

C. ᵕᵕ [1]
   8-9   2

D. — —
   1-2   5
   6-7   1
   10-11   1

III. Trisyllables

A. — — —
   1-3   1

B. — — ᵕ
   2-4   1

C. ᵕ — —
   5-7   2

D. — ᵕ ᵕ
   3-5   4
   7-9   1
   11-13   4

E. ᵕ ᵕ —
   4-6   3
   8-10   6
   12-14   3

F. — ᵕ ×
   (final)   2

IV. Quadrisyllables

A. — ᵕ ᵕ —
   3-6   1
   7-10   1
   11-14   2

B. ᵕ — ᵕ ×
   (final)   2

C. ᵕ ᵕ — —
   8-11   1

One or two unusual features call for comment. The first of these is the rarity of the pyrrhic word compared with the higher incidence

---

[1] A final pyrrhic occurs twice, making the disyllabic line-end the most frequent.

in other "c" type meters, 156 in phalaeceans,[1] sixty-four in the glyconic colon, and fifteen in the pherecratean.[2] Moreover, it does not occur at all at 4-5 which would be the most expected position, particularly when compared to the practice in the meters just named, or in contrast to the two poems of Theokritos where a pyrrhic word at 4-5 occurs ten times. However, in the eight whole lines of Sappho, a pyrrhic word occurs only once, at 12-13. In Alkaios they are not infrequent: four at 4-5, one at 8-9, and four at 12-13. The second distinctive feature is the scarcity of polysyllables. This may very well be related to Catullus' general tendency for using shorter words in a long line, as has been noted previously in connection with galliambics, where in a line which has a potential of nineteen syllables, there are almost no pentasyllabic words and relatively few quadrisyllables.[3] Also, the fifteen-syllable priapean line has fewer polysyllables than disyllables and trisyllables. On the other hand, polysyllabics are common in the one other long line poem, 25, a fifteen-syllable septenarius. Contrasted to Catullan usage, in the Greek examples of asclepiadean major, words of four or more syllables are unusually noticeable. Fourteen out of fifty-seven lines of Theokritos end in a quadrisyllable, while four end in a pentasyllable and one in a six-syllable word (28.6). Alkaios and Sappho also use five- and six-syllable finals, and they are found in the *skolia*. A six-syllable ending occurs once in Horace (1.18.4), a pentasyllable twice (1.11.2, 18.13), and a quadrisyllable twice (1.18.10, 4.10.2). Both Latin authors prefer the disyllabic end, 7/12 for Catullus, and 15/32 for Horace,[4] 58% and 47% respectively. If either author had used the meter more, it might have been possible to draw more specific conclusions as to tendencies. Horace's restrictions are clear,[5] but there is too little from Catullus to reveal more than that he was experimenting, and followed no Greek colometric pattern consistently. The only

---

[1] See Cutt, *op. cit.* (supra 34 n. 2) 8.

[2] See tables pp. 84 and 85 respectively. The percentages out of 230 and 82 cola respectively are 28% and 18%.

[3] See supra 129.

[4] See Zinn II 105-106.

[5] See discussion by Heinze, *loc. cit.*, (supra 145 n. 5) and Zinn I, 25, 44, 46, 63. Most of the comments by Zinn are related to the subject of word-accent which I have not discussed in connection with Catullus' use of the asclepiadean major since it does not seem to play any significant or at least evident role in this meter. Only the first line of the poem shows any high coincidence of word-accent with the fixed long syllable.

regularly recurring feature is the word-end at 10 which is found in all but the last two lines, both of which contain a play on two forms of the same verb:

> .... di meminerunt, meminit fides,
> .... facti faciet tui.

Both lines end with a 3-2 word pattern so that the repetition of syllabic patterning emphasizes the couplet nature of the last two lines and the tight epigrammatic close. Thus it would seem that even here, in such a small sample, Catullus used words with an awareness of their syllabic patterning for particular effect.

Catullus 4, *Phasellus ille*   IAMBIC

DEPLOYMENT OF TRISYLLABLES
Ad pag. 94-95   Total 47

	1	2	3	4	5	6	7	8	9	10	11	12
* 1				2		1						
2	2								4			
3											2	
* 4				4			2					
5	2		2				2					
6	1	1	2			5						
* 7				2		4						
* 8				2		1						
9	4										2	
10	1	2		1							2	
11				2		1				1	2	
12				2	2						2	
* 13				2		1						
14	1	1	2		1	2		5				
15	2				2		1	4				
16	2				2		1	4				
17	1	4							1			
18	1	2			1	1	5					2
19	2				2		2					
* 20				2		1						
21	2					4				1	2	
22	1	2		2		5						2
23	1	2		2		1				1	2	
24				1	1	2						2
25	1	1	2						1	4		
26	2				2							2
* 27				2		1						

	No. of Lines	
7	1	1
6	2	2
	1	1
	0	2
5	3	4
	2	6
	1	4
	0	1
4	3	1
	2	4
	1	1
3	2	1
WORDS	TRISYLLABLES	
Per	Line	

* Smoothest line, beginning and ending with a trisyllable. Note pairing of lines such as 7 & 8, 15 & 16. Same pattern occurs in 1, 13, 20 and 27.

Catullus 50, *Hesterno, Licini* PHALAECEAN

DEPLOYMENT OF TRISYLLABLES

Ad pag. 44-48 Total 35

	1	2	3	4	5	6	7	8	9	10	11
1	■			■			1	4			
2	2		■			1	2		■		
3	1	4				2		4			
4	2		4				■		2		
5	■			■			1	1	1	2	
6	2		■			1	1	2		2	
7	1	2		■			2		■		
8	■						5				
9	1	1	1				2		■		
10	1	2					2			■	
11	1	1	4				■			2	
* 12	■			■			■			2	
13	1	2		■			2		1	2	
14	1	■			■			2		2	
15	5					■			■		
16	1	■			2		■			2	
17	1		4				2		■		
18	1	2			2		1	■		2	
* 19	■			2							
20	1	2		■			■			1	1
21	1	2		2		2		1	■		

WORDS Per Line	TRISYLLABLES	No. of Lines
6	2	3
6	1	4
5	2	5
5	1	2
4	3	2
4	2	1
4	1	1
4	0	1
3	2	2

* Principal Four-Word lines

GRAPHS SHOWING INCIDENCE OF TRISYLLABLES

CATULLUS 4

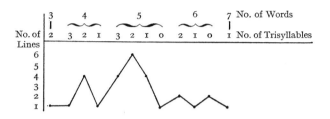

CATULLUS 50

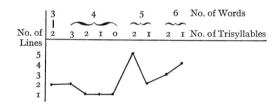

BIBLIOGRAPHY *

Abbott, F. F., "The Accent in Vulgar and Formal Latin," *CP* 2, 1907, 444-460.
Abbott, K. M., "The Grammarians and the Latin Accent," *Classical Studies in Honor of William A. Oldfather*, University of Illinois Press (Urbana 1943) 1-19.
——, "Ictus, Accent, and Statistics in Latin Dramatic Verse," *TAPA* 75, 1944, 127-140.
Ahlberg, A., *Studia de Accentu Latina* (Lundae 1905).
Allen, G., "The Attis of Gaius V. Catullus," *Bibliothèque de Carabas* (London 1892).
Allen, W. S., *Vox Graeca. The Pronunciation of Classical Greek* (Cambridge 1968).
——, *Vox Latina* (Cambridge 1965).
Ardizzoni, A., "Callimaco 'Ipponatteo'," *AFLC* 28, 1960, 3-16.
Arnold, E. V., *Vedic Metre* (Cambridge 1905).
Avallone, R., "Catullo e Aristophane," *Antiquitas* 2, 1947, 11-49.
——, "Catullo ed Euripide," *Antiquitas* 3, 1948, 112-181.
——, *Catullo e i suoi modelli romani* (Salerno 1944).
Axelson, B., "Die zweite Senkung im jambischen Senar der Phaedrus," *Vetenskaps-Societeten i Lund Årsbok*, 1949, 45-68.
Bardon, H., *La Littérature latine inconnue* 1 (Paris 1952).
Beare, W., "The Meaning of Ictus as Applied to Latin Verse," *Hermathena* 81, 1953, 29-40.
——, "The Origin of Rhythmic Latin Verse," *Hermathena* 87, 1956, 3-20.
Becker, P. A., "Die Anfänge der romanischen Verskunst," *ZFS* 56, 1932, 257-323.
Bergaigne, A. & H. V., *Manuel pour étudier le sanscrit védique* (Paris 1890).
Birt, T., *Jugendverse und Heimatpoesie Vergils* (Teubner 1910).
Bitterman, H. R., "The Organ in the Early Middle Ages," *Speculum* 4, 1929, 390-410.
Blass, F., "Die Berliner Fragmente der Sappho," *Hermes* 37, 1902, 456-479.
Bonavia-Hunt, N., *Horace the Minstrel, a Study of His Sapphic and Alcaic Lines* (London 1954).
Bongi, V., "Il Carme 63 di Catullo e il culto di Cibele e di Attis," *La Civiltà Moderna* 7 (Florence 1943).
Bücheler, F., *Kleine Schriften I* (Berlin 1915).
Burger, M., *Recherches sur la structure et l'origine des vers romans* (Paris 1957).
——, "Le Vers accentual en bas-latin," *REL* 37, 1959, 230-246.
Campbell, D., "Galliambic Poems of the 15th and 16th Centuries," *Humanisme et Renaissance* 22, 1960, 490-510.
Christ, W., *Metrik der Griechen und Römer* (Leipzig 1874).
Colin, J., "L'Heure des cadeaux pour Thallus le cinède," *REL* 32, 1954, 106-110.
Collinge, N. E., *The Structure of Horace's Odes* (London 1961).
Commager, S., *The Odes of Horace* (New Haven 1966³).
Crusius, F., *Römische Metrik* (Munich 1959⁴).

* This bibliography does not include all the books and articles mentioned in the footnotes, but only those which had a direct bearing on this study.

Crusius, O., "Die Delphischen Hymnen," *Philologus* 53, 1894, Ergänzungsheft.

——, *Herondae Mimiambi* (Leipzig 1914).

Cutt, T., *Meter and Diction in Catullus' Hendecasyllabics*, Chicago University Dissertation, 1936.

Dale, A. M., *The Collected Papers of A. M. Dale*, ed. T. B. L. Webster (Cambridge 1969).

——, "Greek Metric 1936-1957," *Lustrum* 2, 1957.

——, *The Lyric Metres of Greek Drama* (Cambridge 1968²).

Dale, F. R., "The Attis of Catullus," *G&R* 11, 1964, 43-47.

Davison, J. A., "Double Scansion in Early Greek Lyric," *CQ* 28, 1934, 181-189.

Dawson, C. M., "The Iambi of Callimachus," *YCS* 11, 1950, 1-168.

della Corte, F., "Per il testo delle 'Menippee'," *RIF* ns. 20, 1942, 201-213.

——, "La Poesia di Varrone Reatina recostituita," *AttiTor* Estratto dalle Memorie (Torino 1938).

——, "Rileggendo 'Le Menippee'," *GIF* 1, 1948, 69-76.

——, "Varrone e Levio di fronte alla metrica tradizionale della scena latina," *AttiTor* 70, 1935, 375-384.

——, *Varrone il terzo gran lune romano* (Florence 1970).

——, "Varrone metricista," *Fondation Hardt* 9, 1962, 141-172.

——, *Varronis Menippearum Fragmenta* (Private lithograph Torino 1953).

Drexler, H., "Quantität und Wortakzent," *Maia* 12, 1960, 167-189.

Duckworth, G. E., *Structural Patterns and Proportions in Virgil's Aeneid* (Ann Arbor 1962).

Dunn, G., "The Galliambic Metre," *CR* 7, 1893, 146-148.

Edmonds, J. M., *The Fragments of Attic Comedy* (Leiden 1957).

Elder, J. P., "The Art of Catullus' Attis," *TAPA* 71, 1940, xxxiii-xxxiv.

——, "Catullus' Attis," *AJP* 68, 1947, 394-403.

Ellis, R., *A Commentary on Catullus* (Oxford 1889).

Enk, P. J., "The Latin Accent," *Mnemosyne* s. 4 6, 1953, 93-109.

Fairbanks, A., "A Study of the Greek Paean," *CornellSCP* 12, 1900.

Fairclough, H., "The Poems of the Appendix Vergiliana," *TAPA* 53, 1922, 1-34.

Farina, A., *Ipponatte* (Naples 1964).

Ferguson, J., "Catullus and Horace," *AJP* 77, 1956, 1-18.

Floriani Squarciapino, M., *I Culti orientali ad Ostia* (Leiden 1962).

Fraenkel, E., *Iktus und Akzent im lateinischen Sprechvers* (Berlin 1928).

Garcia, J. F., "La Cesura en el verso 11 del carmen 11 de Catullo," *Emerita* 9, 1941, 160-162.

Geffcken, J., "Leonidas von Tarent," *NJbb* supplbnd. 23, 1897.

Gerhard, G. A., *Phoinix von Kolophon* (Teubner Leipzig 1909).

Giarratano, C., *De M. Val. Martialis Re Metrica* (Naples 1908).

Giri, G., *De Locis qui sunt aut habentur corrupti in Catulli carminibus* (Augustae Taurinorum 1894).

Goodell, T., "Word Accent in Catullus' Galliambics," *TAPA* 34, 1903, 27-32.

Goold, G. P., "A New Text of Catullus," *Phoenix* 12, 1958, 93-116.

Graillot, H., *Le Culte de Cybèle* (Paris 1912).

Greenough, J. C., "Accentual Rhythm in Horatian Sapphics," *HSCP* 4, 1893, 105-115.

Guillemin, A., "Le Poème 63 de Catulle," *REL* 27, 1949, 149-157.

Hack, R., "The Law of the Hendecasyllable," *HSCP* 25, 1914, 107-115.

Hangen, E., "The Syllable in Linguistic Description," *For Roman Jakobson* (The Hague 1956) 213-221.

Hardie, E. R., "The Galliambic Metre," *CR* 7, 1893, 280-281

——, *Res Metrica* (Oxford 1920).

Harkins, P. W., "Autoallegory in Catullus 63 and 64," *TAPA* 90, 1959, 106-116.

Harkness, A. G., "The Final Monosyllable in Latin Prose and Poetry," *AJP* 31, 1910, 154-174.

——, "The Relation of Accent to Elision in Latin Verse Not Including the Drama," *TAPA* 36, 1905, 82-110.

Harsh, P. W., "Early Latin Meter and Prosody," *Lustrum* 3, 1958, 226-233.

——, "Iambic Words and Regard for Accent in Plautus," *Stamford University Publications in Language and Literature*, 7¹, 1949.

——, "Ménandre, Le Diskolos, ed. Martin," *Gnomon* 31, 1959, 577-586.

Havet, L., "Mélanges latines sur la prononciation des syllabes initiales latines," *MemSocLing* 6, 1885-1889, 11-39.

Heidel, W. A., "Catullus and Furius Bibaculus," *CR* 15, 1901, 215-217.

Heinze, R., *Die Lyrischen Verse des Horaz* (Amsterdam reprint 1959).

Hellegouarc'h, J., *Le Monosyllabe dans l'hexamètre latin* (Paris 1964).

Hepding, H., "Attis seine Mythen und sein Kult," *Religionsgeschichtliche Versuche und Vorarbeiten*, 1903, 11.

Herescu, N., "Autour de la 'Salax Taberna'," *Hommages à Leon Herrmann, Coll. Latomus* 44, 1960, 431-435.

Herter, H., *De Priapo* (Giessen 1932).

Highet, G., *Poets in a Landscape* (New York 1965³).

Hudson-Williams, A., "Catullus 11 9-12," *CQ* 46, 1952, 186.

Hurlbut, S. A., *A Series of Mediaeval Latin Hymns*, St. Alban's Press (Washington 1936).

Irigoin, J., "Lois et règles dans le trimètre et le tétramètre trochaïque," *REG* 72, 1959, 67-80.

Kabell, A., "Metrische Studien II, Antiker Form sich nährend," *UppsÅrsskr* 1960, no. 6.

Kalinka, E., *Griechisch-römische Metrik und Rhythmik im letzten Vierteljahrhundert, JAW* 250, Supplbnd. 1935, 290-507; 256, 1937, 1-126.

Kawczynski, M., *L'Origine et l'histoire des rythmes* (Paris 1889).

Kent, R., "The Alleged Conflict of Accents in Latin Verse," *TAPA* 51, 1920, 19-29.

Klotz, A., "Zu Catull," *RhM* 80, 1931, 342-356.

Knight, W. J., *Accentual Symmetry in Vergil* (Oxford 1950²).

Knox, W. A., "The Early Iambus," *Philologus* 87 (1932) 18-34.

——, "Herodes and Callimachus," *Philologus* 81, 1926, 241-255.

Knox, W. A. & Headlam, W., *Herodas* (Cambridge 1922).

Kolář, A., *De re metrica poetarum Graecorum et Romanorum* (Prague 1947).

——, "De Romanorum metris Aeolis, praecipue Horatianis," *LF* 62, 1935, 428-462.

Kollman, E. D., "Remarks on the Structure of the Latin Hexameter," *Glotta* 46, 1968, 293-316.

Koster, W. J. W., "De Glyconei et Pherecratei origine," *Philologus* 80, 1925, 353-365.

——, *Traité de métrique grecque* (Leyden 1966⁴).

Lachmann, K., *Kleinere Schriften* (Berlin 1876).

Lafaye, G., *Catulle et ses modèles* (Paris 1894).

Lambrechts, P., "Attis à Rome," *Mélanges George Smets* (Brussels 1952) 461-473.
——, "Attis. Van Herdersknaap tot God," *Verhand. Vlaamse Acad. voor Wet. van België Kl. der Lett.* 46, 1962.
——, "Les Fêtês 'phrygiennes' de Cybèle et d'Attis," *BIBR* 27, 1952, 141-170.
Laurand, L., "L'Accent grec et latin, remarques et bibliographie choisie," *RevPhil* s. 3, 12, 1938, 133-148.
Law, N. N., *Age of the Rgveda* (Calcutta 1965).
Lehman, L., *Quantitative Implications of the Pyrrhic Stress*, University of Virginia Dissertation, 1924.
Lenchantin de Gubernatis, M., "I Metri eolici della lirica Latina," *Athenaeum* 12, 1934, 239-254.
Leo, F., *Ausgewählte Kleinen Schriften I & II* (Rome 1960).
   1. *Die Römische Poesie in der Sullanischen Zeit*, 249-282.
   2. *Ein Metrisches Fragment aus Oxyrhynchos*, 395-408.
——, "Die plautinischen Cantica und die hellenistische Lyrik," *AbhGöttPhil Hist Klasse*, n. f. 1, no. 7, 1897.
Leon, H. J., "A Quarter Century of Catullan Scholarship (1934-1959)," *CW* 53, 104-113, 141-148, 173-180.
Leutsch, E., "Zu Catullus," *Philologus* 10, 1855, 735-743.
Lindsay, W. M., *Early Latin Verse* (Oxford 1922).
——, *The Latin Language* (Oxford 1894).
Lotz, J., "Notes on Structural Analysis in Metrics," *Helicon* 4, 1942, 119-146.
Lunderstedt, P., "De C. Maecenatis Fragmentis," *Commentationes Philologae Ienenses*, 9¹, 1911, 1-119.
Maas, P., *Greek Metre*, translated by H. Lloyd-Jones (Oxford 1966²).
Mangelsdorff, E. A., *Das Lyrische Hochzeitgedicht bei den Griechen und Römern*, Dissertation zur Erlangung der Doktorwürde Grossherzoglich Ludwigs-Universität zu Giessen (Hamburg 1913).
Marouzeau, J., *L'Ordre des mots dans la phrase latine III* (Paris 1949).
——, "Structure rythmique de la phrase et du vers latin," *REL* 11, 1933, 325-343.
——, "Le Style oral latin," *REL* 10, 1932, 186.
Masson, O., *Les Fragments du poète Hipponax* (Paris 1962).
Means, T., "Catullus LXIII," *CP* 22, 1927, 101-102.
Megoun, H. W., "What Was the Nature of the Latin Caesura?," *TAPA* 63, 1932, xxxvii.
Meillet, A., *Aperçu d'une histoire de la langue grecque*, (Paris 1965⁷).
——, *Esquisse d'une histoire de la langue latine*, (Paris 1966⁷).
——, "Métrique éolienne et métrique vedique," *BSL* 22, 1921, 16-17.
——, *Les Origines indo-européennes des mètres grecs*, (Paris 1923).
——, "La Place de l'accent en latin," *MSL* 20, 1918, 165-171.
Meineke, A., "Ceterorum Poetarum Choliambi," *Fabulae Aesopeae* ed. Lachmann (Berlin 1845).
Mendell, C. W., "Catullan Echoes in the Odes of Horace," *CP* 30, 1935, 289-301.
Meyer, W., "Caesur im Hendekasyllabus," *SBMünch*, 1889, II, 208-227.
——, "Über die weibliche Caesur des klassischen lateinischen Hexameters und über lateinischen Caesuren überhaupt," *SBMünch*, 1889, II, 228-245.

Morelli, G., "Studi sul trimetre giambico," *Maia* 13, 1961, 143-161; 14, 1962, 149-161.
Müller, L., *De Re Metrica Poetarum Latinorum* (Leipzig 1894²).
——, "Zu Catulls Attis," *RhM* 25, 1870, 166-169.
Munro, H. A. J., *Criticisms and Elucidations of Catullus* (Cambridge 1878).
Münscher, K., "Metrische Beiträge," *Hermes* 56, 1921, 66-103.
Needler, G. H., *The Lone Shieling, Origin and Authorship of the Blackwood "Canadian Boat Song"* (Toronto 1941).
Neudling, C. L., "A Prosopography to Catullus," *IowaSCP* 12, 1955.
Norberg, D., *Introduction à l'étude de la versification latine médiévale* (Stockholm 1958).
——, "La Récitation du vers latin," *NPhM* 66, 1965, 496-508.
Norden, E., *Kleine Schriften* (Berlin 1966).
Nougaret, L., *Traité de métrique latine classique* (Paris 1963).
Numberger, K., "*Inhalt und Metrum in der Lyrik des Horaz*," Inaugural Dissertation University of Munich, Faculty of Philosophy, 1959.
Oksala, T., "Catulls Attis-Ballade," *Arctos*, n.s. 3, 1962, 199-213.
O'Neill, E. G., Jr., "The Importance of Final Syllables in Greek Verse," *TAPA* 70, 1930, 256-294.
——, "The Localization of Metrical Word Types in the Greek Hexameter," *YCS* 8, 1942, 105-178.
——, "Word Accents and Final Syllables in Latin Verse," *TAPA* 71, 1940, 335-359.
Onions, J. H., "Adversaria Noniana," *JP* 16, 1890, 89-119.
——, "Noniana Quaedam," *JP* 16, 1888, 162-182.
——, "Verisimilia Noniana," *CR* 3, 1889, 247-249.
Page, D., *Sappho and Alcaeus* (Oxford 1955).
Palmer, L. R., *The Latin Language* (Faber & Faber 1966⁵).
Pascal, C. B., *The Cults of Cisalpine Gaul*, Coll. Latomus 75, 1964.
Pelckmann, J., *Versus Choliambi apud Graecos et Romanos Historia*, Diss. Greifswald (Keil 1908).
Perotta, G., "Il Poeta degli epodi Strasburgo," *StItal*, n.s. 15, 1938, 17-19.
Perret, J., "Un Équivalent latin de la loi de Porson," *Hommages à Léon Herrmann*, Coll. Latomus 44, 1960, 588-594.
——, "Le Mythe de Cybèle, Lucrèce, II, 600-660," *REL* 13, 1935, 332-357.
Pighi, G. B., "Il Canto di Attis," *Rivista Musicale Italiano* 39, 1832, 34-40.
——, "I Ritmi eolici nella metrica greca," Ἔρανος, *Raccolta di scritti in onore del Prof. Casimiro Adami* (Verona 1941) 17-49.
——, "La Struttura del carme LXI di Catullo," *Humanitas* 2, 1948, 40-53.
Pöschl, V., *The Art of Vergil*, Trans. by G. Seligson (Ann Arbor 1962).
Pohlsander, H. A., *Metrical Studies in the Lyrics of Sophocles* (Leiden 1964).
Porter, H. N., "The Early Greek Hexameter," *YCS* 12, 1951, 3-63.
Postgate, J. P., "Ionicus a Minore of Horace," *CQ* 18, 1924, 46-48.
Prakken, D., "Feminine Caesuras in Horatian Sapphic Stanzas," *CP* 49, 1954, 102-103.
Preuss, F. A., "Patterns in Latin Lyric Meters," *CB* 24, 1948, 61-63.
Puccioni, G., *Mimiambi* (Florence 1950).
Puelma-Piwonka, M. *Lucilius und Kallimachos* (Frankfort 1949).
Pulgram, E., "Accent and Ictus in Spoken and Written Latin," *ZVS* 71, 1953, 218-237.
Putnam, J., "Catullus 25,5," *CP* 59, 1964, 268-270.
Quinn, K., *The Catullan Revolution* (Melbourne 1959).

——, "Docte Catulle," *Critical Essays on Roman Literature, Elegy and Lyric*, ed. J. P. Sullivan (Harvard 1962) 31-63.
——, *Latin Explorations* (New York 1963).
Raby, F. J. E., *A History of Christian Latin Poetry* (Oxford 1953²).
——, *A History of Secular Latin Poetry in the Middle Ages* (Oxford 1957²).
Radford, R. S., "The Priapea and the Vergilian Appendix," *TAPA* 52, 1921, 148-177.
Raven, D. S., *Greek Metre* (London 1962).
——, *Latin Metre* (London 1965).
Reitzenstein, R., *Epigram und Skolion* (Giessen 1893).
Reitzenstein, E., "Zur Erklärung der Catalepton-gedichte," *RhM* 79, 1930, 65-92.
Ribbeck, O., "Über Varronischen Satiren," *RhM* 14, 1859, 102-130.
Riccomagno, L., *Studio sulle Satire Menippee* (Alba Sacerdote 1931).
Richardson, L., Jr., "Furi et Aureli Comites Catulli," *CP* 58, 1963, 93-106.
Richardson, L. J., "Greek and Latin Glyconics," *CPCP* 2, 1915, 257-265.
——, "On the Form of Horace's Lesser Asclepiads," *AJP* 22, 1901, 283-296.
——, "Horace's Alcaic Strophe," *CPCP* 1, 1907, 175-204.
——, "On Certain Sound Properties of the Sapphic Strophe as Employed by Horace," *TAPA* 33, 1902, 38-44.
Riese, A., "Kritisches und Exegetisches zu Varros Satiren," *RhM* 21, 1866, 109-122.
Röper, G., "EpimetrumVarronianorum," *Philologus* 9, 1854, 567-573.
——, "M. Terenti Varronis Saturarum Menippearum quarundam reliquiae emendatae," *Philologus* 9, 1854, 223-278.
——, "Varronische Vindicien I," *Philologus* 15, 1860, 267-302.
——, "Varronische Vindicien II," *Philologus* 17, 1861, 64-102.
——, "Varronische Vindicien III," *Philologus* 18, 1862, 418-446.
Rosenmeyer, T. G., Ostwald, M., Halporn, J. W., *The Meters of Greek and Latin Poetry* (New York 1963).
Ross, D. O., *Style and Tradition in Catullus* (Cambridge 1969).
Ross, R. C., "Catullus 63 and the Galliambic Meter," *CJ* 64, 1969, 145-152.
Rossbach, A., *Untersuchungen über die römische Ehe* (Stuttgart 1853).
Rostagni, A., *Storia della letteratura latina I* (Torino 1949).
Rudd, N., "Colonia and her Bridge: A Note on the Structure of Catullus 17," *TAPA* 90, 1959, 258-242.
Rudmose-Brown, T. B., "Some Medieval Latin Metres, Their Ancestry and Progeny," *Hermathena* 53, 1939, 29-58.
Schein, S., *The Iambic Trimeter in Aeschylus and Sophocles*, Dissertation Faculty of Philosophy Columbia University 1967.
Schröder, O., *Aeschyli Cantica* (Leipzig 1916).
——, *Aristophanes Cantica* (Leipzig 1930).
——, *Euripides Cantica* (Leipzig 1928).
——, "Griechische Singverse," *Philologus* Supplbnd. 18, 2, 1924.
——, *Sophoclis Cantica* (Leipzig 1907).
——, *Vorarbeiten zur griechischen Versgeschichte* (Leipzig 1908).
Sedgwick, W. B., "The Trochaic Tetrameter and the Versus Popularis in Latin," *C&R* 1, 1932, 96-106.
Seel, O. & Pöhlman, E., "Quantität und Wortakzent im horazischen Sapphiker," *Philologus* 103, 1959, 237-280.
Showerman, G., "Was Attis in Rome Under the Republic?," *TAPA* 31, 1900, 46-59.

Siefert, G. J., Jr., *Meter and Case in the Latin Elegiac Pentameter*, University of Pennsylvania Dissertation *Language*, suppl. 49, 1952.
Skutch, F., "De Lucilii Prosodia," *RM* n.f. 48, 1893, 303-307.
Sommer, P., *De P. Vergilii Maronis Catalepton* (Halle 1910).
Sonnenschein, E. A., "The Latin Sapphic", *CR* 17, 1903, 252-256.
Soubiran, J., *L'Elision dans la poésie latine* (Paris 1966).
——, "Monosyllables élidés au debout du vers dans la poésie latine archaique," *Pallas* 6, 1958, 39-53.
——, "Recherches sur la clausule du sénaire (trimètre) latin: les mots longs finaux," *REL* 42, 1964, 429-469.
Stowasser, J. M., "Vulgärmetrisches aus Lucilius," *WS* 27, 1905, 211-230.
——, "De Polymetris Senecae Canticis Quaestiones," *Eos* 45, 1951, 93-107.
——, "De re metricae Annaeanae Origine Quaestiones," *Eos* 53, 1963, 153-170.
Strzelecki, L., "De Senecae Trimetro Iambico," *RWF*, s. 3, 20, 1938.
Sturtevant, E. H., "On the Frequency of Short Words in Verse," *CW* 15, 1921, 73-76.
——, "Horace *Carm* 3.30 10-14 and the Sapphic Stanza," *TAPA* 70, 1939, 295-302.
   (For eight other articles on the nature of the Latin word accent, see p. 78 n. 4).
Sturtevant, E. H. and Kent, R. G., "Elision and Hiatus in Latin Prose and Verse," *TAPA* 46, 1915, 129-155.
Tamerle, E., *Der Lateinische Vers ein akzentuierender Vers* (Innsbruck, privately printed, 1938).
Tanner, R. G., "The Arval Hymn and Early Latin Verse," *CQ* 55, n.s. 11, 1961, 209-238.
Thomason, R. F., *The "Priapea" and Ovid: A Study of the Language of the Poems* (Nashville 1931).
Thompson, E. S., "The Galliambic Metre," *CR* 7, 1893, 145-146 (1).
——, "The Galliambic Metre," *CR* 7, 1893, 354-355 (2).
Thomson, D. F. S., "Catullus and Cicero: Poetry and the Criticism of Poetry," *CW* 60, 1967, 225-230.
Todd, F. A., "Passages of Catullus, Martial and Plautus," *CR* 55, 1941, 70-74.
Traglia, A., *Poetae Novi* (Rome 1962).
Tucker, R. W., "Accentuation before Enclitics in Latin," *TAPA* 96, 1965, 449-461.
Tyrrell, R., "Grant Allen on the Attis of Catullus," *CR* 7, 1893, 44-45.
Usener, H., *Beiläufige Bemerkungen, Kleine Schriften* 3 (Stuttgart 1965²).
Vahlen, J., *In Varronis Saturarum Menippearum reliquias coniectanea* (Leipzig 1858).
Vallois, R., "Les Strophes mutilées du péan de Philodamos," *BCH* 55, 1931, 61-364.
Vandvik, E., "Rhythmus und Metrum, Akzent und Iktus," *Symboslo*, Supplbnd. 8, 1937.
Vermaseren, M. J., *The Legend of Attis in Greek and Roman Art* (Leiden 1966).
Verrall, A. W., "The Latin Sapphic," *CR* 17, 1903, 339-343.
Weil, H., "Un Péan delphique à Dionysos," *BCH* 19, 1895, 393-418.
Weinberger, W., "Der lateinische Choliamb," *Serta Harteliana* (Vienna 1896) 117-120.
Weinreich, O., "Catulls Attisgedicht," *Mélanges F. Cumont, AnnPhilHist* 4, 1936, 463-500.
Welcker, F., *Kleine Schriften* (Bonn 1845).

West, A. D., "The Metre of Catullus' Elegiacs," *CQ* 51, 1957, 98-102.

White, J., *The Verse of Greek Comedy* (London 1912).

Wilamowitz-Möllendorff, U. von, "De Versu Phalaeceo," *Mélanges Henri Weil* (Paris 1898) 449-461.

——, "Die Galliamben der Kallimachos und Catulls," *Hermes* 14, 1879, 194-201.

——, *Griechische Verskunst* (Berlin 1921).

——, *Hellenistische Dichtung in der Zeit des Kallimachos* (Berlin 1962²).

Wilkinson, L. P., "Accentual Rhythm in Horatian Sapphics," *CR* 54, 1940, 131-133.

——, *Golden Latin Artistry* (Cambridge 1963).

Zarker, J. W., "Catullus 18-20," *TAPA* 93, 1962, 502-522.

Zicari, M., "Some Metrical and Prosodical Features of Catullus' Poetry," *Phoenix* 18, 1964, 193-204.

Zinn, E., *Der Wortakzent in den lyrischen Versen des Horaz I & II* (Munich 1940).

ARTICLES ON COMPUTERS AND METRICAL STUDIES

Dyer, R. R., "Towards Computational Procedures in Homeric Scholarship," *RELO* 4 (1967).

Halporn, M., "Reflections on Metrics by Computer," *RELO* 2, 1968, 1-11.

Jones, F. P., "A binary-octal code for analyzing hexameters," *TAPA* 97, 1966, 275-280.

——, "Notes on the Input for an Automatic Scansion Program," *RELO* 4, 1968, 5-11.

Ott, W., "Metrical Analysis of Latin Hexameter by Computer," *RELO*, 1966.